Springer Series on Family Violence

Albert R. Roberts, PhD, Series Editor

D0880153

Carol E. Jordan, MS, serves as Director of the University of Kentucky Center for Research on Violence Against Women and holds faculty appointments in the Department of Psychology and the College of Social Work. Ms. Jordan's areas of writing and research interest include the nexus of mental health and the legal system, particularly as it relates to the experience of women. She has published numerous articles, chapters and two books addressing domestic violence, rape, and stalking. Ms. Jordan has 20 years of experience in public policy, legislative advocacy, and program development addressing violence against women, including eight years in the Kentucky Governor's Office.

Michael T. Nietzel, PhD, serves as Provost of the University of Kentucky. Dr. Nietzel's research and teaching interest focus on forensic psychology, jury behavior, origins of criminal behavior, and the evaluation of psychotherapy. He teaches graduate courses in psychotherapy and forensic psychology and is a frequent consultant to attorneys and law enforcement. Nietzel has assisted in jury selection for more than 50 death-penalty trials. He has published more than 75 articles, books and book chapters, and is coauthor of various textbooks on clinical psychology, abnormal psychology, and psychology and the legal system.

Robert Walker, MSW, LCSW, is Assistant Professor at the University of Kentucky Department of Psychiatry and the Center on Drug and Alcohol Research, with conjoint appointments in the College of Social Work and Department of Behavioral Science. He was director of a community mental health center for 20 years and has had an active forensic mental health practice. He is the project director of Kentucky's substance abuse treatment outcome study and co-principal investigator on a National Institute on Alcohol Abuse and Alcoholism study of alcohol use and health among domestic violence victims.

TK Logan, PhD, is an Associate Professor in the Department of Behavioral Science at the University of Kentucky. Dr. Logan has been funded by the National Institute on Drug Abuse (NIDA) and by the National Institute on Alcohol Abuse and Alcoholism (NIAAA), and has completed studies on intimate partner violence and divorce; intimate partner violence and custody outcomes; stalking victimization and perpetration; health and mental health status, barriers, and service use among women; HIV risk behavior; and health, mental health, substance use, and victimization among rural and urban women.

WITHDRAWN

Intimate Partner Violence

A Clinical Training Guide for Mental Health Professionals

Carol E. Jordan, MS
Michael T. Nietzel, PhD
Robert Walker, MSW, LCSW
TK Logan, PhD

 Springer Publishing Company

RC
569.5
.F3
I578
2004

Copyright © 2004 by Springer Publishing Company, Inc.

All rights reserved

No part of this publication may be reproduced, stored in a re-
trieval system, or transmitted in any form or by any means,
electronic, mechanical, photocopying, recording, or otherwise,
without the prior permission of Springer Publishing Company,
Inc.

Springer Publishing Company, Inc.
536 Broadway
New York, NY 10012-3955

Acquisitions Editor: Sheri W. Sussman
Production Editor: Jeanne W. Libby
Cover design by Joanne E. Honigman

04 05 06 07 08 / 5 4 3 2 1

Library of Congress Cataloging-in-Publication Data

Intimate partner violence : a clinical training guide for mental
health professionals / Carol E. Jordan . . . [et al.].— 1st ed.
    p. cm. — (Springer series on family violence)
    ISBN 0-8261-2463-1 1.
    Abused wives—Rehabilitation. 2. Abused women—
Rehabilitation. 3. Abusive men— Rehabilitation. 4. Children
of abused wives—Rehabilitation. 5. Victims of family vio-
lence—Rehabilitation. 6. Wife abuse—United States—
Psychological aspects. 7. Conjugal violence—United
States—Psychological aspects. 8. Family violence—United
States—Psychological aspects. I. Jordan, Carol E. II. Series.
RC569.5.F3I578 2004
616.85'82206—dc22   2004014661

Printed in the United States of America by Vicks Litho & Printing.

To the women whose stories and survivorship have formed the lessons of our last twenty years, and to our colleagues whose work on their behalf has been an extraordinary source of inspiration.

À M et B. Qui sont la meilleur œuvre de notre père, et son meilleur héritage. CEJ

Contents

Preface

This clinical training companion is written with a generalist mental health professional in mind. We draw together research from diverse sources and offer practical applications of those findings in the light of key public policies and legal issues. Although no single book can offer a definitive statement on how to assess and treat intimate partner violence problems, this manual has the goal of putting the complexities into a manageable and empirically justified clinical practice. We attempt to draw clinicians' practices into closer agreement with the consensus of existing research and policy literatures. We also discuss diverse research findings and legal resources with the purpose of improving clinicians' competence and confidence in treating clients for whom intimate partner violence is an issue.

COMMON PITFALLS FACED BY MENTAL HEALTH PROFESSIONALS

Research over the past 2 decades has improved our understanding of how intimate partner violence affects mental health for both victims and offenders. In fact, the associations between violence, mental health, and substance abuse have been shown to be very complex. Mental health problems can increase the risk of violence among offenders and can contribute to greater risk for victims as well. In addition, substance abuse has complex associations with both offender patterns and victimization. The extent of research can be overwhelming and confusing to clinicians who are providing mental health or substance abuse treatment services. In spite of the wealth of new information, the research literature does not always indicate how clinicians should use these findings in treatment. In addition, many new policies, laws, and regulations have been developed nationwide to enhance the protections available to victims. New standards of care and clinical duties have been recommended in response to new research and changed public policies. The net effect of these changes is an increasingly complex legal environment within which treatment services are provided. Clinicians may find themselves practicing at legal and clinical levels without a sure footing in either area.

The challenges posed by intimate partner violence cases expose clinicians to unique potential pitfalls in their practice. The failure to detect abuse or to fully appreciate its potential risks, the application of traditional models of intervention, the lack of clarity on clinical roles in the forensic area, and other pitfalls expose a clinician to the possibility of failing to provide quality care or failing to adequately protect a client's well-being. The latter chapters of this text draw attention to some of the common pitfalls encountered by clinicians in intimate partner violence cases. These include:

1. Practice outside the boundaries of competence
2. Failure to assess intimate partner violence
3. Over and under-reactions to client disclosures of victimization
4. Loss of client privacy by introducing clinical records in court cases
5. Blurred boundaries and overreach by clinicians testifying in court
6. Overreliance on syndromal labels
7. Individual psychotherapy with intimate partner violence offenders
8. Cautions about marital or couples therapy
9. Cautions about alcohol and drug abuse counseling
10. Cautions about pastoral or Christian counseling

This clinical guide offers suggestions in each of these areas in order to help the clinician build a manageable, effective, and defensible practice environment adaptable to the clinical, legal, and ethical complexities that are characteristic of intimate partner violence cases.

CHAPTER SUMMARIES

This clinical training companion is comprised of eight chapters that explore background information, provide suggestions on assessment and basic treatment options for both victims and offenders, and then guide clinicians through the clinical and forensic practice environment associated with intimate partner violence cases. **Chapter 1** provides an overview of the prevalence of violence against women based on research literature. National studies suggest that the victimization of women is very prevalent, that most often the offender is an intimate partner, and that women are more likely to be killed by an intimate partner than by any other type of offender. The research also provides important frequency and severity information with major clinical implications for mental health and substance abuse clinicians. The types of intimate violence experienced by women, including physical and sexual violence, psychological abuse, and stalking, are also described in the chapter. Finally, Chapter 1 focuses on risk factors for victimization, specifically focusing on those associated with lethality and physical injury.

Chapter 2 focuses on mental health and substance abuse as they relate to victimization experiences. Because clinical populations may have higher rates of abuse victimization or perpetration, this chapter explores the ways that abuse can affect mental health and substance abuse. The chapter discusses the prevalence of abuse within clinical caseloads, from general outpatient settings to services for women with severe mental illness. The major findings with respect to the mental health outcomes associated with intimate partner violence are summarized, with a particular focus on depression, suicidality, posttraumatic stress disorder, and substance use and abuse. The acute and chronic physical health implications of victimization for women and the impact of witnessing adult violence on children in the home are discussed.

Chapter 3 reviews clinical characteristics of intimate partner violence offenders and provides information about general types of offending behavior. Research has begun to identify types of offenders, but the clinical value of typologies still appears to be limited. However, understanding the major patterns of offending can help mental health and substance abuse treatment providers in assessing and treating clients with offender behaviors. An overview of key clinical characteristics of offenders, including personality disorders, substance abuse, depression, and other disorders is provided in the chapter.

Chapter 4 discusses effective clinical practice with victims of intimate partner violence. The chapter addresses appropriate screening for current and historic abuse in general client populations and more extensive assessments if a client discloses victimization. Clinicians are encouraged to engage in safety planning with victims, focusing on three key phases: how to identify that risk or danger is increasing, how to identify the specific steps the victim may take upon recognizing those danger cues, and how to maintain safety upon her departure from the offender.

Chapter 5 reviews clinical intervention with intimate partner violence offenders. The chapter discusses the factors associated with risk for violence among offenders and presents information on screening, assessment, and treatment selection for offenders. The chapter also gives cautions regarding the risks attendant to inappropriate treatment and emphasizes the importance of structured group programs for offenders.

Chapter 6 describes the roles and actions recommended for mental health professionals when providing clinical services in cases of intimate partner violence. These recommendations derive from an understanding of intimate partner violence as criminal conduct with serious consequences for victims and offenders. The chapter suggests that mental health professionals have specific clinical duties of care, duties to warn and protect, and duties to report in intimate partner violence situations. Duties of care include being able to identify clients with characteristics associated with violence victimization or perpetration and being able to intervene appropriately. Duties to warn and protect include notifying potential victims of threats and assisting victims with safety planning. Duties to report include reporting child abuse either to protective services or law enforcement as well as reporting spouse abuse to adult protective service agencies.

Chapter 7 describes how the intersection between the mental health and justice systems brings with it unique roles for mental health professionals who must be attuned to the safety of clients and cognizant of how standards of conduct typically applied to clinical practice may change in this area of clinical work. A broader role for mental health professionals in intimate partner violence cases is outlined. The chapter includes recommendations for how mental health professionals can relate more effectively with the court system and describes common pitfalls for clinicians in these cases, particularly as they relate to assessment, confidentiality, roles in court, boundary issues, and the misapplication of common clinical modalities. Finally, the chapter addresses the negative impact clinical work in the intimate partner violence domain can have on clinicians who regularly hear stories of trauma and abuse from their clients.

Chapter 8 provides a modest legal primer for mental health professionals who work with victims and offenders. It focuses on the experience of intimate partner violence victims in the court and the criminal justice remedies and civil orders of protection they find there. Issues that arise in custody proceedings are also discussed.

Each chapter in the clinical training companion begins with an introductory paragraph outlining the topics to be covered. Likewise, each chapter ends with a summary paragraph and a series of questions for readers to use to ensure comprehension of key chapter content.

CONCLUSION

This clinical training companion was developed as a user-friendly resource and aid to the mental health or substance abuse professional who wants to improve clinical practice but who cannot read hundreds of pages of journal articles on the topic. Understanding that clinicians have their clients' best interests at heart, this text was developed to summarize key findings into manageable practice improvements that clinicians can implement in most practice settings. The goal of the book is to provide tools for the introduction of wiser and more empirically supportable practices in mental health and substance abuse treatment settings.

Chapter 1

Scope and Dynamics of Violence Against Women

Current research has important implications for clinical practice, and recently, research attention has focused on the degree to which women are harmed by male violence. **Chapter 1** reviews the literature on the incidence and prevalence of violence against women to raise the awareness of clinicians to both its frequency and severity. National studies reveal that the victimization of women is common, that most often the offender is an intimate partner, and that women are more likely to be injured or killed by an intimate partner than by any other type of offender. **Chapter 1** discusses the use of violence by women, distinguishing these acts from those of primary aggressive partners.

Chapter 1 differentiates the types of violence experienced by women in the context of intimate partner violence: including physical, sexual, and psychological abuse. The chapter also discusses stalking as a form of victimization. The chapter emphasizes a broad definition for violence against women to promote a fuller understanding of the phenomenon and to ensure the inclusion of types of maltreatment that research suggests is most harmful to victims. The sections within **chapter 1** include the following:

- Incidence and prevalence of violence against women
- Intimate partners as aggressors
- Violence perpetrated by women: the myth of mutuality
- Types of intimate partner violence and abuse
- Risk and dangerousness for adult victims

1

"The exact dimensions of violence against women are frequently disputed, yet even conservative estimates indicate that millions of American women experience violent victimization." (Crowell & Burgess, 1996, p. 8)

INCIDENCE AND PREVALENCE OF VIOLENCE AGAINST WOMEN

An important evolution in the understanding of intimate partner violence in the United States has occurred. Research has grown exponentially since the 1960s when the first efforts were initiated. Research findings and changes in public policy over the past few decades have increased general public and treating professionals' awareness of the extent of violence in family and intimate relationships. In the 1960s, studies began to reveal the extent of child maltreatment (Gil, 1970). In the 1970s, largely as a result of the women's movement, researchers began to focus on spouse as well as child abuse (Gelles, 1979), and abuse of the elderly began to receive attention in the 1980's (Steinmetz, 1978). Similarly, in the late 1970's, reports of child sexual abuse began to increase (Finkelhor, 1979, 1984), and research in the 1980s addressed the incidence of rape in marital relationships (Russell, 1982; Shields, Resick, & Hanneke, 1990).

Mental health and substance abuse clinicians must consider research about the prevalence and types of intimate partner violence to better understand characteristics of clinical populations. The data from general population studies can lead to changes in the way that disorders are understood and treated. Current research trends have important implications for clinical practice and, recently, research has focused on the degree to which women are harmed by male violence. The National Violence Against Women Survey (NVAW), a national telephone survey on the incidence and prevalence of woman abuse was conducted recently in households across the country. This study reported that approximately 52% of women reported being physically assaulted in their lifetime and almost 18% reported being victims of rape or attempted rape at some point in their lives.

In addition, 8% reported the experience of stalking victimization. The percent of stalked women increased to 12% if the standard for the level of fear required of victims was decreased (Tjaden & Thoennes, 2000). These findings apply to general household populations and did not include women who were in institutions, who were homeless, or who did not have telephones—an important limitation when applying these data to clinical populations.

In the context of intimate relationships, both the prevalence and severity of violence show differences between men and women. The National Violence Against Women Survey, for example, documented higher lifetime rates of intimate partner violence for women, greater frequency of assaults, and more severe injury (Tjaden & Thoennes, 2000). Following are some of the results of the survey.

Rate of Violence: Lifetime rates of physical assault by intimate are higher for women (25%) than for men (7.6%).

Frequency of Assault: Women victimized by intimate partners experience an average of 6.9 assaults, while men average 4.4 assaults.

Injury Severity: Women experience more chronic and injurious violence than do men; 41.5% of women versus 19.9% of men were injured during their most recent physical assault.

Clinicians who treat women who are members of ethnic minorities should take note of the limited findings about intimate partner violence in culturally diverse populations. In general, minority women, particularly those who live in poverty, are particularly at risk for victimization (Belle, 1990; O'Carroll & Mercy, 1986). In fact, at least one study found that femicide is the leading cause of death in the United States among young African American women aged 15–45 years (Greenfield et al., 1998), though homicide rates are extremely high for African American males as well. In addition, while some studies show little or no significant differences between African American, Hispanic, and other racial and ethnic minority populations (e.g., National Violence Against Women Survey as reported in Tjaden & Thoennes, 2000), estimates from the National Crime Victimization Survey (NCVS) indicate that between 1993 and 1998, African American women experienced intimate partner violence at a rate 35% higher than did White women (Rennison & Welchans, 2000). Other research indicates that more than half the women murdered

(53%) are African American Women (Bailey et al., 1997). Clinicians working with African American women victimized by intimate partner violence must become sensitized to the cultural context within which African American women decide whether to reach out for aid or remain reluctant to report their partner to a system perceived to be biased against African American men (Rasche, 1995). These women may also feel intense social pressure to set aside their individual needs for the survival of the family unit (Billingsley, 1992). Said another way, "If domestic violence service providers and researchers are committed to preventing intimate partner violence among African Americans, they must be prepared to acknowledge and build on the fact that African Americans live a bicultural reality" (Hampton, Oliver, & Margarian, 2003, p. 548).

The complexity of studying violence against Hispanic women derives in part from the fact that this group includes women from many different countries and cultures. Torres (1991) has noted that Hispanics in the United States originate from at least 32 different countries. One example of a key difference between groups is that rates of violence against Mexican-born Mexican American women were lower than for American-born Mexican American women (Sorenson & Telles, 1991). A study with women in a shelter for battered women found no differences in rates of violence across ethnicity but found that Hispanic women reported longer duration of abuse, a tendency to marry at a younger age, greater poverty, lower education, and larger families than other women (Gondolf, Fisher, & McFerron, 1988). Additional research is needed on the prevalence and the unique characteristics of intimate partner abuse in African American, Hispanic, Native American, Asian, and other important groups in order to guide practitioners on issues they may need to factor into effective assessment and treatment.

The incidence and prevalence data provided in this chapter should be of interest not just to criminologists or social scientists, but also to clinical staff. The message to clinicians from these data is that the size of the problem of violence against women is so great that victims and offenders are very likely to be found in the caseloads of any generalist clinician.

INTIMATE PARTNERS AS AGGRESSORS

The findings of the National Violence Against Women Survey and similar studies emphasize that, for women, victimization is most likely to occur in the context of an intimate relationship, not at the hands of a stranger. Historically, studies have shown that a woman is more likely to be assaulted, raped, or killed by a current or former male intimate than by any other type of assailant (Browne & Williams, 1993; Finkelhor & Yllo, 1985; Langan & Innes, 1986; Russell, 1982; Koss, 1992). The National Violence Against Women Survey found that the majority of women responding to the survey said it was an intimate partner who had raped (62%), physically assaulted (72%), or stalked (60%) them after they turned 18 years of age (Tjaden & Thoennes, 2000). In a comprehensive analysis of existing research, intimate partner violence accounted for 21% of violent crime against women compared to 2% for men (Greenfield et al., 1998).

Additionally, studies show that women are more likely to be killed by their intimate partners than by any other type of perpetrator (Kellermann & Mercy 1992; Koss et al., 1994; McGuire & Pastore, 1996) while men, on the other hand, are more likely to die at the hand of a stranger or unidentified assailant (Kellermann & Mercy, 1992; Mercy & Saltzman, 1989). The 1996 National Crime Victimization Survey revealed that three out of every four victims of intimate murder were female (Greenfield et al., 1998). Similarly, among murder victims for every age group, females are much more likely than males to have been murdered by an intimate (Cooper & Eaves, 1996). NCVS reports the following data (Bachman & Saltzman, 1995):

- Nearly 30% of female homicide victims were killed by their husbands, former husbands, or boyfriends.
- Just over 3% of male homicide victims were known to have been killed by their wives, former wives, or girlfriends.
- The rate of intimate-offender attacks on women separated from their husbands was about 3 times higher than that of divorced women and about 25 times higher than that of married women.

The fact that most acts of violence against women are carried out by intimate partners may have an impact on the type of injury sustained by the woman. The severity and repetition of violence in intimate contexts may increase because close partners have ready access to their victims, substantial time with which to commit acts of aggression, and the opportunity to inflict harm in private (Koss et al, 1994). The National Violence Against Women Survey provides evidence for this argument, as women in the study who reported being physically assaulted by an intimate partner had been assaulted an average of almost seven times. In addition, intimate offenders may engage in acts of aggravated or serious violence because they believe that sanctions, or even identification, can often be avoided (Gillespie, 1989). Collectively, these studies lend empirical credence to claims that, as a gender, women are safer on the street than in their own homes.

VIOLENCE PERPETRATED BY WOMEN: THE MYTH OF MUTUALITY

Over the years, studies measuring the incidence and prevalence of violence in intimate relationships have documented the use of aggression by both partners. In national surveys, about as many women as men report having used violence at least one time during their relationship (Straus, 1990). In addition to the documentation of violence by both men and women in general samples, clinicians know that couples often enter treatment programs with reports of both partners' use of violence. In fact, one study found that 71% of couples presenting for general marital therapy reported physical aggression in their relationships within the past year (Cascardi, Langhinrichsen, & Vivian, 1992).

These findings can be interpreted to mean that women and men are equally violent toward partners. In one very crude sense, this may be correct—if one only examines self-reported acts without controlling for frequency or severity. The Conflict Tactics Scale (CTS) (Straus & Gelles, 1979) for example, asks couples to respond to questions about specific acts of abuse as yes/no options. The scale does not probe for injury or harm caused by the acts, merely their presence. Findings from this instrument suggest equal violence by women and men. However, when more thorough assessment is made of violent acts, it is apparent that an "equality" conclusion is incorrect. Men commit assaultive acts within relationships significantly more frequently than do women (21% greater for assault and 42% greater for severe acts of abuse) (Straus, 1989). Further, men are more inclined to engage in multiple aggressive acts within the course of one incident of abuse than are women (Straus et al., 1980; Straus & Gelles, 1990). Another problem with the equality hypothesis is that national surveys do not measure the intent of the actor. They do not distinguish, for example, whether an act of pushing or hitting was in self-defense or a primary act of aggression. They also omit psychological abuse committed in conjunction with physical assault, and they ignore whether the assault was an isolated act or part of a pattern of systematic control and terror against the partner. Finally, not all national incidence surveys document the impact of the abuse on the victim; consistently, women are much more likely to sustain injury during attacks by male partners than the reverse (Stets & Straus, 1990). In a study of couples entering therapy, in 86% of cases both the husband and wife were reported to use aggression, but wives were more likely than were husbands to be negatively affected and to sustain severe injuries. Specifically, 13% of the women sustained substantial injury (e.g., broken bones or teeth or injury to sensory organs), and 34% of the husbands were classified as severely aggressive.

For clinicians, these data mean that violence reported by clients must be contextualized. The simple report by one or both parties that a woman has engaged in an act of violence does not translate into the simple belief that violence in the relationship is mutual. Mutuality of intimate partner violence is, more often than not, another confounding factor that can distort the understanding of the impact of violence on relationships. This is not to say that women are never violent; it is to say that when women commit violence, it likely has very different characteristics and outcomes and that these differences may be clinically important. Mutuality is, more often than not, a myth that is shattered by understanding the context within which the violence has occurred.

TYPES OF VIOLENCE AGAINST WOMEN

Violence against women should be understood by clinicians, not as a singular act or form of abuse, but rather as the aggregate of physically, sexually and psychologically abusive behaviors directed by one partner against another. Generally, when one form of abuse exists, it is coupled with other forms as well. Almost by definition, the infliction of physical assault also involves the infliction of fear. Likewise, sexual assault or exploitation is usually accompanied by other violent acts, and offenders' attempts to control and dominate the victims' environment are also common in cases of physical abuse. Furthermore, intimate partner violence occurs, not as spo-

> The American Psychological Association's Task Force on Male Violence Against Women defined male violence against women as "physical, visual, verbal, or sexual acts that are experienced by a woman or a girl as a threat, invasion, or assault and that have the effect of hurting her or degrading her and/or taking away her ability to control contact (intimate or otherwise) with another individual." (Koss et al., 1994, p. xvi)

radic, discrete inflictions of violence, but rather as continued exposure to multiple forms of abuse. One form of abuse is interspersed with another, giving an overall abusive quality to the relationship.

Understanding violence against women as multiple forms of abuse, not just physical assault, is important for clinicians who must address all the key experiences of a woman that impact her mental health status. For example, if a clinician approaches violence against women with an assumption that it is limited to physical assault, then the experience of psychological maltreatment, which some research suggests is most harmful to victims (e.g., Follingstad et al., 1990), will be overlooked.

Some of the most common forms of violence inflicted on women are defined in the following sections; these include physical, sexual, and emotional or psychological abuse. In addition, stalking is also discussed as a variant of intimate partner violence.

PHYSICAL VIOLENCE AND ABUSE

In the context of a client's violent intimate relationship, clinicians will be told about acts of physical assault resulting in injury or physical pain to the victim. Physical violence includes behaviors such as pushing, shoving, slapping, hitting, kicking, biting, choking, burning, the use of weapons, or other acts that result in injury or death (Crowell & Burgess, 1996). It has been estimated that between 1 in 3 and 1 in 4 women experience physical assault at the hands of an intimate at some point during their lives (Browne & Williams, 1993; Tjaden & Thoennes, 2000a). Although some studies find lower annual rates of partner violence, at least one study found annual rates of partner violence as high as 1 in 12 women (Plichta, 1996). In the Commonwealth Fund Survey, 8% of women experienced physical abuse in the year prior to the study (Plichta, 1996). The National Family Violence Survey also measured acts of severe violence against women and found that, in the year preceding the survey, more than 3 out of every 100, or 1.8 million women, were severely assaulted (defined as being punched, kicked, choked, hit with an object, beaten up, threatened with a knife or a gun, or had a knife or gun used on them) (Straus & Gelles, 1990). Physical assault has also been measured in a national study of college women, with findings that 32% of college women had experienced physical aggression from a date or other intimate partner (White & Koss, 1991). Taken together, the last two decades of national incidence and prevalence studies now provide evidence that as many as 4 million women every year in the United States will experience severe or life-threatening physical assault perpetrated by a male partner (Koss et al., 1994).

Physical assault in a relationship rarely occurs as an isolated event; it is customarily a recurrent feature of the offender's behavior and a chronic trauma for the victim (Cascardi & O'Leary, 1992; Straus, 1990). Some researchers suggest that physical abuse tends to escalate in frequency or become more severe as it continues (Walker, 1984), while others suggest that the rates evidenced early in the relationship tend to stabilize over time (Follingstad, Hause, Rutledge, & Polek, 1992). Although research shows varying patterns of violence in relationships as years progress, a reduction or tapering off of violence is least likely to occur in severely aggressive offenders (Jacobson, Gottman, Gornter, Berns, & Shortt, 1996; Quigley & Leonard, 1996).

Clinicians must also be aware that even in cases in which the physical violence ceases to occur on a regular basis, the infliction of emotional or psychological abuse may persist (Jacobson & Gottman, 1998; Jacobson et al., 1996) and serve as a constant reminder that the offender is capable of physical assault at any time. To the extent that violence is often used by offenders as a means of controlling the victim, the physical assault is no longer needed as an instrument of control, the fear associated with the threat of harm is sufficient.

SEXUAL VIOLENCE AND ABUSE

In addition to physical assault, clients will also describe acts of sexual violence involving nonconsenting sexual encounters in which they have either been pressured, coerced (explicitly or implicitly), or forced into with the partner. Sexual violence includes behaviors such as forcible penetration, vaginally, anally or orally by the offender's sexual organs, other body parts, or objects; and forced sex with other persons (Bachman & Saltzman, 1995; Russell, 1982).

The National Violence Against Women Survey found that 18% of all women reported the experience of completed or attempted rape during their lifetime, with over two thirds of those victims reporting the offender to be an intimate (Tjaden & Thoennes, 2000). Other studies have shown that the lifetime prevalence of sexual violence within intimate relationships is 9% to 14% in the general population of women (Basile, 2002; Finkelhor & Yllo, 1985; Kilpatrick et al, 1992; Russell, 1982). Rates of sexual violence against women are much higher when focusing only on relationships in which other forms of physical violence are also present. For example, 40% to 46% of battered women are reported to have suffered sexual violence by their partner (Campbell, 1989; Finkelhor & Yllo, 1985; Campbell & Soeken, 1999; Shields & Hanneke, 1983).

In the early 1980's, research began to document sexual violence occurring in marital relationships. In one early study, more than twice as many women reported being raped by husbands or ex-husbands than being raped by strangers or acquaintances (Russell, 1982), leading researchers to describe rape by a spouse as one of the forms of sexual coercion a woman is most likely to experience (Finkelhor & Yllo, 1985). Specifically, Diana Russell (1982) found that over 12% of women reported that their husband committed acts against them which would qualify legally as rape. Undoubtedly, this figure is lower than the actual incidence of marital rape; because many victims and offenders hold the belief that rape is an act committed by a stranger, and they are unwilling to label the experience of forced sexual relations with a spouse as rape.

Among the population of women who seek protective shelter from violence, marital rape incidence is found to be even higher at 59% (Shields, Resick & Hanneke, 1990). Important for clinicians is the fact that sexual violence by a spouse is often a repeated victimization, with 69% to 83% of marital rape victims in clinical (Bergen, 1996) and nonclinical (Russell, 1982) samples reporting multiple victimizations. In addition, Bergen (1995) found that spousal rape victims were raped more than 20 times by the same partner. This distinguishes intimate partner sexual assault victims from stranger rape victims (1.3 average rapes) and acquaintance rape victims (1.4 average rapes) (Russell, 1982).

While society has historically downplayed the harm resulting from rape that occurs in the context of marriage, being married to the offender does not decrease the severity of the impact of a rape. To the contrary, victims of rape by partners experience significant physical harm. For example, approximately one-third of women in a clinical sample had been sexually assaulted during pregnancy (Bergen, 1996), and numerous studies have found partner rape to be associated with increased severity and frequency of violence against the victim and an elevated risk for homicide (Campbell, 1989; Campbell & Soeken, 1999; Campbell et al., 2003). Victims of rape by spouses and boyfriends have also been reported to sustain greater physical injuries than victims of rapes committed by acquaintances (Stermac, Del Bove, & Addison, 2001). The degree of violent coercion is not linearly related to the degree of intimacy, however; although spouses and boyfriends were equally likely to use physical violence in at least one study, boyfriends used more coercion, weapons, and physical restraint during the rape than did spouses or acquaintances (Stermac et al., 2001).

The psychological impact of rape by an intimate is also substantial, and involves significant trauma both in the immediate aftermath and over the long term. Contrary to the myth, marital or intimate partner rape is not less traumatizing than being raped by a stranger; in fact intimate partner rape is equal to or more traumatizing than rape by a stranger (Kilpatrick, Best, Saunders, & Veronen, 1988; Riggs, Kilpatrick & Resick, 1992). In addition, studies comparing psychological sequelae in women experiencing only physical violence with women who have been physically battered and raped by an intimate partner find that battered and raped women display higher levels of psychological distress and symptomatology compared to women who were physically battered only (Shields & Hanneke, 1983; Shields, Resick, & Hanneke, 1990; Whatley, 1993). While higher distress levels for these women may be attributable to the fact that relationships involving both physical and sexual violence are also those in which the physical aggression is the most severe (Kilpatrick, Best, Saunders, & Veronen, 1988; Shields & Hanneke, 1983); but it is also the case that research that separates the effects of physical and sexual violence find that rape carries with it the most severe effects. As noted by the authors in one study, "These results suggest that, in the case of intimate partner violence, the severity of sexual violence may account for the bulk of subsequent PTSD symptoms. Even within the context of ongoing physical violence, the experience of sexual violence directly results in more severe PTSD" (Bennice, Resick, Mechanic, & Astin, 2003, p. 92). As will be discussed in chapter 4, it is important for clinicians to assess for the presence of sexual violence and to ensure that treatment plans focus specifically on sexual victimization.

According to researchers in one marital rape study, the victims they spoke to

> " . . . felt an overwhelming sense of shock, followed by a profound sense of despondency. They could not believe that their husbands, who were supposed to have a special regard for them, could have done something so frightening, so humiliating and so demeaning. Compounding the betrayal for many women was the realization that their husbands had no awareness of the effect of the brutal behavior" (Finkelhor & Yllo, 1985, p. 118).

> "In addition to the immediate trauma of marital rape, the victims we talked to reported serious long-term effects. Some were still experiencing them 5 or 10 years after they had divorced their husbands. They talked about an inability to trust. They talked about lingering fear and emotional pain. They talked about terrifying flashbacks and nightmares. They talked about apprehensions about men and sexual dysfunctions—problems that kept them from having a social life, or that interfered with subsequent marriages" (Finkelhor & Yllo, 1985, p. 126).

PSYCHOLOGICAL ABUSE

In the context of a client's violent intimate relationship, clinicians will hear about acts of emotional or psychological abuse. In fact, the vast majority of women who experience physical abuse by a partner are also psychologically maltreated (Follingstad et al., 1990), and physical aggression rarely occurs in the absence of psychological abuse (Henning & Klesges, 2003). In particular, men with antisocial characteristics (as measured by prior arrests for nonfamily violence, nonviolent arrests, deviant peer relations, recent substance abuse, and employment problems) are more psychologically abusive to their partners than are other men (Henning & Klesges, 2003).

"A few researchers have even suggested that learning to cope with the threat of violent victimization is a normative developmental task for females in the United States" (Gilfus, 1995, as cited in Crowell & Burgess, 1996, p. 8).

Because psychological abuse targets a victim's thoughts, feelings, and perceptions, it has the potential of profoundly impacting how a woman views her sense of self, her relationship with her partner, and her relationship to the world around her (Marshall, 1994a). Psychological abuse, through words, facial expressions, gestures, and acts of commission or ommission, can convey severely damaging messages to a woman—but because of their discreet nature, they may never be noticed or viewed as malignant by others around the woman. As noted by one author,

"Defining the nature of abuse to which the battered woman is exposed involves far more than describing simply the acts of violence or even the sequence of events that led to the acute battering. Understanding the battered woman's experience also requires understanding the meaning associated with the abusive context, whether or not, at any particular point in time, the battered woman herself is entirely aware of that meaning on a conscious level." (Dutton, 1992b, p. 6).

Psychological abuse often co-occurs with physical and sexual violence (Browne, 1987; Follingstad et al., 1990; Hart & Brassard, 1991; Sabourin et al., 1993), and the early presence of psychological abuse tends to result in physical abuse within the first few years of the relationship (Murphy & O'Leary, 1989; O'Leary, Malone, & Tyree, 1994). Specifically, psychological abuse consists of such behaviors as the following (Follingstad et al., 1990):

- ridicule, harassment, and name calling, designed to erode the woman's self-esteem and to cause her to believe that she is not worthwhile;
- isolation, designed to separate a woman from her family or other support systems and to control with whom she has contact,

- restraint, designed to prevent a woman from access to bank accounts, finances, and other resources and to thwart her independence,
- extreme jealousy or possessiveness acompanied by excessive monitoring of behavior and repeated accusations of infidelity,
- verbal threats of harm, abuse, or torture directed at the woman, the children, or other family of the woman, or the woman's friends,
- threats to abandon, leave, divorce, or initiate an affair with another woman if the victim does not comply with the wishes of the offender, and
- damage or destruction of a woman's possessions or personal property.

Psychological abuse can be thought of as an "ongoing process in which one individual systematically diminishes and destroys the inner self of another" (Loring, 1994, p. 1) and as "a process of deliberate intimidation intended to coerce the victims to do the will of the victimizer" (Jones, 1994, p. 88). These views of psychological abuse suggest that the clinician should focus, not just on the offender's conduct, but on his intent and on the adverse consequences or effects that behavior has on the mental health of the victim.

Psychological abuse is often used to instill fear and a pervasive anxiety that gives the offender greater control over the partner. When coupled with physical violence—even if they are rare episodes—the threats take on added force. In these cases, the victim's anticipatory anxiety resulting from threats can be as debilitating as the violence itself. In fact, some research suggests that psychological abuse is a better predictor of a woman's fear of subsequent violence than the severity of the earlier violence itself (Marshall, 1999), and, for some victims, threats can have a more paralyzing effect than acts of outright violence—particularly when the threats involve the victim's children or when they are punctuated with occasional violent acts. Finally, the offender's unpredictable juxtaposition of physical violence and psychological abuse with loving behaviors may increase the victim's uncertainty about herself and her perceptions (Marshall, 1994b).

Clinicians should be sensitive to a client's report of psychological abuse, not only because it may portend the concurrent or future presence of physical abuse (Stets, 1990), but also because psychological victimization can have significant impact on the mental health of the client. In fact, many of the negative effects previously attributed to physical assault may actually be byproducts of coexisting psychological abuse (Engels & Moisan, 1994; Marshall, 1994b). Self-reports from some battered women describe the psychological abuse, particularly ridicule, as the most painful form of abuse they experienced (Follingstad et al., 1990). Fear of the offender and the risk of harm to which he exposes the victim may influence a woman to remain in the violent relationship because she comes to believe that leaving the offender will increase her risk of harm (Jacobson & Gottman, 1998).

Psychological maltreatment is often used by an offender as a means of establishing control over the victim, as expressed by Herman 1992, p. 77):

"The methods of establishing control over another person are based upon the systematic, repetititve infliction of psychological trauma. They are the organized techniques of disempowerment and disconnection. Methods of psychological control are designed to instill terror and helplessness and to destroy the victim's sense of self in relation to others. Although violence is a universal method of terror, the perpetrators may use violence infrequently, as last resort. It is not necessary to use violence often to keep the victim in a constant state of fear. The threat of death or serious harm is much more frequent than the actual resort to violence.

In addition to inducing fear, the perpetrator seeks to destroy the victim's sense of autonomy. This is achieved by scrutiny and control of the victim's body and bodily functions. The perpetrator supervises what the victim eats, when she sleeps, when she goes to the toilet, what she wears. When the victim is deprived of food, sleep, or exercise, this control results in physical debilitation. But even when the victim's basic physical needs are adequately met, this assault on bodily autonomy shames and demoralizes her."

STALKING IN THE CONTEXT OF INTIMATE PARTNER VIOLENCE

Stalking, like most forms of psychological maltreatment, is intended to control the victim or inflict fear in her. It is broken out as a separate form here because it has just begun to receive empirical attention in the violence against women field. The first national study to specifically measure the prevalence of stalking found rates higher than expected - revealing a rate of 8% for women (12% when using a lower standard of fear in the definition) and 4% for men (Tjaden & Thoennes, 2000). A recent analysis of over 100 studies of stalking-related phenomena revealed an even higher prevalence rate, with 23.5% of women and 10.5% of men having experienced stalking (Spitzberg, 2002). As has been the pattern with every other form of abuse described in this chapter, most often women are stalked by someone known to them (77% of cases), with over two thirds of stalkers being current or former intimate partners (Tjaden & Thoennes, 2000). There is also evidence that intimate stalkers pose more risk than stalkers who have no current or prior relationship with the victim: in a study comparing intimate to nonintimate stalkers in a police sample, intimate stalkers were more dangerous and more likely to act on their verbalized threats to the victim (Palarea et al., 1999).

National studies show that stalking often occurs concurrently with other forms of violence against a partner (Logan, Leukefeld, & Walker, 2000; Spitzberg & Rhea, 1999; Tjaden & Thoennes, 2000). In the National Violence Against Women Survey, 81% of women who were stalked by a current or former partner were also physically assaulted by that individual and 31% also experienced sexual violence (Tjaden & Thoennes, 2000). Other studies have found that stalking is related to verbal and physical forms of abuse (Bjerregaard, 2000; Coleman, 1997) and sexual coercion (Spitzburg & Rhea, 1999). A study of severely battered women also found a link between physical assault and stalking (Mechanic et al., 2000). The National Violence Against Women Survey also documented a relationship between stalking and controlling and other emotionally abusive behavior on the part of the offender. Specifically, offenders who stalked were more likely than those who did not stalk the victim to exhibit jealousy, possessiveness and to limit the victim's contact with other people (Tjaden & Thoennes, 1998).

It also appears that the degree of dangerousness of a case may increase when stalking is present (Coleman, 1997; Meloy, 1998). In a study of femicide cases, 23.4% of the women in the study who had been murdered by a current or former partner had been stalked prior to the fatal crime (Moracco et al., 1998); and in a 10-state study of actual and attempted intimate partner femicide, a majority of victims experienced at least 1 episode of stalking in the year proceeding their death (76% of femicide and 85% of attempted femicide victims) (McFarlane et al., 1999). In addition, femicide victims in this study who were physically abused prior to the murder were also far more likely to be stalked than were non-physically abused women, again documenting the pairing of stalking and violent behavior.

Given the frequency of violent behavior on the part of stalkers, it is not surprising that stalkers often have criminal histories. Between 39% and 66% of stalkers have committed prior criminal offenses (Harmon, Rosner & Owen, 1995; Jordan, Logan, Walker, & Nigoff, 2003; Meloy, 1996; Mullen & Pathé, 1994; Mullen, Pathé, Purcell & Stewart, 1999), and protective order histories among stalkers are also common (Jordan et al., 2003; Logan, Nigoff, Walker & Jordan, 2002).

RISK AND DANGEROUSNESS FOR ADULT VICTIMS

One of the most significant challenges of clinical practice in the intimate partner violence domain is that often clients are at risk of violence and harm. Victimization is most often a chronic, repeated form of trauma, such that revictimization of a client during the course of therapy is a distinct possibility. Clients can be at risk of multiple forms of victimization that can grow in severity over time. As a result, an understanding of the factors associated with risk to a woman client is an important component of effective clinical care.

In one of the most comprehensive studies to date of risk associated with intimate partner femicide, key markers of a victim's risk were identified. These included the offender's access to a gun; previous threats with a weapon; having the offender's stepchild in the home; and physical estrangement or separation, especially from an offender with particularly controlling traits (Campbell et al., 2003). Other significant risks included stalking, forced sex, and abuse of the victim during her pregnancy. Protective factors identified within the study included the victim and offender never having lived together and the offender having been arrested before for his violence (Campbell et al., 2003).

Research has identified several other risk factors associated with physical, sexual, psychological abuse, stalking, and homicide:

Separation: An important contextual factor to consider when evaluating or assessing risk is separation. This is a key point for clinicians, as a significant percentage of women do leave violent relationships; in fact, research shows that intimate partner violence can play an important role in a woman's decision to leave (Amato & Rodgers, 1997; Kurz, 1996). Contrary to publicly held opinions about battered women, a significant percentage of women do not stay in violent relationships, as evidenced by one study that found that 38% of the women in the sample had separated within 2 years (Jacobson, Gotman, Gortner, Berns, & Shortt, 1996); and a second study in which almost two thirds (63%) of the battered women in the study had left the abuse at the time of the 2-year follow-up (Campbell, Miller, Cardwell, & Belknap, 1994).

There is evidence that the point of separation from a violent relationship poses one of the most dangerous times for a woman. Women separated from their spouses are 3 times more likely to be victimized than divorced women and 25 times more likely to be victimized than are women still married to the violent partner (Bachman & Saltzman, 1995). Studies of intimate homicides show that murder is frequently preceded by a history of physical and other domestic abuse and often involves a recent attempt at or completion of separation by the victim (Arbuckle et al., 1996; Wilson & Daly, 1993; Ellis & DeKeseredy, 1997; Sev'er, 1997; Stark & Flitcraft, 1996; Browne & Williams, 1993; Campbell, 1992). In a 10-state study of cases involving the murder of the woman, separation was identified as a risk marker for femicide (Campbell et al., 2003). In a study of intimate partner violence homicides in Ohio, more than half of the victims were killed at the point of separation (Campbell, 1992); and in a study of men incarcerated for killing their female partners, over half the murders occurred when the men were separated from their intimates (Stout, 1993). The time frame for separation is another important factor in intimate partner violence homicides, with most occurring within the first 1 to 2 months following separation (Stout, 1993; Wilson & Daly, 1993; Wallace, 1986).

A study of women in a battered women's shelter found that one-third of the victims had been physically assaulted during separation, with half of those assaults occurring within the first 10 weeks of the initial separation and most of the assaults being severe (e.g., the victims were kicked, raped, choked, stabbed, and/or shot) (Fleury, Sullivan, & Bybee, 2000). Estranged wives are also four times more likely to report that husbands raped, assaulted, or stalked them than were women living with husbands (Tjaden & Thoennes, 2000). The National Violence Against Women Survey found a higher rate of stalking after the relationship ended, with 43% of victims reporting post-relationship stalking, 21% reporting stalking during the relationship, and 36% reporting stalking during and after the pendency of the relationship (Tjaden & Thoennes, 2000). Other research shows that 46% of stalking victims are physically attacked after leaving an intimate relationship, and that 86% experience physical injury as a result (Brewster, 2000). In addition to escalated risk of continued physical assault and stalking, separation often entails ongoing psychological abuse of women (Hotton, 2001; Logan, Walker, Jordan, & Campbell, 2004).

Exposure to Parental Violence: A woman's chances of physical injury from intimate partner violence increase if her partner's father had ever been violent toward his mother; or if her father had ever been violent toward her mother (Thompson et al., 2001; Saunders, 1995).

Timing of Assault: A woman's chances of physical injury increase if the violence in her relationship began prior to marriage (Thompson et al., 2001).

Presence of Children: A woman's chances of physical injury from intimate partner violence increase if children are present at the time of the incident (Thompson et al., 2001).

Alcohol: A woman's chances of physical injury increase if the offender was drinking at the time of the assault (Thompson et al., 2001). This finding has also been reported by other researchers who found that women whose partners abused alcohol were more than 12 times as likely as women whose partners did not to incur acute injury as a result of the violence (Kyriacou et al., 1998). In cases of sexual assault, substance use by male offenders has been associated with increased both physical violence (Abbey, Clinton-Sherrod, McAuslan, Zawacki, & Buck, 2003; Ullman, Karabatsos, & Koss, 1999) and victim injury (Coker et al., 1998; Martin & Bachman, 1998).

Prior Abuse: If the same partner has previously victimized a woman, her chances of physical injury increase (Thompson et al., 2001);

Firearms and Violence Against Women

Women (and men) are more likely to be murdered with a firearm than by any other means (Kellermann & Mercy, 1992). The risk of homicide in the home by an intimate partner is 7.8% higher if a firearm is kept in the home. (Kellermann et al., 1993)

Fear of Death: Women in relationships who report fearing for their lives are also the women most likely to sustain physical injury from their partners (Thompson et al., 2001). In other words, a victim's perception of vulnerability or lack of safety as expressed through her fear often indicates an actual level of danger, and, if expressed in a counseling session, should guide clinicians to discuss protective remedies.

Emotional Abuse: A woman's chances of physical injury from intimate partner violence increase if she reported that her partner had engaged in moderate or high levels of emotional abuse against her; in other words, severe emotional or psychological abuse often occurs in tandem with physical abuse in these cases (Thompson et al., 2001).

Generalized aggression: A woman's chance of physical injury from intimate partner violence increases if the offender is violent both toward family members and toward persons outside the family (Campbell, 1986; Farr, 2002; Holtzworth-Munroe & Stuart, 1994; Saunders, 1995).

Weapons: A woman's chance of physical injury is associated with use or threatened use of a weapon (Campbell, 1986); in other words, if a woman discloses in a counseling session that her partner threatened her with a weapon, clinicians should address the potential of her elevated risk.

Forced Sex: A woman's chance of physical injury is associated in the research with having been forced by the offender to have sex (Campbell, 1986; Campbell, 2003).

Threats to kill: offenders who overtly threaten to kill a woman are also those more likely to routinely inflict physical injury on her (Campbell, 1986).

Control of the Victim's Activities: A woman's chance of physical injury is associated with an offender controlling the victim on a daily basis (Campbell, 1986).

Offender Threats of Suicide: a woman's chance of physical injury is associated with threats by the offender to commit suicide (Campbell, 1986).

Chapter 1 reviewed the literature on the incidence and prevalence of violence against women; noting that the victimization of women is common, that most often the offender is an intimate partner, and that women are more likely to be injured or killed by an intimate partner than by any other type of offender. **Chapter 1** clarified misconceptions related to the use of violence by women against their partners and described the types of violence experienced by women in the context of intimate partner violence. Readers should be able to answer the following questions following a review of **chapter 1:**

- How prevalent are crimes of violence against women?
- What should a working definition of violence against women include?
- What is the most common type of relationship between victims and offenders in cases of femicide?
- If a client discloses that she is being stalked by her partner, what are the primary clinical concerns?
- A domestic violence victim comes to your office for services a week after separating from a violent husband. What are your clinical concerns?
- What are some key risk markers for future physical assault or death of a victim?

Chapter 2

Clinical Effects Associated
With Victimization

Chapter 2 focuses on why intimate partner violence is a pressing concern for the mental health community. The chapter opens with a discussion of the prevalence of abuse within clinical caseloads, from general outpatient settings to services for women with severe mental illness. **Chapter 2** then summarizes the literature concerning the psychological effects of victimization, particularly focusing on depression, suicidality, posttraumatic stress disorder, and substance use and abuse. Physical health implications for victims and the impact on children of witnessing violence in the home are also discussed. The sections within **chapter 2** include the following:

- Victimization experiences among women in mental health populations
- Mental health effects for women victimized by intimate partner violence
- Substance use among intimate partner violence victims
- Physical health impact of victimization
- Impact of intimate partner violence on child witnesses

VICTIMIZATION EXPERIENCES AMONG WOMEN
IN MENTAL HEALTH POPULATIONS

Historically, victimization was not understood as a significant contributor to mental health problems. Research and clinical experience

Common Psychological Effects of Domestic Violence

- fear and terror
- low self-esteem
- difficulty concentrating
- difficulty with trust and intimacy
- sexual difficulties
- anxiety
- problems with memory
- cognitive confusion
- depression
- anger and irritability
- shame and embarrassment
- health concerns
- nightmares
- increased startle response and physiological arousal
- numbing and avoidance

Report of the American Psychological Association's Presidential Task Force on Violence and the Family (1996)

of the past 2 decades, however, have highlighted the mental health adversities for women victimized by crime, particularly when perpetrated by intimate partners. Even as mental health professionals have begun to develop specialized interventions for intimate partner violence, the literature has shown that crime victims are not a new population for mental health providers. Violent crime is a significant contributor to mental health problems, with as much as 10% to 20% of mental health care expenditures in the United States being attributable to crime (Cohen & Miller, 1998).

In addition to causing mental health problems, victimization is common among women with severe mental illnesses. While intimate partner violence may not cause major mental disorders, it is clear that women diagnosed with a severe mental illness (SMI) have an additional vulnerability to victimization. In a recent review of studies on physical and sexual violence against women with SMI, between 51% and 97% reported experiencing lifetime physical and sexual assault from intimate, family, or other offenders, with many of those reports including multiple acts of victimization (Goodman, Rosenberg, Mueser, & Drake, 1997). Lifetime experiences of victimization for women with SMI are so common, in fact, that one researcher (who found that 87% of the women in her study had such an experience) suggested that "victimization appears to be the norm for this sample" (Goodman et al., 2001, p. 623).

In addition to lifetime experiences of harm, clinicians must be alert to recent experiences of violence for women with SMI. In one study, for example, almost 80% of recently hospitalized women had been physically assaulted by a partner or relative in the past 12 months (Cascardi et al., 1996), and in a second study, over one third of the women reported either physical or sexual assault in the past year (Goodman et al., 2001). The findings of this study, in comparison to the National Violence Against Women Survey, mean that women with SMI are 16 times more likely to experience violent victimization than are general community samples of women (Goodman et al., 2001).

The next section summarizes research findings concerning the mental health effects of intimate partner violence victimization, particularly depression, suicidality, PTSD, and substance use and abuse. Research has documented extremely divergent patterns of intimate partner violence and differences in the reactions of victims based on those varying experiences (Follingstad, Brennan et al., 1991; Snyder & Fruchtman, 1981).

MENTAL HEALTH EFFECTS FOR WOMEN VICTIMIZED BY INTIMATE PARTNER VIOLENCE

Victims of intimate partner violence may suffer both acute and chronic mental health problems, including depression, anxiety, dissociation, cognitive impairments, and substance abuse, and in fact, most of the major non-organic forms of mental distress and disorder have been associated with the interpersonal victimization of women (Briere & Jordan, in press). Violence by a spouse or partner is as psychologically traumatizing for the victim as is stranger-perpetrated assaults (Riggs et al., 1992). Further, although even one episode of violence can inflict psychological trauma on a victim, in the areas of physical and sexual violence and stalking, abuse is often repetitive, and severity and repetition of violence are associated with greater psychological impairment (Follingstad, Brennan et al., 1991).

As discussed earlier, the specific form of abuse experienced by a victim may relate to the psychological effects she experiences. In addition to effects resulting from physical violence, for example, adverse mental health sequelae have been found in women victimized by sexual assault (Kilpatrick et al., 1997; Campbell & Soeken, 1999; Mackey et al., 1992; Kilpatrick, Resick, & Veronen, 1981). The magnitude of the impact on a victim is predicted by both objective and subjective characteristic of the sexual assault incident and can be seen in a wide range of psychological symptoms (Koss et al., 1994). Symptoms evolve over time and include anxiety, depression, sexual dysfunction, and interpersonal difficulties (Ellis, 1983; Hanson, 1990; Lurigio & Resick, 1990; Resick, 1990).

In addition to physical and sexual assault, the experience of being stalked can have profound effects on the mental health of a victim, including anxiety, depression, sleeplessness, anger, intense stress, and symptoms of trauma (Davis, Coker, & Sanderson, 2002; Pathé & Mullen, 1997; Hall, 1998; Spitzberg et al., 1998; Mechanic, 2000). Some studies report that victims compare the experience of being stalked for long periods of time to psychological terrorism. In one study of victims, 83% reported that their "personalities had changed" and that following the crime they experienced several negative feelings, including feeling paranoid, easily frightened, more aggressive, and less trusting (Hall, 1998). Although stalking may lead to physical violence, in the majority of cases, it is the fear of violence and the protracted and unpredictable nature of the victimization that appears to have the greatest effect on the victim (Davis, Coker, & Sanderson, 2002). For example, the average length of a stalking victimization has been estimated to be 24 months (Tjaden & Thoennes, 1998), and for intimate partner violence victims, the stalking often occurs both during relationship and after separation (Tjaden & Thoennes, 1998; McFarlane et al., 1999). Stalking victims may also suffer psychologically because they frequently experience multiple forms of abuse when stalked. For example, the National Violence Against Women Survey found that 81% of stalking victims were also victims of physical assault, and 31% were also sexually victimized (Tjaden & Thoennes, 2000). Among the deleterious effects of stalking is the isolation that results from a victim's chronic fear and mistrust of others (Mullen et al., 2000). This reaction may reflect the victim's attempt to reduce her level of fear or to gain control of her environment, but the negative side effect is to reduce social supports and her ability to reach out for help. As will be discussed in Chapter 4, these issues become relevant when the clinician works with the victim in safety planning.

Finally, as noted earlier, victims often report that psychological abuse has the greatest negative impact on their well being (Follingstad et al., 1990). Psychological abuse increases risk for depressive symptoms among women, even in the absence of physical violence (Migeot & Lester, 1996; Vitanza et al., 1995).

Intimate partner victimization has many complex associations with mental health problems. While research has provided much support for an association between abuse experiences and mental health problems, the exact cause—effect relationships of violence and depression, anxiety, PTSD, and other problems remain unclear. For example, victimization can occur to three individuals, but only one might develop PTSD. A second might suffer from depression, and a third might evidence no overt symptoms at all. In addition, beyond differences in specific types of problems resulting from victimization, individual differences exist in severity, duration, and resultant disruption in daily life. Post-victimization effects for any singular victim are mitigated or exacerbated by a number of factors, including the direct effects of the victimization experience and its various characteristics, historical variables and other victim-specific factors that existed prior to the victimization, and the social and cultural context in which the violence took place (Briere & Jordan, in press).

Clinicians will see the behavioral, cognitive, and emotional consequences of victimization in the lives of their clients, but it is important to avoid the temptation to pathologize victims. Some authors have expressed a justifiable concern that a focus on psychological effects or characteristics can lead to victim blaming (e.g.: Schechter, 1987), an unintended consequence clinicians are cautioned to avoid. This discussion of mental health problems cautions against excessive focus on disorder among victims; rather, it encourages sensitivity to the kinds of emotional and psychological problems that can result from victimization.

Characteristics of the individual victim are salient to how she may react to abuse. For example, prior trauma history may exacerbate psychological difficulties for women facing intimate partner violence (Dutton, 1992a; Foa, Cascardi, Zoellner, & Feeny, 2000). In addition, for a clinician to understand a client's psychological reaction to intimate violence, he or she must look beyond the specific type of abuse experienced to incorporate the woman's perception of her circumstances. In other words, a victim's perceived vulnerability to physical and psychological danger and her perceived loss of control or power may worsen the psychological effects of victimization. The influence of these perceptions is powerful and is distinguishable from those effects resulting strictly from the type of physical abuse she experienced (Smith, Tessaro, & Earp, 1995).

DEPRESSION AND SUICIDALITY

Intimate partner violence victims suffer high rates of depression. Although the causes of any mental disorder are numerous and complex, victimization poses a special risk factor for depression (Gleason, 1993). In one study, 83% of women leaving a domestic violence shelter reported depressive symptoms (Campbell, Sullivan & Davidson, 1995). Other studies with samples of women in shelters have found rates of depression ranging from 28% to 47% (Khan, 1993; Orava et al., 1996; Sato & Heiby, 1992; Surtees, 1995; West et al., 1990). Studies of women seeking treatment in health clinics and inpatient programs have also shown rates of depression, with 69% of abused women in one chart review study evidencing depression (Carmen et al., 1984). In a study using a national sample of battered women, researchers found that of the 37.5% of women who had high levels of depressive symptoms, 16.5% had experienced violence at the hands of their partner in the past year (Plichta & Weisman, 1995).

The degree of depression is significantly related to the frequency and severity of the abuse (Migeot & Lester, 1996; Vitanza et al., 1995; Cascardi & O'Leary, 1992; Follingstad et al., 1991). For example, in a study of women seeking therapeutic help from a domestic violence agency, researchers found that as the severity of abuse increased, depressive symptoms increased (Cascardi & O'Leary, 1992).

The physical and emotional effects of intimate partner violence and threat may improve once the victim is no longer in the dangerous relationship. In a study of 234 battered women, most perceived their physical and emotional health as deteriorating from the initial stages of the relationship, worsening during the time of abuse, and improving once the relationship ended (Follingstad, Brennan et al., 1991). In one study that followed abused women for over 2 years, 91% of the sample had clear patterns of decreased depression following the end of the abusive relationship (Campbell et al., 1994). Similarly, women have been found to be significantly less depressed after a stay in a domestic violence shelter (Campbell, Sullivan & Davidson, 1995).

There is also some evidence, at least among battered women exiting shelters, that those women most at risk for long-term depression can be identified early and that they can benefit from social supports as mitigators of depression (Anderson et al., 2003). Although these studies suggest that the removal of violence from the life of a woman can reduce levels of depression, clinicians must also be alert to the stressors associated with leaving a relationship that can exacerbate rates of depression in their clients. Levels of depression and PTSD in women who have separated from an abusive relationship can equal or even exceed those of women who are still involved in the violent relationship (e.g.: Herbert, Silver, & Ellard, 1991; Lerner & Kennedy, 2000). The act of separation from a relationship can bring with it multiple secondary stressors, including continued or intensified attacks from the offender; significant reduction in financial status and social support; grieving over the loss of a relationship, the strain of single parenthood; and numerous other factors. The experience of separating from a partner in the context of victimization may compound the intensity and difficulty of separation as it is experienced by women leaving non-violent relationships (Logan, Walker, Jordan & Campbell, 2004). In other words, making life-altering decisions while experiencing fear and threat to physical integrity not only increases the typical levels of stress associated with separation, it also creates an experience that is fundamentally very different. When this is the case, rather than a return to pre-trauma levels of functioning, clinicians should be prepared to address a spiral of increasingly negative changes in psychological well being for some women.

Finally, although it is clear that depression and victimization are associated, the exact nature of the relationship and the way in which depression will be manifested in any singular victim is complex and may also reflect factors such as childhood physical and sexual abuse experiences and other historical variables, concurrent exposure to other stressors, the sense of self within the relationship, and the social and cultural context in which the violence took place (Briere & Jordan, in press; Campbell et al., 1997; Carlson, McNutt, & Choi, 2003).

Intimate partner violence is also a significant risk factor for suicidal behavior among women (Abbott, Johnson, Koziol-McLain, & Lowenstein, 1995; Bergman & Brismar, 1991; Kaplan, Asnis, Lipschitz, & Chorney, 1995; Roberts, Lawrence, O'Toole, & Raphael, 1997; Stark &

Flitcraft, 1996). In a sample of women seeking help at an emergency room, those who reported prior intimate partner violence were much more likely than were women without an abuse history to have made suicide attempts (26% versus 8%) (Abbott, Johnson, Koziol-McLain, & Lowenstein, 1995). Similarly, in a study of clients in an outpatient mental health setting, physical abuse in adulthood was significantly related to increased rates for lifetime suicide attempts (Kaplan et al., 1995). Golding (1999) found a mean rate of 23.7% of battered women had attempted suicide, compared to .01%–4.3% in the general population of women (Moscicki et al., 1988). Across studies included in the review, the highest attempted suicide rates occurred among psychiatric patients and domestic violence shelter residents. Finally, in a study of African American women who had experienced interpersonal violence within the past year, several risk factors differentiated women who made suicide attempts from those who did not, including high levels of depressive symptomatology, hopelessness, drug use, and a history of childhood abuse or neglect (Thompson, Kaslow, & Kingree, 2002).

POSTTRAUMATIC STRESS REACTIONS

Research on trauma has greatly increased over the past two decades. One result of this research is that there is no simple picture of PTSD, its cause, or its treatment. Unlike most other psychiatric disorders, the criteria for PTSD include an anchor event or mental construct of a fearful event. The importance of this criterion is to place emphasis on an environmental trigger for the disorder. This attention to an external force allows the behaviors or symptoms seen in women suffering from abuse to be contextualized as a response to the trauma of the abuse experience rather than as some intrapsychic weakness on the part of the victim. Similarly, many symptoms attributed to women harmed by violence may in fact be part of a posttraumatic stress reaction rather than the manifestation of a more chronic mental disorder (Dutton, 1992c; Herman, 1992).

Specifically, clinicians may witness clients describing fear and terror, flashbacks during which prior episodes of violence are relived, marked expressions of denial and avoidance, loss of memory for aspects of the traumatic incident, constricted affect, psychic numbing, chronic anxiety and hypervigilance, difficulty sleeping, nightmares, and marked physiological reactivity (Dutton, 1992b). However, the complexity of the victimization experience brings challenges to clinicians attempting to understand a client's symptoms within the PTSD framework. First, as noted by Koss et al. (1994):

> "Providers may be particularly confused when periods of denial—an integral part of survival for most individuals faced with ongoing aggression—are interspersed with expressions of extreme fear or desperation at the dangers being faced. Recognizing the potential for at least some posttraumatic stress responses to be present in any individual exposed to physical attack, threat, or rape gives clinicians and researchers a basis from which to evaluate seemingly contradictory or inconsistent responses." (Koss et al., 1994, p. 91)

"Extreme traumatic stressors," which are included in the criterion definition of PTSD, are very characteristic of the experience of a woman victimized by violence from a partner; and stressors inflicted by a person are particularly likely to cause acute psychological distress (Davidson & Baum, 1990). The construct of posttraumatic stress is also useful with victims of intimate partner violence, because it encourages a focus on the cause of the stress (the outside coercion of a violent partner) rather than on an attributed "weakness" of the woman. In addition, this approach emphasizes that many of the current psychological experiences of the victim are normal human responses to a traumatic event, a message that can be very reassuring for victims.

Women victimized by rape, stalking, or domestic violence frequently present symptoms of PTSD (Mechanic, 2000; Pathé & Mullen, 1997; Kilpatrick & Resnick, 1993; Kilpatrick et al., 1997; Astin, Lawrence & Foy, 1993). In a study of women seeking treatment for battering, 84% were diagnosed with PTSD on the Clinician-Administered PTSD Scale (Kubany, Leisen, Kaplan, & Kelly, 2000). A recent review of multiple studies reported a mean prevalence PTSD rate of 63.8% compared to lifetime prevalence in general populations of women of 1.3% to 12.3% (Golding, 1999). A review of 11 studies documented prevalence ranging from 31% to 84% (Cascardi et al., 1999). The disparity across these studies is likely attributable to sample differences (shelter samples evidence higher rates than community samples) and assessment methods (self-report measures showed higher rates than clinician-administered scales).

As noted earlier for general mental health effects, the cognitive, psychological, and behavior responses of women who experience intimate partner violence are not singular or standardized. In fact, although some types of criminal victimization are associated with higher rates of PTSD (Kilpatrick & Resnick, 1993), generally the same list of psychological outcomes can be seen by clinicians for each of the major forms of interpersonal violence (physical, sexual, etc.). Yet, while all of these PTSD-related symptoms may be seen in a victim of intimate partner violence, any given victim is unlikely to evidence all these reactions, and studies indicate that victimized women vary considerably in the severity of their post-victimization reactions.

It is important for clinicians to identify those factors related to a client and her experience that will impact the likelihood of her suffering post trauma and other types of abuse-related reactions. Generally, research on the severity of abuse experiences considers four key factors:

- characteristics of the victim,
- severity of the trauma experience,
- characteristics of the victim's reaction to the trauma, and
- the presence of social support following the event.

As to individual characteristics, posttrauma reactions are more prevalent in women than in men (e.g.: Breslau, Davis, Andreski, & Peterson, 1991). In fact, lifetime prevalence of PTSD for women was twice that for men in a major epidemiological study, the National Comorbidity Study (Kessler, Sonnega, Bromet, Hughes, & Nelson, 1995). Research has also suggested that the actual susceptibility to PTSD may be related to genetic and other preexisting factors (Shalev, 1996; True & Pitman, 1999). Hence, certain people may carry higher risk factors for developing PTSD following an abusive event; however, these individuals might never have developed any mental health problems in the absence of an abusive experience (Shalev, 1996). A history of exposure to trauma may also predict how a victim experiences the current trauma (Kilpatrick, Resnick, Saunders, & Best, 1998). Generally speaking, greater severity of PTSD symptoms are likely in individuals who have a prior trauma experience (Ozer, Best, Lipsey, & Weiss, 2003). As a result, a woman experiencing intimate partner violence who presents with psychological symptoms may be suffering not only from the current events, but also from earlier victimization experiences that have their own negative effects. The effects of these different incidents may be additive (i.e., the woman's current symptomatic state may reflect historic but continuing symptoms, plus those symptoms arising from a current assault), or may be interactive (i.e., effects of the earlier trauma may magnify the impacts of the latter trauma, or the latter trauma may trigger a resurgence of symptoms from the earlier assault) (Briere & Spinazzola, in press).

A history of psychological problems, including depression, may also complicate a woman's recovery from violence. Prior adjustment problems are associated with higher PTSD symptoms following trauma (Ozer, Best, Lipsey, & Weiss, 2003). Family psychiatric history, intelligence, childhood adversity, and trauma are also individual characteristics that impact how a person responds to trauma (Brewin, Andrews, & Valentine, 2000).

As to the severity of the trauma, the likelihood of developing PTSD following a traumatic event appears to increase when the victim experiences the stressors under conditions of perceived life threat, injury, substantial force, extreme fear or terror, and a sense of helplessness at the time of the traumatic event (Davidson & Foa, 1993; Herman, 1992; Ozer, Best, Lipsey, & Weiss, 2003; Resnick, Kilpatrick, Dansky, Saunders, & Best, 1993). In an analysis of 12 studies of cases where the victims perceived that their life was in danger during the traumatic episode, perceived life threat was a more robust predictor of PTSD for interpersonal violence victims than for combat veterans (Ozer et al., 2003). In addition, among severely battered women, the severity and recency of violence and verbal abuse have been found to be related to PTSD (Dutton, 1992c; Houskamp & Foy, 1991; Saunders, 1994). Trauma characterized by unpredictability or a victim's lack of control—perhaps because they violate expectations of a safe environment—are also believed to increase vulnerability to PTSD (Foa et al., 1992).

Third, a woman's reactions at the time of the traumatic event (peritraumatic reactions) may be important predictors of later symptoms of PTSD. Extreme anxiety, fear, horror, panic, and/or negative emotional reactions (e.g., helplessness, guilt, and shame) have been suggested as important predictors of the likelihood of experiencing PTSD (Bernat, Ronfeldt, Calhoun, & Arias, 1998). In addition to peritraumatic emotional responses, individuals who have dissociative experiences during or immediately after the traumatic event tend to have appreciably higher levels of PTSD symptoms (Ozer et al.,

2003). Although peritraumatic reactions will be an important assessment item, clinicians should be cautious not to interpret a woman's severe reactivity to a trauma experience as an affect-regulation problem or characterologic hyperresponsiveness, when, in fact, that response may well be an interaction between prior trauma exposure and current victimization experiences (Briere & Spinazzola, in press).

Finally, more recent reviews of posttrauma research have begun to focus on the degree of support experienced by a victim following exposure to trauma. In general, individuals who report lower levels of perceived social support after the traumatic event report higher levels of PTSD (Ozer et al., 2003). Isolation from family, friends, and support systems has been identified as a specific form of psychological abuse experienced by the majority of victims of intimate partner violence (Follingstad et al., 1990). Therefore, clinicians should assess the degree of social support and formal or informal support system that are available to clients and that can be incorporated into treatment planning.

Although posttrauma reactions in victims of intimate partner violence are common, use of a PTSD diagnosis for intimate partner violence cases is not without challenge. The diagnosis of posttraumatic stress disorder emphasizes a discrete traumatic event and symptoms that follow. Prolonged and repeated traumas, by the very nature of their chronicity, may have unique long-term effects and have been described with terms such as *complex PTSD* or *complicated PTSD* (Herman, 1992). Not only is the nature of intimate partner violence chronic and ongoing, the threat of further traumatization is realistic. As a result, trauma-related behaviors seen by clinicians may be normalized reactions to chronic exposure to threat and the anticipation of future trauma, not just a reaction to a prior event (Dutton, 1992b; Foa, Cascardi, Zoellner, & Feeny, 2000). Put another way, victims may show clinical symptoms in a realistic anticipation of future trauma, not just as a reaction to a prior victimization (Dutton, 1992b).

Further, a diagnosis of PTSD does not automatically inform clinicians of treatment implications. For example, in one study, 81% of the battered women and almost 63% of the women experiencing only verbal abuse met diagnostic criteria for PTSD (Kemp, Green, Hovanitz, & Rawlings, 1995). These very different abuse experiences resulted in the same diagnosis but called for different treatment approaches.

In sum, part of the complexity of postvictimization responses in women suffering violence arises from the equivalent complexity of interpersonal violence (i.e., it comes in different forms, with differing levels of predictability and with differing levels of severity and frequency). It is generally not enough for a clinician to know that a woman was raped or battered when assessing the etiology of a mental health problem; it is also important to ascertain the frequency, severity, duration, and other characteristics of her experience(s), and whether other forms of victimization also occurred. This fact emphasizes the need for thorough assessment by clinicians, as discussed in later chapters.

ANXIETY AND OTHER FEAR-RELATED EFFECTS

In the same way that depression has been found to have a higher prevalence in battered women compared to the general population of women, studies also find comparatively higher rates of anxiety (Gleason, 1993). Numerous studies have also documented heightened anxiety in women victimized by intimate partner violence (Folingstad et al., 1991; Kemp, Green, Hovanitz, & Rawlings, 1995).

SUBSTANCE USE AMONG VICTIMS OF INTIMATE PARTNER VIOLENCE

In addition to the mental health effects of victimization, clinicians will see a complex relationship between the abuse experienced by their clients and the use of substances. While studies have for some time identified a relationship between offending behavior and substance abuse (Leonard & Quigley, 1999; Maiden, 1997; Roizen, 1997), studies also now suggest a significant association between victimization and substance use (Arellano, 1996; Kilpatrick et al., 1997; Kilpatrick et al., 2000). As mentioned above in discussing mental health problems among victims, there are cautions about exploring substance abuse among victims to avoid blaming victims for their exposure to abuse. Lifestyle choices, cyclical patterns of abuse experiences and victimization and related associations should be understood as behaviorally related but not causal: in other words, a woman's behavior or lifestyle choice does not cause her victimization. It is important, however, to examine substance use as a contributing factor for victimization and as a concern for clinical treatment approaches for persons with victimization. For example, one study found from a sample of women from community health clinics that 46.3% of women reporting partner violence also reported current drug or alcohol abuse compared to 15.3% of women not reporting intimate partner violence experiences (McCauley et al., 1995). In that victimization and substance use often co-occur in the life of a woman, they should be comprehensively addressed in treatment.

Women typically have lower rates of alcohol and drug abuse than do men (Robins & Regier, 1991). For example, lifetime prevalence of alcohol abuse or dependence is estimated at 23.8% of men and 4.6% of women (Robins & Regier, 1991). Similarly, data from the National Comorbidity Survey showed that a women's lifetime prevalence of alcohol abuse is 6.3%, and drug abuse is 3.5% (Kessler et al., 1994; Kessler et al., 1995). Prevalence rates among women suffering intimate partner violence, however, appear to be much higher. For example, in one study, 51% of the battered women, compared to 28% of the control group of women, were high consumers of alcohol (Bergman et al., 1987), and in a second study, women in abusive relationships were significantly more likely than were women in nonabusive relationships to abuse alcohol (Barnett & Fagan, 1993). Similarly, alcohol consumption rates have been estimated to be about five times greater among victims of intimate partner violence than among the general population of women (Grant et al., 1994; Robins & Regier, 1991). In addition to showing the prevalence of substance use among victim populations, research has also examined rates of victimization history among substance abusing women. Prevalence rates for intimate partner violence experiences among clinical samples of substance-using women range from 41% to 80% of women (Bennett & Lawson, 1994; Dansky, Saladin, Brady, & Kilpatrick, 1995; Miller & Downs, 1993). In addition, it appears that women entering treatment for drug abuse problems have high rates of physical and sexual abuse experiences (Covington, 1997; Dunn et al., 1994; Gil-Rivas et al., 1996; Miller & Downs, 1993).

Not only are substance use and victimization frequently associated, when they do coexist, substance use often changes the nature of the victimization experience. For example, some research suggests that substance using offenders use weapons more often than do nondrinking offenders, and victims of substance using offenders are more likely than other victims to be injured (Brecklin, 2002). The association of drinking on the part of the offender and more severe injury to the victim has been found in numerous studies (Martin & Bachman, 1997; Pernanen, 1991). In addition, in a study of intimate partner violence cases ending in homicide of the woman, drug abuse on the part of the offender was "associated with patterns of intimate partner abuse that increase femicide risk" (Campbell et al., 2003, pg. 7).

Substance abuse patterns and victimization may be related in complex and interactive ways. First, women with substance use problems may be more vulnerable to victimization than nonsubstance abusing women because they suffer an impaired ability to detect predatory assailants or because of increased exposure to potential offenders because of lifestyles associated with substance use (Acierno et al., 1999; Testa & Livingston, 2000). Illegal and legal drugs may be used in situations that carry their own independent risks for harm, such as bars or drug exchange situations. In other words, independent of the chemical properties of the substances, the proximity to drug-taking culture means an increased risk of harm (Cohen & Felson, 1979; Hindelang, Gottfredson, & Garofalo, 1978). Second, evidence exists that alcohol has a negative effect on judgment (Norris, Nurius, & Dimeff, 1996; Peterson, Rothfleisch, Zelazo, & Pihl, 1990; Testa & Parks, 1996), and as a result, substance use can impair decision-making, which may increase a woman's vulnerability to revictimization. In addition, alcohol use can impair inhibition or increase impulsive behavior (Fillmore & Vogel-Sprott, 1999; Fillmore Dixon, & Schweizer, 2000) such that a woman who is intoxicated may downplay the risks in a specific situation or be more likely to make impulsive decisions that increase her vulnerability to victimization. It is also the case that certain types of offenders may target substance-abusing women due to their perceived increased vulnerability (Kilpatrick et al., 1997). It is important to note that the substance use—victimization relationship may not be the same for alcohol as for drugs. In at least one study examining whether victimization led to assault, the association was supported for drug use but not for exclusive alcohol abuse (Kilpatrick et al., 1997).

A second key interaction between victimization and substance use is that women may use substances to self-medicate for the physical and emotional pain they experience from the victimization (Beckham et al., 1998; Khantzian, 1990, 1997; McCormick & Smith, 1995; Wills & Filer, 1996; Wills & Hirky, 1996). This phenomenon has been called chemical avoidance (Briere, 1989) and describes the relieving effect substances can have in removing the negative emotions that often accompany or follow a victimization experience. Substance abuse has serious negative consequences for women even if, in the short term, it helps to relieve physical and emotional pain. Notably, in that the probability of a behavior's reoccurring is increased if it alleviates an aversive situation, the frequency of substance use behaviors are expected to increase if they are effective in diminishing the painful effects of victimization (Kilpatrick et al., 1997).

In addition to associations with repeat victimization, the coping strategy of substance abuse can contribute to mental health problems, increasing the need to use substances to reduce the mental health problems, and thereby creating yet another type of vicious cycle (Kushner, Abrams, & Borchardt, 2000; Newcomb, Vargas-Carmona, & Galaif, 1999; Swendsen & Merikangas, 2000). For example, as was discussed, PTSD often results from victimization experiences, and the experience of posttrauma symptoms has been shown to be associated with the increased risk of substance abuse (Breslau, Davis, Peterson, & Schultz, 1997; Chilcoat & Breslau, 1998; Epstein, Saunders, Kilpatrick, & Resnick, 1998; Stewart, 1996). Similarly, a review of data from a national probability sample of adult women found that experiencing a crime increased the risk of developing alcohol problems, and PTSD was an additional major risk factor for alcohol problems within the victimized groups (Kilpatrick & Resnick, 1993). Thus, women who experience victimization and who develop PTSD may be at greater risk for developing alcohol problems. Further, in an analysis of multiple factors including interpersonal trauma (adult violence and childhood sexual abuse), substance abuse, and mother's alcohol use, each of these three experiences predicted the severity of a woman's later alcohol use (Clark & Foy, 2000). These studies illuminate the complexity of issues facing clinicians who work with victims, and these findings must be incorporated into assessment and treatment if these programs are to be effective and safe.

PHYSICAL HEALTH IMPACT OF INTIMATE PARTNER VIOLENCE

Intimate partner violence is directly linked to a number of negative physical health consequences for women, the most obvious being

Women suffering intimate partner violence often attribute physical health problems to the physical and psychological abuse they suffer at the hands of their partners (Eby et al., 1995).

that the physical infliction of violence can be a "direct pathway" to acute injuries on the part of a woman (Coker et al., 2000). In the National Violence Against Women Survey, women physically assaulted by an intimate had been assaulted an average of almost 7 times, and approximately 1 in 3 women sexually and/or physically assaulted since age 18 reported being physically injured during their most recent assault (Tjaden & Thoennes, 2000). In a hospital emergency room study, more than one third of women seeking emergency medical care for violence-related injuries had been injured by a current or former spouse (Rand & Strom, 1997). Not surprisingly, as a result, common locations for injuries among battered women are the face, neck, upper torso, breast, or abdomen (Campbell et al., 2002), a fact that should encourage clinicians to assess for the presence of intimate partner violence when these injuries are visible. While these types of injuries are common, however, studies which have attempted to discern a certain "pattern" of injury in victims of intimate partner violence have not been successful, a finding leading to a recommendation for universal screening for intimate partner violence in health care settings (Plichta, in press).

In addition to the short-term consequences of acute injury, women also suffer chronic effects from being victimized by intimate partner violence, including pain or discomfort from headaches, back pain, fainting, seizures or related central nervous system complaints (Campbell et al., 2002; Coker et al, 2000; Diaz-Olavarreita, Campbell, Garcia de la Cadena, Paz, & Villa, 1999; Leserman, Li, Drossman, & Hu, 1998; Plichta, 1996). Chronic pain, miscarriage, irritable-bowel syndrome, and psychosomatic and somatic complaints have also been associated with victimization (Coben et al., 1999; Dutton et al., 1997). The likelihood of closed head injury for victims has not been adequately researched, but there is some evidence suggesting a risk of this type of injury, as well as postconcussional symptoms such as headache, fatigue, dizziness, insomnia, difficulty concentrating, and memory problems (Slagle, 1990). Victims of intimate partner violence are more likely than other women to have gynecological symptoms, including sexually transmitted diseases, vaginal bleeding or infection, fibroids, pelvis pain, and urinary tract infections (Campbell et al., 2002; Coker et al., 2000; Leserman et al., 1998; Letourneau, Holmes, & Chasendunn-Roark, 1999; Plichta, 1996). Although many of the acute and chronic health problems noted above result from the infliction of physical injury on a woman, intimate partner violence can also harm a woman's health due to the associated psychological maltreatment she experiences. Through this more indirect pathway of psychological abuse and chronic stress, other symptoms and illnesses evidenced in women include; hypertension; functional gastrointestinal disorders and appetite loss, viral infections, and cardiac problems (Coker et al., 2000; Leserman et al., 1998).

Finally, abuse of many women does not cease even during pregnancy; and profound health consequences are the result (Gazmararian et al., 1996; Helton, McFarlane, & Anderson, 1987; McFarlane, Parker, Soeken, & Bullock, 1992; Plichta, 1996). Abused pregnant women are more likely to use substances and less likely to obtain prenatal care than are nonabused women (Plichta, in press). Low birth weight has been associated with violence before and during pregnancy (McFarlane, Parker, & Soeken, 1996), and miscarriage and spontaneous abortion have also been found in abused pregnant women (McFarlane et al., 1992). Women who suffer abuse during pregnancy are at increased risk of homicide (McFarlane, Parker & Soeken, 1995); in fact, homicide is the leading cause of mortality in women in the immediate pre- and postdelivery time period (Dannenberg et al., 1995; Fildes, Reed, Jones, Martin & Barrett, 1992). Similarly, physical abuse during pregnancy is associated with a victim's experiencing more severe abuse in general from her partner (Campbell, 1995).

The acute and chronic impact of intimate partner violence often results in increased health-care utilization by victims. Research suggests that victims see primary-care physicians, specialists, and emergency room physicians more frequently than do nonvictims (Kendall-Tackett, 2003), an increase that does not occur prior to the onset of violence, and that includes visits for more than just treatment of abuse-related injuries (Kimerling & Calhoun, 1994).

IMPACT OF INTIMATE PARTNER VIOLENCE ON CHILD WITNESSES

Historically, children have been the "forgotten victims" of intimate partner violence, based on the mistaken belief that children can

I couldn't lift the baby up or anything. She would cry, and I would feel so bad because I couldn't pick her up, and I couldn't feed her . . . because I couldn't move my arm."

Quote from a battered woman as reported in Hilton (1992, p. 80)

somehow escape direct exposure to the violence and its effects. In reality, however, national surveys find that 11%–20% of adults report witnessing violent partner incidents (Henning et al., 1996; Straus & Smith, 1990), and at least 3.3 million American children between the ages of 3 and 17 years are exposed to marital violence each year (Carlson, 1984).

More recent estimates have reached much higher, including estimates based on the National Family Violence Survey's projection that 10 million American children have been exposed to intimate partner violence (Straus, 1992), and a survey of undergraduate college students showing that 17.8 million children were exposed to intimate partner violence during their childhoods (Silvern et al., 1995). In addition, 50% of men who frequently assault wives also assault their children (Suh & Abel, 1990; Bowker, Arbitell & McFerron, 1988), and when considering cases in which police responded to a domestic disturbance call, children were directly involved 9%–27% of the time (Fantuzzo, et al., 1997). Intimate partner violence has been shown to occur disproportionately in homes with children under the age of 5 years (Taylor, 1994). In addition to incidence, studies show that children who witness intimate partner violence are most often exposed to multiple occurrences. Studies with adults who recall witnessing intimate partner violence during their childhoods are aware of an average of 9 instances (Straus, 1992). (While studies show that multiple incident exposure is most commonly reported by children, it is likely that adults who report retrospectively about their childhoods are more likely to remember violence if it occurred multiple times.)

Children's exposure to intimate partner violence includes cases in which children witness adult violence, cases in which they are also targeted for abuse, and cases where a child is injured by stepping in to protect a victimized parent. Studies find a relationship between witnessing and experiencing violence in the home (Litrownik, Newton, Hunter, English, & Everson, 2003), with the overlap between violence against adults and the physical or sexual abuse of children in the home reaching 30%–70% of cases (Suh & Abel, 1990; Bowker, Arbitell & McFerron, 1988). There is also substantial evidence from shelter samples that intimate partner violence often co-occurs with child abuse (Appel & Holden, 1998; Jouriles & Norwood, 1995; Moore & Pepler, 1998; O'Keefe, 1995). In one study, children were not only witnesses to violence in the home, 45% of women in the study reported that children were often the focus of the argument that preceded the act of violence against them (Hilton, 1992). Adolescents in homes with intimate partner violence are also at heightened risk for physical abuse compared to adolescents in nonviolent homes (Tajima, 2002). Abuse of the mother usually precedes violence against the child, and a positive correlation exists between the severity of abuse directed at spouses and children (Bowker et al., 1988; Stark & Flitcraft, 1988).

The effects of intimate partner violence on a child witness are manifested in emotional, behavioral, cognitive, and physical spheres of the child's life (Edleson, 1999; Graham-Bermann & Levendosky, 1998). Some children withdraw and show internalized behavioral and emotional difficulties, such as somatic disorders, insomnia, heightened anxiety, depression, guilt, and damaged self-esteem (Graham-Bermann, 1998; Hughes & Graham-Bermann, 1998; Jaffe, Wolfe, & Wilson, 1990; Hughes, 1988; Pynoos & Eth, 1984). In a study examining the effects of intimate partner violence on preschoolers' intellectual functioning, researchers found that child witnesses had significantly poorer verbal abilities than did nonwitnesses (Huth-Bocks, Levendosky, & Semel, 2001). Children's reactions to witnessing domestic abuse may also be aggressive in nature: for example, child may model the offender and act out with parents, siblings, peers or other social relationships (Hughes & Graham-Bermann, 1998; Margolin, 1998; Straus, Gelles, & Steinmetz, 1980). When the attention of both adults in the home is focused on intimate partner conflict and violence, children may also be neglected and at risk for developing psychological adjustment problems (Straus et al., 1980). Studies show that, on the average, approximately 35–45% of children who witness violence in the home score in the clinical problem range on standardized measures of psychopathology (Hughes, 1997). Children who both witness adult violence and are themselves physically abused show higher levels of distress (Hughes, Parkinson, & Vargo, 1989) and exhibit more behavioral problems (O'Keefe, 1995) than do children without violent exposure or only one type of violent experience. When child witnesses are compared to children experiencing direct maltreatment, in fact, each type of abuse experience has been found to produce unique negative outcomes for the children involved (Edleson, 1999). Adding to the complexity is that children not only experience different forms of violence concurrently, as noted, they also experience multiple episodes of traumatic incidents (Saunders, 2003).

Posttrauma symptoms are often seen in child witnesses of violence, in large part due to the overstimulation and terror to which they are routinely exposed (Silvern & Kaersvange, 1989). In fact, numerous studies now document posttraumatic stress in child witnesses to intimate partner violence (Kilpatrick & Williams, 1997; Lehmann, 1997; Mertin & Mohr, 2002). In a study of children whose mothers had been residents in a woman's shelter, distressing thoughts, conscious avoidance, hypervigilance, and sleep difficulties were the most common experiences, with 20% of the children meeting the criteria for a diagnosis of posttraumatic stress disorder (Mertin & Mohr, 2002).

Clinicians working with children from homes where there is intimate partner violence should conduct a comprehensive assessment of the child. Before the impact of the child's experiences can be understood, the clinician must know if children saw violent behavior (incidents) and how often they saw it (chronicity); also, the clinician needs to know details of violent incidents the children saw (severity), and who was responsible for the incidents. These reports can come in part from nonoffending parents, but studies suggest that mother and child reports of whether the child was witness to the violence are not always consistent; in other words, parents may not always understand what their children see, hear, or understand (Jouriles, Mehta, McDonald, & Francis, 1997; Sternberg et al., 1993). Assessment should include the levels of exposure to different types of violence (e.g., the witnessing of intimate partner violence and of physical abuse of a child), as studies show that these different experiences can predict subsequent aggressive and anxious/depressed problem behaviors in children (Litrownik, et al., 2003). Specifically, child psychological and physical victimization predicts aggressive behavior, whereas only psychological victimization and witnessing adult violence has been found to predict anxious and depressed behavior in children (Litrownik et al., 2003). In addition, understanding the different types of violence experienced is important, as the impact on a child may be caused by just one form of the abuse experienced or it may result from the cumulative or compounded effects of being exposed to multiple forms of abuse.

The severity of violence witnessed should also be assessed, as research suggests that child witnesses encounter serious levels of abuse. For example, one third of women in a study who reported witnessing intimate partner violence as a child had seen fathers kick, bite, hit with fists; 6% had seen mothers "beat up," 3% had witnessed choking and threats with weapons; and 1% had seen use of knives or guns (Henning et al., 1996). Most children in shelters have witnessed acts of severe violence (Hilton, 1992; Holden & Ritchie, 1991), and in a study of sheltered women who had been raped by a partner, 18% reported that their children had witnessed that violent act (Campbell & Alford, 1989).

Finally, clinicians should assess for the presence of risk factors associated with abuse to the child, and protective factors available in the child's environment that can mitigate the impact of the abuse experience. The presence of young caregivers, low education level or income, and lack of a social support network for the victim compound the risk for child maltreatment associated with intimate partner violence (Cox, Kotch, & Everson, 2003). Protective factors associated with child witnesses overcoming the adversity include parental competence (Graham-Bermann & Levendosky, 1998); the mother's mental health (Hughes & Luke, 1998; Jaffe, Wolfe, & Wilson, 1990); and the presence of social supports (Hughes, Graham-Bermann, & Gruber, 2001).

Chapter 2 discussed the prevalence of abuse in clinical caseloads and summarized the mental health effects of intimate partner violence, focusing on depression and suicidality, posttrauma reactions, anxiety and other mental health problems, and substance abuse. The physical health effects of victimization were also discussed, as was the impact of intimate partner violence on child witnesses. Readers should be able to answer the following questions following a review of **chapter 2:**

• What are the characteristics of intimate partner violence most likely to be associated with posttrauma reactions?

- What are the characteristics of stalking victimization that are likely to be associated with negative mental health effects?
- What is the relationship between victimization and substance abuse?
- What areas of assessment should be addressed when interviewing a child who has witnessed intimate partner violence?

Chapter 3

Clinical Characteristics of Intimate Partner Violence Offenders

Chapter 3 reviews clinical characteristics of intimate partner violence offenders and provides information about general types of offending behavior. While research has begun to identify types of offenders, the clinical value of typologies still appears to be limited. However, understanding the major patterns of offending can help clinicians assess and treat clients with offender behaviors. **Chapter 3** provides an overview of key clinical characteristics of offenders; including personality disorders, substance abuse, depression, and other disorders. The sections within **chapter 3** include the following:

- Typologies of intimate partner violence offenders
- Mental health, substance abuse, and other clinical characteristics of intimate partner violence offenders

TYPOLOGIES OF INTIMATE PARTNER VIOLENCE OFFENDERS

Historically, attempts to understand the characteristics of offenders of intimate partner violence have relied on comparisons of maritally violent versus nonviolent men, an approach that suggests that the batterers are a homogeneous group. Instead, it is now clear from research and clinical practice that intimate partner offenders are heterogeneous and have varying patterns and motivations for violence, as well as varied personality and psychological traits.

As a way of promoting better understanding of violent and abusive behavior, research has suggested typologies of intimate partner violence offenders. Part of the impetus for this research has been to rectify earlier misunderstandings of intimate partner violence as merely a communication disorder among partners in a relationship. Although typologies have been developed in part with a belief that they lead to more appropriate treatment (Huss & Langhinrichsen-Rohling, 2000), existing typologies may actually be more helpful as guides to patterns of abuse and offender traits associated with those patterns rather than as profiles that can be applied to specific cases. There are few offenders who fit entirely into one classification since most offenders have complex histories and complex patterns of violence that include multiple forms of abuse. As with diagnostic classifications, these types have uncertain boundaries, and, with the exception of the offenders with antisocial personalities, it may be that little is gained by trying to apply these in a diagnostic sense. The typologies can, however, help clinicians understand the scope and pattern of abusive behavior that offenders can exhibit. In addition, the listing of traits associated with these types can prompt clinicians to explore more behaviors when clients give partial evidence of intimate partner violence perpetration.

Many typologies of batterers differentiate offender types along three dimensions: (1) frequency and severity of violence, (2) victimization targets—that is, family only or people in general, and (3) psychopathology status. In regard to the first dimension, while frequency and severity of violence are two distinct behaviors, they have generally been considered together in typologies and are believed to be positively correlated (Holtzworth-Munroe & Stuart, 1994). In other words, offenders who inflict the most serious injuries are also more likely to commit abuse frequently, and more frequent abusers are more likely to inflict serious injury. In assessment, evidence of severe injury or very frequent acts of violence should suggest to a clinician that the other characteristic needs assessment as well.

Second, the types of targeted victims can be important in distinguishing different offender types. This criterion differentiates between offenders whose violence is directed generally to others, including strangers and acquaintances, or to family members only (Holtzworth-Munroe & Stuart, 1994; Saunders, 1992). Researchers note that offenders who are more generally violent have been found to engage in more severe violence than do family-only offenders (Holtzworth-Munroe & Stuart, 1994). Hence, clients who appear to be more generally violent should be assessed for severity and frequency of violent acts.

Third, as will be discussed in the following section, the existence of psychopathology or personality disorders (specifically including antisocial personality disorder, posttraumatic stress, and borderline personality organization) has been documented in battering men (Hamberger & Hastings, 1991; Saunders, 1992). Personality disorders and psychopathology are thought to be common among domestic violence offenders, with one study reporting that only 12 out of 99 men in a court-ordered treatment program showed no evidence of either personality disorder or other psychopathy (Hamberger & Hastings, 1986). Huss and Langhinrichsen-Rohling (2000) have proposed that psychopaths represent a significant subgroup of batterers who respond uniquely to punishment and treatment. These authors also suggest that psychopathic batterers inflict the most severe and most frequent physical and emotional abuse against their partners.

OFFENDER SUB-TYPES

Holtzworth-Munroe and Stuart (1994) conducted a review of existing typologies in the literature and developed a model using the three dimensions just described to identify subtypes of batterers: family only, generally violent/antisocial, and dysphoric/borderline:

Family-Only Batterers

Family-only batterers are believed to engage in the least severe violence against their partners and may be the least likely to engage in systematic psychological abuse or sexual violence. Violence committed by this subtype of batterers is generally targeted at members of the offender's family, not at persons outside, a factor that may result in less experience or contact with the criminal justice system. Family-only batterers appear to evidence little psychopathology and

Holtzworth-Munroe & Stuart Offender Typology

1. Family-only offenders;
2. Dysphoric-borderline offenders
3. Generally violent antisocial offenders (Holtzworth-Munroe & Stuart, 1994)

either no personality disorder or a passive-dependent personality disorder. If all battering men are considered (both those from the community and those from treatment groups) Holtzworth-Munroe and Stuart hypothesize that this subtype likely constitutes up to 50% of violent partners.

Generally Violent/Antisocial Batterers

Generally violent/antisocial batterers engage in moderate to severe violence against their partners, including both psychological abuse and sexual violence. Offenders in this subtype engage in the most extrafamilial aggression and have the most extensive history of criminal conduct and related court involvement. Generally, violent/antisocial batterers are likely to have problems with alcohol and drug abuse, and they are the most likely to have an antisocial personality disorder or psychopathy. Holtzworth-Munroe and Stuart hypothesize that this subtype likely constitutes up to 25% of violent partners. This type of offender trait is very different from the emotionally unstable, borderline-like offenders who lose control of their emotions. Antisocials in this classification use violence purposefully in order to dominate and get their way. Their violence is poorly explained by any hypothesis other than their perceived needs for dominance over others.

Dysphoric/Borderline Batterers

Dysphoric/borderline batterers engage in violence that can range from moderate to severe. Their violence against their partners can also include both psychological abuse and sexual violence. While the violence committed by this subtype is primarily targeted at family members, some extrafamilial violence and criminal conduct may also be exhibited. Dysphoric/borderline batterers are the most psychologically distressed and emotionally volatile of the three subtypes, evidencing borderline and schizoidal personality characteristics. These batterers may also have problems with alcohol and drug abuse. It is estimated that this subgroup constitutes approximately 25% of batterer samples. The dysphoric offender is a likely candidate for admission to mental health clinics and substance abuse programs due to their evident emotional problems. As with other clients with poor emotion regulation, they may explain or rationalize their behavior as a result of extreme emotion rather than harmful intent. They may also try to explain their violence as a product of alcohol or drugs and may express remorse when threatened with loss of the relationship.

While this conceptualization of offender types has been widely disseminated, its predictive validity remains uncertain. Holtzworth-Munroe and colleagues (2003) studied the typologies in their sample for 1.5 and 3 years to observe the stability of the types over time. One of the questions to be resolved by the follow-up study was to ascertain whether the less severe group, the family-only violent men, was simply earlier in their development toward violence. In other words, the types might represent phases on a temporal continuum rather than stable types related to overall character or disorder among the men. However, this study supported the idea that the three major types are relatively stable over time, suggesting that those who present with higher levels of violence (borderlines and generally violent males) remain more violent over time than family-only violent males (Holtzworth-Munroe, et al., 2003). Findings relating to the persistence of antisocial traits are consistent with research on childhood conduct disorder and its prediction of adult abusive behavior and substance abuse (Magdol, Moffitt, Caspi & Silva, 1998). Also among the findings was support for the addition of a low level antisocial type (Holtzworth-Munroe, et al., 2003).

MENTAL HEALTH, SUBSTANCE ABUSE AND OTHER CLINICAL CHARACTERISTICS OF INTIMATE PARTNER VIOLENCE OFFENDERS

Male intimate partner violence offenders have been assessed in comparison to nonviolent males to examine differences in clinical characteristics and prevalence of mental disorders. While research has found conflicting evidence about the severity of mental disorders among offenders, there is a consensus in the literature about a greater likelihood of mood disorders, substance abuse, and personality disorders among offenders than among nonviolent males. Also, while research has generally supported the idea that offenders have more mental health and substance abuse problems than nonviolent males, there is little support for the idea that mental disorders or substance abuse directly cause intimate partner violence. Rather, these conditions may be seen as risk factors that contribute to violence in complex ways. Some researchers have found "less" pathology among batterers than was expected (Gondolf, 1999). However, Gondolf's (1999) findings of 25% of the 840 batterers in his study having "severe" mental disorder and 39% having narcissistic or antisocial tendencies suggests a high rate of emotional problems among intimate partner violence offenders. In the 1999 study, Gondolf compared batterers to the clinical population used to norm the Millon Clinical Multiaxial Inventory I-III (MCMI-III) and to a clinical population of substance abusers. Hence, the findings for batterers were lower on most measures compared to these other clinical populations. However, these prevalence rates of mental disorder are much higher than the epidemiological estimates for males in the general population.

Among the mental disorders that are commonly cited in the literature on intimate partner violence offenders, personality disorders, substance abuse, and depression appear to be the most significant. These three disorder groups have considerable co-occurrence and share a general likelihood of affective instability. In exploring mental disorders among intimate partner violence offenders, it is important to be reminded of the limitations of research findings to date. Most studies have focused on clinical populations of offenders or ones who have been identified by the criminal justice system and thus may not be representative of all offenders. However, for mental health and substance abuse treatment clinicians, these findings may sensitize assessment and treatment regarding the extent and degree of violence among clinical populations.

PERSONALITY DISORDERS

Early research reported evidence of personality disorders among male domestic violence offenders (Hamberger & Hastings, 1988).

There has also been evidence of borderline personality disorder (BPD) as well as antisocial personality disorder (ASPD). This is not surprising, since both of these disorders have social and relationship disturbances as key criteria for the diagnoses (American Psychological Association [APA], 2000). Other studies have supported the finding of BPD among intimate partner violence offenders by examining violent males, maritally discordant males, and happily married males with more of the violent males reporting BPD and related symptoms (Murphy, Meyer & O'Leary, 1993). In addition, studies using the construct of borderline personality organization rather than the Diagnostic and Statistical Manual's *(DSM's)* diagnostic criteria for BPD, have reported prevalence of these traits among offenders Dutton (1995b, 1998). However, clinicians should approach these studies somewhat cautiously, since it is unclear how these data contribute to treatment. For example, the criteria selected by Dutton (1994) for the borderline personality organization include a fragile sense of self, intolerance of abandonment, impulsivity, intense anger, and a demanding style with others—particularly with the partner on whom they are dependent. These personality traits appear to be simply descriptive of offender traits in general and may represent a different clinical language for offender behavior and personality. In addition, other research with over 800 domestic violence offenders from different jurisdictions and treatment settings has found a low percentage of batterers with borderline personality disorder, but a high percentage of batterers with narcissistic and antisocial traits as measured by the MCMI-III (Gondolf, 1999). The issue is further confused by a lack of consensus in the literature about the prevalence of personality disorders among batterers. Based on available research, sampling differences appear to have a major affect on prevalence findings, since studies of other clinical populations show higher ratings of borderline and antisocial personality among offenders compared to controls (Wonderlich, Beatty, Christie & Staton, 1993).

Antisocial personality disorder may represent a limited percentage of intimate partner violence offenders, but this group may also represent a particularly dangerous type of offender. In an important study of very violent couples, a study that excluded couples with only pushing or shoving as the physical violence expressions, a significant difference among types of offenders emerged that was associated with greater stealth of perpetration. Named the "cobras," these offenders had traits that have been identified with antisocial

males that included lower physiological arousal to conflict and violence (Jacobson & Gottman, 1998). Antisocial males have long been
identified as having lower heart rates than do nonantisocial males
and lower physiological reactivity to violence and threats of aggression (Raine, 1996). There are at least 16 studies among noninstitu-
tionalized antisocials that present these same findings about lower
heart rate across the age spectrum from 8 to 10 year old boys to
teenaged boys and girls, thus suggesting it an enduring dispositional
trait (Raine, 1996). In fact, this relationship even extends to differenti-
ating among criminals wherein the more violent the male, the lower
the heart rate (Raine, 1996). The domestic violence study found the
same pattern in that the more planful, stealthy offenders had the
lower physiological reactivity (Jacobson & Gottman, 1998). In more
psychological terms, this lower heart rate and lower arousal rate
suggest that these offenders have less fear, less ability to process
negative events, and less ability to foresee negative consequences
to their violence. Of all the "type" descriptions that could be clinically
useful, this finding about cold, calculating offenders may be most
important. The identification of low-reactivity antisocial offenders
may be one of the more important "types" to bear in mind in clinical
practice, since these traits are so clearly associated with extreme
violence.

Two other clinical areas that are often associated with BPD, attachment disorders and trauma related symptoms, have also been examined by researchers studying intimate partner violence offenders
(Dutton, 1995a; 1995b; 1998). Consistent with the application of borderline personality organization, Dutton identified disrupted attachment and excessive fear of rejection or abandonment, both of which
have been associated with attachment disorders (Bowlby, 1977). The
idea of attachment disorder may help explain offenders' dependency
and jealousy regarding their partners. Partner-assaultive men have
been identified as more dependent than are nonviolent men who
have discordant relationships (Murphy, Meyer & O'Leary, 1994).
Dutton, Saunders, Starzomsky, and Bartholomew (1994) reported
that nonviolent males have far more secure attachments than violent
males and that attachment problems were related to trauma symptoms and borderline personality organization. Trauma symptoms
among offenders raises an additional clinical complexity for most
clinicians, since trauma suggests a treatment approach using empathy and support, whereas treatment for offender behavior suggests

a more confrontive and focused approach. These clinical approaches tend toward opposite directions; hence, a consideration of trauma as the shaping diagnostic characteristic of offenders should be approached cautiously.

While the narcissistic, borderline, and antisocial personalities share a conceptual fit in the B cluster of personality disorders, the description of their characteristics in the intimate partner violence offender literature seem quite different and even polarized with the borderline narcissist at one end and the antisocial at the other. The trauma/attachment disorder portrait suggests intense emotionality and rage, while the antisocial type appears cold and emotionally unreactive; perhaps unattached versus experiencing insecure attachments. However, other studies have had difficulty distinguishing adequately among borderline and antisocial types, since many intimate partner violence offenders scored high on both personality scales (Waltz, Babcock, Jacobson, & Gottman, 2000).

DEPRESSION

Intimate partner violence offenders have reported high levels of depression, with depression levels showing an almost linear relationship with levels of violence (in other words, the greater the depression, the more extreme the violence), suggesting an important relationship between depression and levels of aggression (Maiuro, Cahn, Vitaliano, Wagner, & Zegree, 1988; Pan, Neidig, & O'Leary, 1994). When depression is accompanied by trait hostility, the risk of violence is greater. In fact, current thinking suggests that hostile depression may involve personality and substance abuse as well (Flett & Hewitt, 2002). This would suggest that clinicians might be vigilant about their understanding of depression since it may intersect in very complex ways with personality, substance abuse, and violence. The picture of sad or withdrawn depression is very different from the type of depression identified in these offender studies.

SUBSTANCE ABUSE

Research shows a strong correlation between substance abuse and intimate partner violence. Rates of alcohol abuse and dependency among offenders are two to seven times higher than for males in the general population (Grant et al., 1994). Studies of intimate partner violence offenders in treatment also show high rates of alcohol usage (Barnett & Fagan, 1993; Julian & McKenry, 1993; Telch & Lindquist, 1984). Similarly, men seeking treatment for alcoholism have higher rates of violence perpetration than do men in the general population (O'Farrell, Van Hutton, & Murphy, 1999). Finally, chronic alcohol abuse by offenders, rather than acute intoxication, is a better predictor of battering (Tolman & Bennett, 1990).

In addition to research showing a general correlation between substance abuse and intimate partner violence, studies now also document the frequency of alcohol use during violence incidents. In one study, husbands were significantly more likely to report drinking alcohol in conjunction with episodes of physical aggression than in episodes involving only verbal conflicts (Leonard & Quigley, 1999); and 22% of males and 10% of females in another study reported consuming alcohol prior to the most recent and most severe occurrence of domestic assault (Kantor & Straus, 1987).

Use of alcohol during domestic violence incidents is associated with increased severity of injury to victims (e.g.: Roizen, 1997). In a study of almost 400 battered women, researchers compared four domestic violence incidents involving substance abuse with four incidents without the concurrent use of alcohol and found that offenders abusing alcohol were more likely to inflict injury on the victim than were offenders with no alcohol use (Eberle, 1982). Similarly, another study found that over a quarter of victims were injured when the offender was drinking, compared to 13% when no drinking was involved in the incident (Pernanen, 1991). Finally, Brecklin (2002) found alcohol use by offenders was associated with greater likelihood of physical injury and marginally associated with more medical-attention seeking by the victim.

While there is extensive research on substance abuse and violence, directly applicable and clinically useful information is limited. The major findings suggest very complex relationships between violence, substance abuse, personality disorder or traits, depression, cognitive functioning (particularly frontal-lobe activity), and context. Substance abuse adds considerable complexity to the understanding of aggression in intimate partner violence offenders. While it is tempting to see the specific drug or alcohol as a cause of violence, this interpretation is not supported by the evidence. The intuitive understanding of substance use on violence is shaped by anecdote, not empirical evidence, which suggest many different contributing, exacerbating, or potentiating roles for substances in the expression of aggression (Pernanen, 1991; Roizen 1997). Even when substance abuse is very evident in a case, it is unlikely to be the cause of the violence; other factors such as personality or the executive functioning of the frontal lobes may be more explanatory (Pihl & Hoaken, 2002).

Substance abuse has been associated with antisocial personality and both have been shown to have possible common genetic bases (van den Bree, Svikis, & Pickens, 2000). The two disorders represent risk factors for the other, but also may share genetic contributions that affect emergence of both problems—at least for some variants of alcoholism (Cadoret, O'Gorman, Troughton & Heywood, 1985; Pickens, Svikis, McGue, & LaBuda, 1995). There is limited research on the heritability of substance abuse other than alcohol.

IMPULSIVITY

There is a large body of research on impulsivity, which has been associated with intimate partner violence and related problems such as excessive anger, rage, and explosive behavior (Webster & Jackson, 1997). As is evident from the earlier discussion, some offenders present with deliberative violence that is anything but impulsive. However, the borderline/narcissistic types may well exhibit impulsivity. Impulsivity, in this context refers primarily to the clinical use of the term, which is a way of saying that cognitive or behavioral impulses are poorly regulated or managed among some intimate partner violence offenders. The term may have very different meanings in legal contexts, where it may be used to mitigate willful actions (Ogloff, 1996). Impulsive violence has also been associated with biological correlates such as low serotonin levels and low metabolism of glucose in the frontal lobes of the cerebral cortex (Raine et al., 1994; Volkow et al., 1995). The clinical usefulness of impulsivity as an explanation for violent behavior is uncertain. The awareness of psychobiological dysregulation such as deficient serotonin turnover and glucose metabolic problems (Virkkunen & Linnoila, 1996) does little to guide clinical decision-making or treatment options. However, it can be important to understanding the relative persistence of impulsive traits, given the biological contributions to the problem. While serotonin is a likely impulse inhibitor (Coccaro & Kavoussi, 1996), there is little evidence that serotonin-enhancing agents reduce impulsive aggression.

ANGER AND INTIMATE PARTNER VIOLENCE

Many communities have developed anger management groups for intimate partner violence offenders. These programs have arisen with an understanding of offending behavior that appears unrelated to the majority of research literature on offender traits. To date, the understanding of anger and its role in intimate partner violence perpetration is limited primarily to rather enduring anger traits as opposed to temporary states of anger. Anger management approaches do not appear to always differentiate between these two types of anger. Anger management, and the use of anger models to explain offender behavior, has been limited due to very small sample sizes (McCarthy-Tucker, Gold, & Garcia, 1999) from narrowly defined clinical populations or from literature that is clinical in nature (Escamilla, 1998; Sanderlin, 2001). In addition, given the high rates of co-occurring substance abuse among male offenders referred for anger management (Easton, Swan, & Sinha, 2000), it has been difficult for research to differentiate anger effects related to substance use or withdrawal versus trait anger or state conditions.

Trait anger is associated with personality type (Beasely & Stoltenberg, 1992; Flett & Hewlitt, 2002). One of the expressions of narcissism or borderline personality is an expectation that reality should conform to the individual's schema for how it should be (Rothschild, Dimson, Storaasil, & Clapp, 1997). When reality fails to meet the demands of the schema, the individual experiences anger or even rage. These offenders tend to have the expectation of an other-person-oriented perfectionism (Eckhart, Barbour & Davidson, 1998). This pattern is abundantly evident in the emotional abuse patterns of belittling and castigating others who do not conform to the offender's standard of perfection. The perfectionism is not turned toward self, but only toward the partner. This trait sets the stage for virtually continuous anger that can manifest itself in verbal abuse if not violence (Flett & Hewitt, 2002; Maiuro, Cahn, Vitaliano, Wagner, & Zegree, 1988). In addition, there is evidence of anger that is part of an overall depressive personality (Flett & Hewitt, 2002).

FAMILY OF ORIGIN ISSUES

Research about the specific contribution of family of origin violence to adult intimate partner offending is still very limited (Wall & McKee, 2002). However, research suggests that adult intimate partner violence has some association with a child's witnessing violence between parents (Widom, 1989). In addition, in a study with college males, witnessing father-to-mother severe physical aggression was predictive of mild and severe aggression in dating relationships (Cantrell, MacIntyre, Sharkey, & Thompson, 1995).

The primary way to understand family of origin violence contributing to an adult's own offending behavior is to see it at as learning or modeled experience. A boy witnesses violence in the home and learns that this is the way that men relate to their partners. Often the lesson is also that little negative consequence results from violence, and that, in fact, violence is a successful way of gaining control in the family. This then forms a template for adult behavior later on. There has been extensive research on social learning theory or social cognitive theory (Bandura, 1986; Wall & McKee, 2002) that would support this type of model for intimate partner violence (Widom & Toch, 2000). In the case of intimate partner violence, however, a number of other contributing factors also exist, including family-of-origin substance abuse that has been strongly associated with the development of antisocial and aggressive traits in child development (Loeber, Farrington, Stouthamer-Loeber, & Van Kammen, 1998). Disorder in family lifestyles, coercion, parental depression and/or anxiety, and other factors also contribute to family-influenced aggression and antisocial traits (Loeber, et al., 1998). Likewise, a review of studies that report batterers' retrospective accounts of their family background, suggested that later physically violent behavior (adolescent and adult violence, physical abuse of one's children, and violence toward spouses and partners) was associated with multiple family problems such as earlier physical abuse, childhood neglect, and exposure to adult violence (Malinosky-Rummell & Hansen, 1993). While these studies and others provide information about intimate partner offenders tending to have witnessed intimate partner violence during their childhood, their childhood experience alone should not be seen as predicting a violent adulthood.

Social learning theory adds one more dimension to the biopsychosocial contributions toward later violence, and it brings the concept of agency into the picture (Bandura, 1999). Agency is the capacity to act upon the environment and to have awareness of self as an actor (Bandura, 1999). In other words, social cognitive theory applied to offenders suggests that intimate partner violence is in part a result of learning a way of acting toward others, but, at the same time, being more than a passive transmitter of aggression. This aspect of social learning is sometimes overlooked in the rush to discover specific parental behaviors that could have modeled aggression toward partners.

One of the problems in focusing on family of origin violence for clinicians is that the number of clients who have grown up in extremely disordered, substance abusing, and violent families is very great. However, most clients with this background do not go on to inflict physical violence on adult partners. Hence, it is important to assess family-of-origin issues very carefully, since they can be misleading contributing factors in offenders' behavior, and to see these issues as some of the many influencing factors in the historical experience of the offender.

SUMMARY OF CLINICAL CHARACTERISTICS

This brief review of clinical characteristics of intimate partner violence offenders suggests that several major disorders are most likely to be associated with offender behavior. It is also evident that these disorders have complex interactions, with each one contributing to increased severity or problems in the other. Substance use disorders exacerbate depression; depression may contribute to personality; personality type is related to substance abuse; impulsivity is closely related to personality disorder, criminality, and substance abuse.

Chapter 3 reviewed clinical characteristics of intimate partner violence offenders and provided information about general types of offending behavior. The Chapter provided an overview of key clinical characteristics of offenders including personality disorders, substance abuse, depression, and other disorders. Readers should be able to answer the following questions following a review of **Chapter 3**:

- What does the literature cite as the three most common mental disorders in men who are violent with an intimate?
- What is the clinical implication when depression is accompanied by trait hostility?
- What is the role of anger in cases of intimate partner violence, and how do anger traits differ from angry states? How are these two approached clinically?
- Does substance abuse cause intimate partner violence? Why or why not?

Chapter 4

Clinical Responses to Women Victimized by Violence

Chapter 4 discusses effective clinical practice with victims of intimate partner violence. The chapter addresses appropriate screening for current and historic abuse in general client populations and more extensive assessments if a client discloses victimization. **Chapter 4** also encourages clinicians to engage is safety planning with victims, focusing around three key phases: how to identify that risk or danger is increasing, identification of the specific steps the victim will take upon recognizing those danger cues, and methods for maintaining safety upon her departure from the offender. Finally, **chapter 4** discusses key clinical issues for victims of partner violence. The sections within **chapter 4** include the following:

- Screening for intimate partner violence and abuse history in the clinical setting
- Safety planning with intimate partner violence victims
- Assessment in preparation for treatment intervention
- Support groups for women victimized by intimate partner violence
- Clinical intervention for women victimized by intimate partner violence

SCREENING FOR INTIMATE PARTNER VIOLENCE AND VICTIMIZATION HISTORY IN THE CLINICAL SETTING

SCREENING

As has been discussed in earlier chapters, the mental health impact of violence and the presence of victimization history among women who seek mental health care have been demonstrated. It does not follow, however, that clinicians view victimization history as clinically relevant, that they routinely screen for abuse, or that they detect abuse in their clinical caseloads (Jordan & Walker, 1994; Saunders et al., 1989). When researchers asked clinicians in one study how they would respond to cases involving partner abuse, the majority did not identify violence as a presenting problem (Hansen, Harway, & Cervantes, 1991). Evidence exists that women will respond to abuse inquiries: In a study comparing intake procedures, fully twice the number of clients disclosed victimization history in response to a direct question as compared to a conventional intake interview (Saunders et al., 1989). Similarly, in a chart-review study, disclosures of abuse history increased 10-fold when clinicians asked direct questions of psychiatric emergency-room patients (Briere and Zaidi, 1989). Finally, fewer than 5% of couples seeking marital therapy will respond spontaneously about the presence of intimate partner violence, but over two-thirds (66%) report some form of violence in response to a written self-report measure (O'Leary, Vivian, & Malone, 1992). If clients are not directly and sensitively assessed, the ability of the clinician to adequately identify abuse, evaluate lethality, and structure appropriate interventions will be lost.

Asking simplistic questions may not be a sufficient intervention on the part of a clinician, as evidence exists that victims of intimate partner violence minimize the extent of the abuse when it is disclosed to clinicians or researchers (Dutton, 1992b; Walker, 1994). Also key to safe and appropriate intervention is that women most likely to minimize the disclosure of violence may also be those who have experienced the most severe violence and those who have the most accepting attitudes toward violence (Dunham & Senn, 2000). In the study just referenced, it was also the case that the longer the women waited to disclose, the more they were likely to minimize.

As a result, clinicians need to show particular levels of sensitivity and insight when interviewing clients.

While authors of this manual and other writers emphasize structured assessment and abuse-specific inquiry, clinicians should be cautioned against using confrontation or insistent approaches to promote disclosures by women. It would be an error to pressure women to disclose prior to their attaining a degree of comfort in the clinical setting and sufficient trust of the clinician. Inherent in the experience of violence at the hand of an intimate is a trust violation, such that client readiness to disclose frightening or intimate details may be delayed. In addition, clinicians will want to avoid giving the impression to any client that she is expected to have something traumatic to disclose (Briere, 1997).

The use of close-ended questions by clinicians specific to the assault of women has been recommended (Gondolf, 1998). One advantage of asking specific questions that call for "yes" or "no" responses, is that this approach introduces the vocabulary of abuse and validates these experiences merely by asking about them. Open ended questions can be used in follow-up to the initial closed ended ones. In addition, effective screenings should include behavioral descriptions when assessing for partner violence, as many women may reframe their experiences as "not getting along" or "fighting with" their partners rather than applying a term such as battering or domestic violence (Briere, 1997). Similarly, they may not apply those terms if they self-attribute blame for the abuse and confusion regarding definitions of abuse may "arise from psychological defenses against acknowledging traumatic events" (Briere, 1997, p. 82). Given these factors, it is advisable for clinicians to avoid simply using a list of traumatic events, but, rather, to describe such behaviors in a way that the understanding is unambiguous (Briere, 1997).

Some evidence exists that a specific screening tool applied in a general clinical setting will significantly increase the clinician's ability to access information regarding a client's abuse history (Warshaw, 1989). While the scientific validity of a brief set of screening questions has not been fully tested, several items have been suggested (Gondolf, 1998), such as the following:

Screening Questions

1. Are you in any way fearful of your partner?
2. Does your partner have angry outbursts or temper tantrums?

3. Has your partner stopped you from going places or seeing people?
4. Has your partner threatened to harm you, your children, or your relatives?
5. Has your partner ever pushed, grabbed, slapped, or hit you?
6. Has your partner ever pressured you into sexual acts against your will?

Follow-Up Questions

(Each screening question with a positive response should be followed with probes for the most recent incident, duration, frequency, effect, and response to the incidents (Gondolf, 1998)).

1. When was the most recent incident?
2. How long has this been going on?
3. How often has it happened in the last six months?
4. How has it made you feel?
5. How has it hurt you physically?
6. What help or assistance have you sought?
7. How do you feel about calling the police or going to court to receive assistance?

Clinicians need to take extra care in assessing for psychological abuse, as some research suggests that victims may be less able to identify or name that experience. As discussed in earlier chapters, psychological abuse can have extremely detrimental effects, but while physical abuse is easily identifiable and victims know that physical acts have been used to harm them, some suggest that victims of psychological abuse may have more difficulty identifying the fact that abuse is occurring (Loring, 1994) and may therefore be less adept at defending themselves against this form of victimization (Marshall, 1994a).

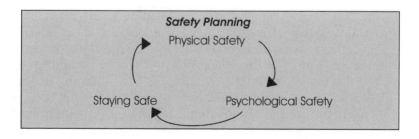

If clinicians positively assess the presence of abuse in the current or historic life of a client after use of a screening instrument, a more detailed abuse history seeking detail on the extent and impact of the victimization is called for. Numerous tools for assessing abuse history are available, including the Conflict Tactic Scale (Straus, 1979) and the Danger Assessment Scale (Campbell, 1986; 1995; Stuart & Campbell, 1989). The Danger Assessment Scale, one of the most commonly used risk instruments, is a 15-item questionnaire compiled from research on homicide and serious injury of victims of intimate partner violence (Campbell, 1986). Its ease of use comes from the brevity of the instrument and from the fact that it elicits information solely from the victim (Goodman, Dutton, & Bennett, 2000). There is growing empirical evidence of the predictive usefulness of the Danger Assessment Scale. For example, in one study, women who had been abused while pregnant scored significantly higher on the instrument than did women who had been abused prior to but not during pregnancy (McFarlane, Parker, & Soeken, 1995); and in a pilot study of women in the justice system, the Danger Assessment Scale contributed to the prediction of short-term reoccurrence of abuse by arrested offenders (Goodman, Dutton, & Bennett, 2000).

Finally, numerous instruments exist that provide a structured interview format for assessing trauma (Wilson & Keane, 1996), including the Traumatic Events Scale (TES) created by Elliott (1992), and the self-administered Trauma Symptom Inventory created by Briere (1995). More in-depth assessment is discussed later in this chapter.

Clinicians should be sensitive to the after effect on the victim of completing a thorough assessment. For some victims, having the opportunity to fully disclose the nature of their abuse experience in the safety of the therapy setting is, in and of itself, therapeutic. Some women may also be provided additional insight and understanding as they see the full extent of their own victimization. That type of greater understanding can facilitate safety planning and future decision making for the women. Clinicians should be mindful, however, that for others, full disclosure may be attended by an overwhelming sense of anger, shame, fear, or panic. In addition, describing abuse experiences in detail may give the effect of recreating the earlier trauma in the session or in the hours and days that follow the disclosure. A client's reaction to the recounting of abuse experience and the perceived risk she faces should guide the clinician in dosing the pace of disclosure during the assessment process.

3 Phases of Comprehensive Safety Planning

1. Identification that risk or danger is increasing.
2. Identification of the specific steps the victim will take upon recognizing danger cues.
3. Methods for maintaining safety upon the victim's departure from the offender.

SAFETY PLANNING WITH INTIMATE PARTNER VIOLENCE VICTIMS

At the outset and throughout the duration of the clinical relationship, clinicians must be prepared to engage in crisis stabilization with victims of intimate partner violence that uniquely attends to safety planning. Safety planning is a process of engaging a victim in planning for both physical and psychological safety. It should not be a singular or one-time event but, rather, should be an on-going process throughout the time the client is receiving services. As contextual and clinical factors associated with a case change, the detail of the safety plan will need to accommodate the increase or decrease of danger potential (e.g.: contextual factors such as the offender's loss of a job, initiation of stalking the victim, or his increase in alcohol consumption; or clinical factors, such as her growing depression or the beginning of suicide ideation, would necessitate changes in the safety plan developed by the victim and the clinician).

Safety planning with victims should incorporate risk information the clinician has gleaned from screening and intake procedures. In limited instances, police reports or other collateral information will be available to guide safety planning, but the primary source for information and risk appraisal will be the woman herself. Research suggests that incorporating into risk assessments and safety planning the predictions made by women regarding their own safety can be extremely useful (Gondolf & Heckert, 2003). In studies with women whose partners were receiving treatment in offender programs, their predictions regarding the offender's likelihood of reassault were the single best predictor of severe violence (Weisz, Tolman, & Saunders, 2000) and significantly improved prediction accuracy above and beyond standardized instruments (Heckert & Gondolf, 2002).

Physical safety planning for victims involves developing detailed, prearranged plans for ensuring her safety and that of her children (Hart & Stuehling, 1992). Comprehensive planning should fully encompass three key phases: identification that risk or danger is increasing; identification of the specific steps the victim will take upon recognizing danger cues; and methods for maintaining safety upon her departure from the offender. Recognizing cues or signs of potential danger include both characteristics of the offender and characteristics of the prior circumstances of abuse. For example, the clinician should help the victim identify those behaviors and traits of the offender that have been associated with violence in the past (e.g., increase in substance abuse; expression of anger or increased tension; or introduction of external sources of stress, such as job loss). It is also helpful to note for the victim those behaviors in which she may engage that may make her more vulnerable to her partner's use of violence against her, specifically including substance abuse. The identification of circumstances or context associated with prior abuse may include listing locations where the prior abuse has happened, a time of day, when other certain peers of the offender were present, or possibly the context of an argument between the couple.

After the victim has identified offender and context-related cues, the second part of the safety plan involves identifying steps she will take if cues are identified. Steps may include keeping access to money, an extra set of car keys, knowing how to escape from a residence or workplace, and having a previously arranged method of contacting children and other family members or friends to inform them of the danger situation. Some experts provide the following common elements for safety plans (Hart & Stuehling, 1992):

- practicing quick exists
- always keeping purse and care keys near the door
- hiding an extra set of keys and money
- storing important documents in a safe place
- keeping a suitcase packed and stored in a safe place at home or at a friend's home
- teaching children how to call the police and fire departments
- setting up a code word or signal for children or friends or both so they will know it is time to begin the safety plan
- knowing the phone number for a battered women's shelter

The Essential Protection Resource: Shelters for Battered Women

One of the primary protective resources for victims of intimate partner violence is a protective shelter. Clinicians should be familiar with the shelter in their communities, as these programs provide safe housing, advocacy, support groups, crisis hotlines, and other critical services for victims and their families.

Clinicians should also work very concretely with victims to list safety resources such as police agencies, crisis hotlines for shelters, adult protection agencies, and the courts. Clinicians should educate victims regarding the process of how to access orders of protection from the court or should refer the victim to advocates who can provide that critically needed information (see chapter 8 for information on legal remedies for victims). In studies that should encourage clinicians to refer victims to advocates for assistance, battered women who worked with advocates reported being more effective in accessing resources than did the women without advocates, reported higher quality of life and social support, and experienced lower partner revictimization rates (Sullivan, 1991; Sullivan & Bybee, 1999).

Clinicians and their clients cannot rely on a standardized list of concrete steps every victim should take, because any safety plan must be developed individually, taking into consideration the context of the woman's environment. For example, calling law enforcement agencies may increase the protection for one woman, but may bring retribution and elevated violence from the offender for another. Some victims may benefit from telling their employers about the risk posed to them by their partners, but clinicians are cautioned to be aware that other women may lose their employment and thus increase their economic dependence on the offender by disclosing to a supervisor.

Engaging in the safety planning process is, in effect, a structured way to assist a woman with problem-solving coping skills. Numerous studies suggest that it is good for women suffering from intimate partner violence to engage in problem-focused coping (Arias & Pape, 1999), both because it increases her safety and because the process itself can lessen depression and related sequelae. Notably, however, studies have found that this relationship may only hold true when social supports are actually available for the woman (Kocot & Goodman, 2003). Otherwise, creating plans when she does not understand the resources available to her and when she perceives herself as having few social supports may actually exacerbate her feelings of being overwhelmed and, thereby, worsen her mental health status. This effect should, again, encourage clinicians to conduct safety planning with victims and also ensure to the extent possible that they have access to a victim advocate.

In additional to planning for a woman's physical safety, effective safety planning should always include an assessment of her mental state or psychological stability, the outcome of which should influence clinical intervention and, subsequently, any safety plan. This includes assessing for any suicide risk or potential homicidal thoughts against the offender. The presence of depression is important, as intense sadness or hopelessness may impede the victim's effectiveness in safety planning or even her belief that she is worth protecting. In addition, denial and avoidance symptoms associated with posttrauma reactions may impair a victim's ability to monitor her environment for danger cues. Safety planning should also attend to risk of increased substance use if that is a clinical issue for the victim.

The third part of an effective safety plan involves developing steps to keep a victim and her children safe after her separation from the offender. This is particularly important in light of the fact that a victim's risk of harm does not end when she separates from the offender, as previously discussed—rather, it may escalate. Effective safety planning, as a result, attends not just to the safe escape from violence, but also to the safe *separation* from the violent partner. Clinicians should continue to focus on contextual factors with the victim: including ensuring that she understands (1) how to access orders of protection from the court, (2) steps to take if the conditions of an order are violated by an offender; (3) steps to take if the offender begins to stalk the victim or her children; and (4) management of legal issues. In addition, victims who are employed may need assistance knowing how and when to approach supervisors and colleagues regarding their circumstances and how to weigh sharing details to ensure safety while at the workplace versus exposing themselves to risk of job loss if an employer is not supportive. Another unique aspect of safety planning with victims is teaching documentation of offender conduct that could be used in a court proceeding. Particularly in stalking cases in which evidence of a pattern of repeated conduct or behavior is most often necessary to convict the offender, clinicians can aid the victim by recommending that she keep such evidence as logs of phone calls, copies of letters, or photographs of the offender outside the workplace or residence of the victim (Davis, Coker, & Sanderson, 2002).

Comprehensive Trauma Assessment Protocol

a) Pretrauma functioning
b) Trauma exposure
c) Social supports
d) Comorbidity
e) Potential malingering or secondary gain
f) Posttraumatic stress response

Briere (1997)

ASSESSMENT IN PREPARATION FOR TREATMENT INTERVENTION

The discussion of assessment thus far has focused narrowly on identifying and moderating risk for a victim. If the clinician will assume a treating role, a fuller and in-depth assessment phase is also recommended as a means of understanding the nature of the abuse, its attendant effects, and the strengths and capacities of the victim to recover her preabuse functioning. Briere (1997) recommends a comprehensive trauma assessment protocol that addresses six domains or measures: (1) pretrauma functioning, (2) trauma exposure, (3) social supports, (4) comorbidity, (5) potential malingering or secondary gain, and (6) posttraumatic stress response. Inquiry into the pretrauma functioning of the victim will assist a clinician in determining whether depressive or other symptoms existed prior to the current violence or appear to result from it. In addition, prior abuse experiences will be clinically relevant in determining what may worsen or mediate the client's current experience: Women with childhood abuse experiences, for example, may not only suffer from the current violence, but the current abuse may trigger memories and symptoms associated with the prior victimization. Finally, it will be of use to know whether a client has suffered previously from depression, suicidality, or substance abuse, as these may be more acute areas of risk in the current situation as a result. Briere's comprehensive assessment protocol suggests assessment in each of the following areas to ascertain pretrauma functioning:

Previous psychological symptoms and disorders

Previous psychiatric or psychological treatment

Alcohol and drug abuse history

Prior occupational functioning

Criminal and incarceration history

Pre-victimization social adjustment

Evidence of pretrauma personality disturbance

Relevant medical history (e.g.: history of brain injury or disorder)

Specific questioning and assessment around the current abuse experience is important, as it is not sufficient to know that the client is a victim of interpersonal violence in order to design an appropriate intervention. As has been discussed in prior sections, the frequency, severity, duration, and other factors significantly impact the sequelae that will be experienced by the victim. As a result, it is important to assess with some specificity the nature of the abuse (severity, frequency, duration); it's immediate impact (any physical injury), and the victim's perception of the experience (degree of fear, presence of terror, perceived risk of death, perceived risk to the children). Assessment in the area of social supports is important in safety planning and in identifying strengths in the victim's environment. As a clinical matter, it has also been shown that the presence of support systems following a traumatic event can decrease the experience of PTSD symptoms (Ozer et al., 2003). Comorbidity relates to concurrent mental health and substance abuse problems that will impact the victim's ability to protect herself from violence and her ability to fully recover from the current experience.

SUPPORT GROUPS FOR WOMEN VICTIMIZED BY INTIMATE PARTNER VIOLENCE

The most commonly utilized modality of clinical intervention for victims of intimate partner violence is group work (Tutty, Bidgood, & Rothery, 1993). Support groups offer a remedy for the isolation experienced by many intimate partner violence victims, and they provide an opportunity for information sharing. Some authors have argued for the support group model as an anecdote to more inappropriate modalities such as traditional marital or family therapy, which ignore the differential power structure inherent in these relationships (Pressman, 1989; Tutty, Bidgood, & Rothery, 1993). The literature is limited in describing the efficacy of support groups for women in violent relationships, but most studies suggest that these groups are less structured, less didactic, and more focused on the emotional process for the woman as compared to groups for men who batter, and that client gains can be realized (Tutty, Bidgood, & Rothery, 1993). Support groups with psychoeducational components can also provide a mechanism by which women can learn about the dynamics of abusive relationships, parenting skills, assertiveness skills, and anger management (Dutton, 1992b).

While specific models vary, general goals for support group work with women experiencing partner violence have been identified (Pressman, 1984) and tend to focus on the following:

- the future safety of the woman
- reduction of self-blame and learned helplessness
- enhancement of self-esteem
- an understanding of why battering occurs, including an exploration of sexism and beliefs about male-female roles
- opportunities for the ventilation of anger around being victimized
- opportunities to express grief at the loss of a relationship
- building support networks that reduce isolation

TREATMENT SERVICES FOR VICTIMS OF INTIMATE PARTNER VIOLENCE

THE FIRST TREATMENT APPROACH: USING WHAT WORKS, AVOIDING WHAT DOESN'T

As was discussed in chapter 2, clinicians who see the consequences of intimate partner violence in the clinical setting should avoid pathologizing victims. This perspective should inform treatment planning, with the understanding that no change in a woman will, in turn, change the offender's behavior: The control of violence rests with the individual who chooses to perpetrate it. Clinicians should also take care not to pathologize behaviors that have been used to cope with routine physical and psychological aggression but, rather, should understand those behaviors in their context. Some authors have suggested that such psychological mechanisms as denial, dissociation, and alterations in personality style are strengths rather that signs of pathology in that they help the victim to survive the exposure to abuse (Dutton, 1992b). Similarly, Briere suggests a phenomenologic perspective in working with survivors of trauma whereby such behaviors are seen as adaptive responses to victimization. These behaviors may be maladaptive outside the context of the victim's experience of intimate partner violence but can be important, in helping her withstand the abuse to which she was exposed (Briere, 1989). Grounding clinical decisions in this type of philosophy will help ensure effective interventions more than any single clinical technique or modality of treatment.

Effective clinical intervention will also be more likely if the clinician creates an accepting therapeutic environment within which the victim feels believed. Strong therapeutic relationships are more likely if a clinician does not overreact to abuse disclosures with facial expressions or exclamations of horror, or with judgmental reactions regarding the offender. Clinicians can also create productive treatment environments by conveying a sufficient level of competence (e.g.,"I have worked with a number of women who have had the type of experience you are describing"), by emphasizing the client's strengths, and by not communicating just one solution to her experience (e.g., "You clearly can't go back to him.").

COMPREHENSIVE TREATMENT PLANS

An evaluation of the extent of victimization, attendant risk, and the psychological sequelae experienced by the victim, will be the building blocks for a comprehensive treatment plan. Treatment plans should include interventions targeting four key areas:

Behavior. Interventions in the behavioral domain of the client should attend to increasing safety through the safety planning steps discussed earlier.

Cognition. Interventions in the cognitive domain of the client should address her beliefs about the causation of the abuse, perceptions, cognitive schemas, self-esteem, expectations, self-efficacy, and attributions.

Emotion. Treatment plans should include attention to the emotional domain of the client, including such reactions as terror, fear, anger, depression, anxiety, alcohol or drug abuse; and other areas of distress. Notably, it is not possible to completely eradicate emotional trauma reactions if the client continues to be exposed to ongoing violence, as these may be realistic reactions to imminent threat, and the client may not be safe in addressing the psychological effects of victimization outside the therapy setting. In addition, introspective therapies should not replace safety planning.

Interpersonal Relations. Finally, treatment should also include the impact on the client's interpersonal relationships (other than the offender), including any difficulty trusting, fear of intimacy or other dysfunctions.

SUBSTANCE USE AND VICTIMIZATION:
A DUAL FOCUSED TREATMENT NEED

There has been limited research on the interface between victimization and addiction treatment (Bennett & Lawson, 1994; SAMSHA, 1998). Programs often do not screen for both victimization and substance abuse problems, many programs do not have cross-trained staff who are well versed in both substance use and trauma, and cross referrals are not common among substance abuse and domestic violence programs (Bennett & Lawson, 1994; Collins, Kroutil, Roland, & Moore-Gurrera, 1997). There are many reasons for the lack of coordinating treatment between substance abuse and victimization including fundamental differences in treatment philosophies. Substance abuse program counselors often focus on the main goal of abstinence while domestic violence program primarily focus on safety (Substance Abuse and Mental Health Services Administration [SAMHSA], 1997). In addition, addiction treatment is often approached as if addiction were a disease, whereas victimization is not a disease, but rather a life situation (Bland, 1997).

Although there have been difficulties in coordinating treatment efforts in the past, there has been increased effort and progress toward integrated treatment models. A recent review of the literature suggests there are some basic principles that can be used to facilitate more effective treatment for women who are experiencing both substance abuse problems and victimization (Logan, Walker, Cole, & Leukefeld, 2002): (1) It is important to engage in comprehensive and ongoing assessment to address the extent of victimization, risk of revictimization, and substance abuse; (2) in the course of treatment, clinicians should focus on integrated and comprehensive interventions that address factors contributing to the woman's presentation of substance abuse and recent or ongoing victimization, including lifestyle risk factors, early trauma factors, and co-occurring mental health problems. For example, Sullivan and Evans (1994) suggested a five-stage model of treatment for the co-occurrence of current intimate partner violence and substance abuse that moves from a focus on the immediate crisis and safety issues to increasing long-term safety while maintaining abstinence from substance abuse. Their approach includes a focus on changing client self-perception from an addicted victim to a recovering survivor. Although this model lacks empirical evidence of success, the approach combines safety planning and recovery philosophies coherently; and (3) clinicians are advised to expand the breadth of services for women with co-occurring problems through cross-program referrals to target the individualized needs of women with victimization and substance-abuse histories.

Chapter 4 discussed effective clinical practice with victims of intimate partner violence. The chapter addressed appropriate screening and assessment techniques and encouraged clinicians to engage is safety planning that incorporates how to identify the risk or to perceive that danger is increasing, identification of the specific steps the victim will take upon recognizing those danger cues, and methods for maintaining safety upon her departure from the offender. Finally, **chapter 4** discussed clinical intervention with victims of partner violence. Readers should be able to answer the following questions following a review of **chapter 4:**

- What makes assessment for psychological abuse particularly challenging?
- What are the advantages of a structured interview format with victims of Intimate partner violence?
- What might be the effects on a client of a thorough assessment that includes disclosure of significant abuse?
- What are the three key stages to plan for in a comprehensive treatment plan?
- What are the goals of support groups for victims of intimate partner violence?

Chapter 5

Clinical Responses to Intimate Partner Violence Offenders

Chapter V reviews clinical approaches for assessment and treatment of intimate partner violence offenders. Mental health and substance abuse clinicians should first screen their clients for indicators of intimate partner violence. If there are indicators of violent behavior, clinicians should then assess the extent of violence and the level of danger posed by the behavior. The chapter explores screening questions as well as risk assessment factors of offending behavior and suggests clinical responses to the problem. The sections within **Chapter V** include:

- Screening for intimate partner violence among offenders in clinical settings
- General approaches to assessment
- Risk assessment in cases of intimate partner violence
- Clinical approaches with intimate partner violence offenders

SCREENING FOR INTIMATE PARTNER VIOLENCE AMONG OFFENDERS IN CLINICAL SETTINGS

The general client assessment process that is used in mental health and substance abuse treatment settings often overlooks intimate partner violence. Traditional mental health and substance abuse treatment settings routinely explore suicidality, the history of severe mental disorders, and the risks associated with substance use, as well as the risk of poor treatment compliance as a way of identifying clients who may need risk-management attention. While violence in general is screened for and assessed, intimate partner violence is less likely to be a focus of traditional assessment. Furthermore, identification of clients with intimate partner violence behaviors is made more difficult by their tendency to minimize or deny their violent conduct (Jacobson & Gottman, 1998). If clients are not overtly lying about their conduct, their self-reports of violence can still be distorted by post-offense shame or embarrassment. Client minimization may arise from a desire to manage impressions, or it may be associated with cognitive dissonance wherein the offender does not identify with the outcomes of his behavior (Sugarman & Hotaling, 1997; Szinovacz & Egley, 1995). In addition, the typical clinical focus on symptoms of mental disorders and substance abuse may leave little time for a close exploration of intimate partner violence. In fact, it remains unclear whether intimate partner violence offending should be seen as a clinical phenomenon, or simply as illegal behavior (Jacobson & Gottman, 1998). However, the identification of intimate partner violence offenders may be one of the more important clinical risk assessment functions since the risk of serious harm resulting from this behavior is very great.

This chapter describes screening and identification, assessment, and general treatment guidelines for clinical practice with clients who have intimate partner violence behaviors. In general, this chapter is written for clinical practice where intimate partner violence is not the primary program focus—that is, it is written for more general clinical practice. Clinicians who routinely work with court-referred clients seeking mental health or substance abuse treatment may need a more rigorous screening and assessment. Clinicians in programs that target domestic violence typically move directly into assessment of the level of danger since clients are already identified as being offenders. In general practice, however, clients may seek treatment for a variety of problems, and clients may not disclose violence unless specifically prompted. When intimate partner violence is not a part of the referral circumstance, it may be discovered only as treatment issues evolve, and it may take weeks or months before the clinician is aware of the behavior pattern. Clinicians in these cases may have to dramatically rethink their understanding of clients when intimate partner violence has not been identified early in treatment. However, when intimate partner violence is the focal presenting problem, clinicians may be more prepared for risk management and appropriate treatment. This chapter will prepare clinicians for the essential assessment and treatment responses relating to intimate partner violence among clients who are offenders.

As a general rule, clinicians who specialize in services to clients whose presenting problem is intimate partner violence have a higher duty to provide services that meet applicable clinical and program standards for specialty practice. On the other hand, clinicians in generalist settings or in practices focused on traditional mental health or substance abuse problems may have less duty to provide treatment specifically targeting violent behavior. However, generalist clinicians have important duties to refer high risk clients to specialty programs and to treat clients in ways that do not inadvertently exacerbate aggressive behavior. Their duties to refer clients to more appropriate programs may be an alternative treatment or an adjunct to current treatment.

Intimate partner violence offenders can emerge in any number of ways in clinical caseloads. For example, a clinician might be treating a client for anxiety and depression for several weeks and only learn about the client's violent behavior when he gets arrested for an assault. Also, a clinician might be treating a couple for relationship problems or problems relating to their child's behavior, only to discover—six weeks into treatment—that the unspoken issue has been sexual and/or physical violence in the marriage. Intimate partner violence can emerge in any client, and clinician vigilance about the behavior is recommended throughout the treatment process.

Although any client in mental health or substance abuse treatment might have a history of intimate partner violence, there are several referral conditions that suggest a greater likelihood of it. Court-referred clients (including those referred for other crimes and violations like drug possession or driving under the influence) are more likely to have antisocial traits that are associated with greater risk for intimate partner violence. Clients with substance abuse problems should be screened for intimate partner violence since the literature suggests complex associations between substance use and aggression (Pihl & Hoaken, 2002). Since B cluster personality disorders have been associated with impulsivity, substance abuse, and interpersonal conflicts (APA, 2000), clients with these disorders should be screened carefully for intimate partner violence behaviors as well. Screening questions can be difficult to manage early in treatment when clinicians are attempting to develop rapport and a therapeutic relationship with clients. Questions about the perpetration of intimate partner violence are, by nature, confrontational and have the feeling of being accusatory. Questions that are asked in risk screening and assessment can be perceived as intrusive and focused on "wrong doing" by clients. Hence, clients may feel "cross-examined" when using these questions. However, clinicians should not avoid violence related topics simply to preserve a comfort zone around the interview.

SCREENING FOR INTIMATE PARTNER VIOLENCE

Clinicians can use five simple questions in screening for a likelihood of intimate partner violence perpetration in a client (see page 80). The tone of questions should be matter-of-fact and integrated with other less pejorative issues, and the style should not be probative or investigatory in nature. Clients who respond, "yes" to any of these questions should be considered for a more focused assessment with regard to the extent and characteristics of their use of violence. Even if clients only endorse the first question about losing control of anger, it may be important to follow up with additional questions at a later time in treatment when defensiveness may be reduced. Male clients who report "losing control" in regard to anger may be laying groundwork for rationalizing violent behavior that will emerge later in treatment.

GENERAL APPROACHES TO ASSESSMENT

After screening for intimate partner violence and upon getting positive responses to one or more of the screening items, clinicians should focus on a more in-depth assessment of violent behavior. Several factors should be taken into account when beginning an assessment of intimate partner violence. First, if clients have been court referred, they are in a higher risk group and risk assessment should be conducted even in the absence of overt presenting prob-

Sample Screening Questions for General Mental Health or Substance Abuse Client

Begin with an "envelope" within which you can ask questions related to intimate partner violence, such as: "Mr. Smith, I would like to turn to situations in which you have been in conflict with a girlfriend or spouse. These questions will focus on situations that may involve anger or physical force. . . . "

• Has there ever been a time when you thought you lost control of your anger with a partner?
• Has there ever been a time when you yelled, cursed, or said demeaning things to hurt your partner?
• Have you ever talked to her in a way that "put her down"?
• Has there ever been a time when you used physical force with your partner, such as:
  — Shoving
  — Slapping
  — Hitting
  — Using something as a weapon
• Has there ever been a time when, in having sex, your partner would have described it as being against her will?

lems of intimate partner violence. Other clients who have clinical problems that place them in a higher risk group should also be assessed thoroughly even if there are few initial indications of violent behavior. Clients who are in treatment for issues that have little to do with intimate partner violence or related behaviors should be assessed for offending behavior only if there are positive responses to the screening items described.

ASSESSMENT STYLE

An assessment for intimate partner violence is difficult under most clinical situations, and a clinician's style can greatly influence the quality of information obtained. Each of these interviewing recommendations can promote better information sharing and development of rapport with clients. The style that is used to interview and assess for intimate partner violence needs to be focused and serious, though not "investigatory" in nature. Clinicians must adopt a questioning posture that is consistent with their own typical style but should consider the following recommendations. The interview style and approach should include

- a matter-of-fact, nonjudgmental, and nonsensational manner of relating;
- a sense of appropriate proportionality to the questions (they should not greatly exceed the extent of the behavior problem so as to belabor the point);
- a firm and focused approach that does not follow client diversions into other topics;
- "funneling" from general situations into specific acts;
- the use of specific, concrete terms rather than generalities to describe harmful acts;
- the use of questions that allow for self-observational responses, such as "have you ever found yourself doing . . . ";
- a rehearsed and ritualized menu or checklist of abuse areas to be sure that key behaviors or risk factors have not been overlooked;
- considerate, attentive listening to all client responses;
- asking clients for "clarification" when they give contradictory answers rather than directly challenging the contradictions; and
- a summary statement given to clients that conveys what has been heard.

A matter-of-fact, nonjudgmental, and nonsensational manner of relating.   Intimate partner violence can provoke strong feelings from most persons, including clinicians. While mental health and substance abuse clinicians are taught to make professional use of feelings and to not allow them to "leak" into clinical process, this often requires self-discipline, practice, and supervision to accomplish. The reason why a nonjudgmental approach is so important is that if offending clients receive punishing affective reactions from clinicians, they can be likely to avoid disclosing violent behavior. Likewise, avoiding identification with or sympathy for contrite batterers is important. However, a careful and tactful use of understanding and empathy can help overcome denial and minimization (Gondolf, 1998). Empathic responses can be mixed with more matter of fact questioning in order to facilitate both open communication and obtaining risk information (Saunders, 1982; 1999).

Appropriate proportionality to questions.   Questions should be developed around the major factors of risk for intimate partner violence and around behavior patterns exhibited by clients. The questioning should not belabor topics that are simply more interesting to the clinician or that appear more sensational. The questions should target all areas of potential abuse and should expand where there is evidence of greater problem. However, extensive probing of behaviors when clients give little evidence of violence can reduce client engagement in the interview. The extent of questioning should be proportionate to findings—that is, clinicians should not overdo it in the absence of indicators of risk factors.

A firm and focused approach.   Clinicians should maintain a nonemotional, persistent focus on intimate partner violence issues. Clients may try to divert attention to the victim's role in situations or to other areas. The response should be to refocus by ignoring the diversion content and returning to a follow-up question that is back on track.

Funneling from general situations to specific acts.   Straus and Gelles (1990) developed the Conflict Tactics Scale (which has since been modified to include more items) to measure intimate partner violence. They structured the questionnaire in the context of "conflict," a general term that can mean everything from harmless disagreement to physical harm. A funneling approach is recommended in assessment as well. Aside from the overall context for all questions, it can be helpful to return to this framework periodically in the questioning process.

The use of specific, concrete terms.   The interview language should be "clinical" around abuse issues and should not skirt sensitive terms. For example, in asking questions, concrete behaviors (often in closed-ended questions) should be considered such as, "When you said you were 'rough' with your wife, did you use your fist to hit her or use some other object"? Another example would be: "Describe the incident when you slapped her." These concrete terms should be preferred over general questions such as, "Were you ever abusive toward your wife?" or "What happened in that rough incident?" In general clinical practice, clinicians should use close-ended questions parsimoniously, as they can lead to very distorted responses. With offenders, however, the use of concrete examples in the question can convey that clinicians are familiar with these behaviors and are not naíve about them. Furthermore, the use of specific and direct questions with offenders has been found to elicit higher rates of abuse disclosure. Gondolf and Foster (1991) examined a sample of substance abuse clients in which only 5% of clinical records documented intimate partner violence but nearly 40% of the men admitted to having assaulted their spouse when asked a direct question as part of the research survey (Gondolf & Foster, 1991).

Self-observational Responses.   A particularly helpful way of promoting self-disclosure of negative behavior is to use questions that give clients a way to "report" behavior without pressuring them to "confess" to crimes. Clinicians can accomplish this by using the phrase "Did you find yourself doing . . . ". At one level, this language might seem unnecessary, but, in fact, it is also teaching clients to pay attention to their behavior—to observe themselves and note their problem behaviors. The questioning is styled in this manner: "Have you ever found yourself so angry that you simply blew up and hit her?" Or, "Did you find yourself being even more physically violent than you thought you would be?" Even though these questions are close ended, they afford an opportunity for endorsement in ways that are less punitive and, therefore, may be more acceptable for clients. An open-ended version is also helpful such as: "When she said that, what did you find yourself doing?"

A rehearsed assessment agenda.   Since risk assessment of intimate partner violence is so complex and challenging, it can be useful to have a rehearsed checklist of key elements to use with every client. This is not the same thing as following a rigid question-by-question reading of a psychosocial form. Clinicians can use a rehearsed set of *topic areas*, without subjecting clients to too much paperwork. The temptation to complete a form can easily result in superficial "checking" the presence of symptoms without attending to the specific qualities of client behavior.

A considerate, attentive listening stance.   As difficult as it can be, it is also important to use a considerate, polite, and attentive manner in assessing intimate partner violence. Many offenders are innately sensitive to being "dissed" and to even subtle cues of disrespect or inattention. Inattentive clinical styles can perpetuate client biases about indifferent and arbitrary authorities and can lead to unproductive use of services as well as poor assessment information.

The use of "clarification."   Rather than challenging clients to admit that they gave conflicting answers, it can be helpful for clinicians to act confused and to "need clarification" about different answers. By framing the questions as clinician confusion rather than client error or deception, clients may feel freer to approximate truthful responses. By providing "help" to clinicians, clients experience an illusion of more control of the interview and may feel less threatened about resolving conflicting responses.

A summary statement to clients.   Within each of the major domains of assessment, it can be helpful to summarize for clients what has been disclosed in the session. This is a way of clarifying for clients what is being registered and put on the table for consideration in treatment. This summarizing approach can set the stage for treatment planning.

RISK ASSESSMENT IN CASES OF INTIMATE PARTNER VIOLENCE

Risk assessment is a method for learning about clients' risk for dangerous or harmful behavior. In assessing risk for intimate partner violence, the focus can include a wide range of clinical and environmental factors. The central function of the risk assessment is to collect information that can inform treatment plans and risk management plans to reduce the likelihood of future violent acts.

RISK ASSESSMENT VERSUS CLINICAL DIAGNOSIS

Risk assessment makes use of diagnostic information, but it is not the same thing as a clinical diagnosis. Clinicians often use diagnoses to explain clients' behavior, but this practice has many limitations in capturing the risk for intimate partner violence, since this behavior can emerge against the backdrop of many different disorders and even among persons without any diagnosis. Risk assessment focuses on specific areas that research has shown to be associated with intimate partner violence.

Risk assessment can be enhanced by using actuarial methods rather than individual or subjective clinical judgments. Actuarial or statistical methods of risk assessment have long been used in the mental health field to assess risk and clinical changes resulting from treatment (Harris, Rice, & Quinsey, 1993; Miller & Morris, 1988; Milner & Campbell, 1995). These approaches are similar to those of insurance companies that set rates based on relative risk factors. A smoker, for example, has a greater likelihood of having heart disease than does a nonsmoker, even though in individual cases, a nonsmoker might die of a heart attack at age 40 and a smoker might live to age 85 with no cardiac symptoms. Considered across groups of people, however, the odds are that smokers are more likely to have heart disease. In addition, clinicians can use actuarial instruments such as the violence Risk Appraisal Guide (VRAG) (Quinsey, Harris, Rice & Cormier, 1998) to further assess risk. The VRAG combines elements from other instruments along with structured history collection to estimate risk of future violence across a wide range of offender types (Quinsey et al, 1998). In addition to this actuarial instrument, there are also measures of intimate partner violence such as the Conflict Tactics Scale (CFS) (Straus & Gelles, 1988) and other measures of anger and hostility that may further clarify the clinical picture with offenders. These anger instruments include the Danger Assessment Instrument (Campbell, 1986) and the Spousal Risk Assessment (SARA) (Kropp, Hart, Webster, & Eaves, 1999). The Novaco Anger Inventory, consisting of 25 items, has demonstrated validity and is clinically easy to administer (Huss, Leak, & Davis, 1993).

The Multidimensional Anger Inventory (Siegel, 1986) has assessed higher levels of anger among maritally violent than nonviolent males (Dutton, Saunders, Starzomski, & Bartholomew, 1994). In addition, a 36-item anger management scale that assesses escalating strategies, negative cognitions, self-awareness, and calming strategies has recently been developed and tested among college students (Stith & Hamby, 2002).

SOURCES OF INFORMATION

Clinicians may use any number of data collection tools such as the ones mentioned above or the Conflict Tactics Scale (Strauss & Gelles, 1990). These instruments allow for the collection of the same information on all clients and can be useful for understanding clients' behavior in more specific terms. In addition to formal assessment or measures, clinicians need to listen to victims' statements about violent behavior. Some authors believe that victims have a unique ability to predict their partner's violence, as they know the offender better than anyone else (Hart, 1994; de Becker, 1997). At least one study showed that survivor predictions of future violence were strongly associated with actual violence occurring (Weisz et al., 2000). Research has found that victims and offenders both under-report compared to police records, but that victims report more violence and more injury results of violence than do offenders (Heckert & Gondolf, 2000). As noted in chapter 4, however, a victim suffering from psychological trauma may be less able to accurately assess danger (Campbell, 1995), or she may minimize the danger as a way of coping with the threatening situation in which she finds herself (Dutton & Dionne, 1991). While there may be limitations in victims' assessments of their own risk, this perspective should be sought when making risk assessment decisions related to offender conduct. Many offender treatment programs use partner victim reports to corroborate offender statements about their violent conduct and to monitor ongoing safety concerns (Mederos, 2002).

Most risk assessment will be done as part of clinical interviewing. In these situations, as stated above, it is important to have at least a structured agenda of areas to cover in the interview. While it is not clinically imperative to use the same questions with every client (as would be the case using instruments), it is critical to cover the same domains with each client. A modular risk assessment framework may be helpful for clinicians in order to ensure that all major risk areas are covered with each client.

Monahan and Steadman's (1994) framework consisting of four-risk domains offers an easily implemented structure that still supports clinical flexibility in interviewing. This model for risk assessment, applied to intimate partner violence, explores dispositional, historical, clinical, and contextual factors associated with intimate partner violence. The four domains are as follows:

"Dispositional" Risk Factors   are those reflecting the offender's predispositions, traits, and tendencies. As such, they include the more enduring characteristics or styles of the offender. Hostility and impulsivity are examples of key dispositional risk factors. Hostility as a temperamental, constitutional trait often finds expression in anger. Anger, as a precursor to aggression, is a subjective emotional state that results from the combination of a state of physiological arousal, cognitions of antagonism, and an inclination to act in an antagonistic or confrontational way toward another person (Novaco, 1994). Anger as a state—that is, as a momentary reaction to negative events—is not necessarily clinically important. Trait hostility, however, results in continual states of anger that can motivate violence. Research provides support for the idea that trait hostility, interacting with alcohol abuse, predicts marital aggression (Heyman et al., 1995). Although most events associated with anger are typically aversive, or something most individuals would choose to avoid, some offenders may "engineer their own anger experiences by deliberate exposure to either internal or external stimuli; the arousal of anger may be satisfying as well as being functional" (Novaco, 1994, p. 33). Persons with trait hostility may derive a reward from anger and be more easily provoked to anger as well. A second important dispositional factor associated with aggression is impulsivity. Barratt (1994) describes three subfactors of impulsiveness: (1) motor impulsiveness, which involves acting without thinking; (2) cognitive impulsiveness, which involves making quick decisions; and (3) nonplanning impulsiveness, which involves a lack of concern for the future.

"Clinical" Risk Factors   include the various types and symptoms of mental illness or disorder. While research shows that having a major mental illness is associated with a significant increase in the prevalence of violence, having a substance abuse diagnosis poses a much greater violence risk—particularly under extreme contexts when offender coping strategies are no longer effective (Pihl & Hoaken, 2002). In one study of recent violence, the risk among substance abusers was more than twice that of persons with mental disorder and several times higher than that of persons with no identified disorder at all (Swanson, 1994). In addition, substance abuse interacts with personality in ways that can increase the risk of aggression (Flett & Hewett, 2002). Studies have shown that person-

ality disorders are more prevalent among intimate partner violence offenders than among nonviolent married men. Importantly, personality disorders are also among the clinical risk factors identified in Monahan and Steadman's model. Violent behavior, in fact, is included in the criterion of two personality disorders: borderline personality disorder and antisocial personality disorder (DSM-IV, APA, 1994). In addition, some researchers suggest that "repetitive violence is more likely to stem from relatively enduring personality traits" than from situational or unpredictable crises (Litwack & Schlesinger, 1987, p. 211). According to Widiger and Trull, "Many of the persons who abuse their spouses will meet the DSM III-R criteria for antisocial or borderline personality disorder, and research on the aggressive correlates of these personality disorders would support their construct validity. However, personality disorders are not necessarily predictive of future violence among intimate partner violence offenders. The personality traits that are most important and useful in understanding spouse abuse are only partially or indirectly represented in the DSM III-R diagnostic constructs (e.g., impulsivity, hostility, aggression, and lack of empathy)" (Widiger & Trull, 1994, p. 219). In addition, while psychopathic personality traits have predictive value for aggression (Hart, Hare, & Forth, 1994), they must be explored in the context of substance abuse and overall cognitive functioning (Pihl & Hoaken, 2002).

"Historical" Risk Factors   refer to events that have occurred in the offender's past that predispose him or her to violent acts in adulthood. The more extensive the offender history of violence, the greater the likelihood of continued violence. Likewise, a history of violence that involves more serious harm and injury predicts future violence. Also, having witnessed spousal violence during childhood may be a risk factor for certain males (Rossman, 2001; Cantrell et al, 1995; Widom, 1989; Rosenbaum & O'Leary, 1981). However, these factors must be explored judiciously, since many persons witness violence but never become perpetrators of aggressive behavior.

"Contextual" Risk Factors   include factors or characteristics of the offender's current environment that are facilitative or conducive to violence. Gondolf (2002) used this conceptualization to assess reassault in intimate partner violence offenders by assessing situational factors that contributed to violence risk. Among the salient

contextual factors is the status of offenders' relationships with their partners. Separation has been identified as one of the more lethal risk factors. The first few days and weeks after separation are particularly high risk. In addition, research suggests that easy access to weapons increases the potential for lethality in violent episodes. Another contextual factor is victim use of alcohol or drugs. Victim substance use has been found to be associated with greater likelihood of future victimization. Furthermore, given research on victim risk factors, social isolation of victims and their substance use should be carefully explored in assessing risk.

These risk domains might be best understood as a nested system of factors with multiple interactions among them. The risk factors are not simply additive; risk assessment must consider the interactions of factors such as substance abuse with personality, with executive functioning of the frontal lobes, and intersections of these with situational factors as well.

In addition to these domains of risk, clinicians should explore the specific history of abusive behavior in the four broad areas described earlier in the book (emotional, physical, sexual, and environmental). This includes asking about specific behaviors like those included in the Conflict Tactics Scale. Sample items from the Conflicts Tactics Scale are illustrated in the text box below.

Sample Items from the Conflict Tactics Scale plus Stalking Items

- I insulted or swore at my partner—to assess emotional abuse
- I twisted my partner's arm—to assess physical abuse
- I made my partner have sex without a condom—to assess sexual abuse
- I used force (like hitting, holding down, or using a weapon) to make my partner have oral or anal sex—to assess for greater physical violence
- I punched or hit my partner with something that could hurt—to assess physical abuse
- I slapped my partner—to assess physical abuse
- I used threats to make my partner have sex—to assess sexual abuse and threats

- I followed or spied on my partner—to assess stalking (environmental abuse)
- I showed up at my partner's place of work or other places where I thought she would be—to assess stalking

The risk assessment combines information about specific abusive behavior with more global dispositional, clinical, historical, and lifetime and current contextual findings. All factors should be considered without a need to cull out *the* salient focus. Substance abuse presents a difficult problem in assessment of intimate partner violence not unlike the problems it presents in other clinical assessments. There is always a desire to discover the primary problem and focus exclusively on it. This tendency becomes problematic when clinicians seek to know which *single* problem is primary; substance abuse or intimate partner violence. Essentially, clinicians formulate case-specific theories to explain offenders' behavior and may select substance abuse as the primary problem for treatment as a way of indirectly treating intimate partner violence. This approach, while intuitively sound, is poorly supported by research understandings of the contribution of substance use to violence (Pernanen, 1991, Roizen 1999). Even when substance abuse is very evident in a case, it is unlikely to be the cause of the violence; other factors, such as extreme personality traits or impaired executive functioning of the frontal lobes, may be more explanatory (Pihl & Hoaken, 2002). The recommended way to treat co-occurring conditions is to use integrated approaches that address both problem areas simultaneously (Minkoff 2001a; 2001b).

HOW TO USE RISK ASSESSMENT FINDINGS

Clinicians should use findings from a risk assessment interview to help direct or redirect treatment plans and other interventions. The discovery of high levels of risk should suggest an immediate need for interventions that can reduce risk for both victims and offenders. Plans to reduce risk can include traditional clinical treatment, but the more important consideration is for safety planning. Safety planning for victims has been discussed in earlier chapters; however, it has important implications for offenders as well as for victims. Safety

A High Risk Case

Dr. Smith was interviewing a 29 year old man who comes to treatment because he is depressed. He reports a history of heavy cocaine use two years ago, but only alcohol use currently. His live-in girlfriend had just told him to leave their apartment. He came for counseling to set the stage for couples counseling, hoping to get her back. In the assessment, he alluded to being in "juvenile court as a kid". He admitted to being "way too emotional—like, I get carried away and do stuff I don't want to do". He gradually admits to having been "far too hard on Jill", and clarifies later by saying he had once threatened her with a gun to keep her home. He has an unstable employment record and takes offense often during the questioning process and says he feels "like I'm on trial or something". He has two DUI convictions and left high school at age 18 while still in the 11th grade. He owns two handguns and reports liking target practice. His last words on leaving the session were, "I can't live without her and I don't want anyone else to have her either."

plans can include steps to help offenders inhibit their usual impulses or plans to be aggressive. This can include the use of "time-outs" as a way of deferring action until "cool down" time has been achieved. Time-outs are methods for recognizing warning signs of aggression and taking a break from the situation until anger or the need to control has subsided (Wexler, 2000).

When clinicians have assessed extensive patterns of intimate partner violence in mental health or substance abuse clients, the plan should include referral to a batterer treatment program to better target clients' special needs. In cases in which the violence appears to be acute—more related to specific stressors—and where it lacks extensive history, clinicians may choose to add behavior management to the existing treatment plans. "Treatment as usual" should be carefully reexamined, however, since traditional client-centered and supportive psychotherapy may result in inadvertent support for offenders' perspective on their relationship and behavior. While clinicians are unlikely to overtly endorse clients aggressive behavior, they may provide support for clients' reported feelings of being victimized—distortions that play a major role in fueling the violent behavior. Upon learning about clients' violent conduct, clinicians should avoid inadvertent support for perpetration patterns.

The risk assessment findings provide clinicians with a general level of risk in each case. Clinicians should be particularly vigilant about the cardinal risk signs: trait hostility and anger, heavy substance use, childhood conduct disorder, high impulsivity and a context of recent relationship dissolution or separation. In the case above, "Dr. Smith" faces a difficult case, having begun a counseling session that he thought was focused on depression or a loss of a relationship. Had he not done a risk assessment, Dr. Smith might have proceeded to provide support to the client by reflecting his sadness and anger at losing the relationship. But now, with risk assessment information in hand, he can step back and focus instead on the patterns that are associated with violence and can begin a risk reduction treatment plan. This case presents risks in all four domains: (1) predisposing (hostility and impulsivity), (2) historical (childhood antisocial and DUIs), (3) clinical (substance abuse); and (4) contextual (separation from girlfriend).

In the case following, Ms. Wilson has assessed her client and found few indicators of risk for violence. The one episode reported immediately led to guilt and withdrawal from further contact. Other aspects of her client's life are relatively stable, and he recognizes what is realistic and what is not. His risk is moderate—particularly compared with the man in the earlier scenario. By contrast, his risk factors are potentially high in only two domains: (1) clinical (depression and anxiety), and (2) contextual (recent divorce). However, this client recognizes the meaning of the divorce and seems to accept it, rather than believing he can influence his ex-wife to return.

A Lower Risk Case

Ms. Wilson interviews a 38-year-old man who has just been divorced. He reports thinking about his ex-wife constantly and feeling very depressed and anxious. He has had trouble at his job of 8 years because his concentration is poor right now. He admits that during the divorce process, he slapped his ex-wife once and immediately felt bad about it. He left home that evening and did not contact her for several weeks after that. Currently, he would like to try to get back with his ex-wife but knows this is impossible. He has 2 years of college and has only worked for two employers since getting out of school. He says his father was a violent man and that he does not want to become like his father. He admits to drinking beers on the weekend, but never gets drunk. He wants to be able to get over the loss of the relationship.

CLINICAL INTERVENTIONS WITH INTIMATE PARTNER VIOLENCE OFFENDERS

INTRODUCTORY CAUTIONS

As has been discussed, treatment of intimate partner violence offenders should be thought of as a clinical specialty that requires training in identification, assessment, and treatment approaches. As with other specialty practices, generalists may not only fail to properly assess and treat these problems, but, in using traditional mental health approaches, can inadvertently provide rationalizations for offender behavior. These guidelines are intended to provide basic guidance both for clinicians in general mental health and substance abuse practice who are not providing intimate partner violence offender treatment programs. Clinicians who are just getting started in clinical work with offenders may benefit from these recommendations. The guidelines include two very different sets of objectives given the differences in treatment settings and clinical missions. Unlike victim-related mental health or substance abuse problems, there is less assurance that individual symptom reducing approaches will be effective. In fact, the concern is the opposite—that without a thoughtful approach, traditional mental; health or substance abuse treatment could complicate intimate partner violence behaviors by providing "clinical rationales" that offenders can use to excuse or explain their behavior.

ON-GOING SAFETY PLANNING

As was discussed in chapter 4 with respect to victims, safety planning for offenders is not a one-time event. In fact, safety planning needs to be a continuing focus throughout the duration of treatment. Safety planning has a different thrust for offenders than for victims. With victims, safety planning is devoted to reducing the likelihood of serious injury or other harm by strategizing methods for avoiding the offender or establishing contingencies for managing crises. With offenders, safety planning is a method for reducing the likelihood of committing violent acts and of reducing the harm caused by aggressive behavioral styles. Safety planning can include teaching social skills related to impulse inhibition, such as the use of time-outs, but it should not be confused with treatment of the major factors that drive violent behavior. Time-outs and related methods do nothing to solve the causes of violent behavior; they merely contain it and make the situation safer (Wexler, 2000).

In essence, safety planning is a contingency strategy. Gondolf (1998) suggests safety planning in the form of working with offenders to help them identify their own strategies for avoiding abuse. According to Gondolf, "Avoidance strategies are usually based on the selective control that most batterers exercise: Most batterers hit their partners only at certain times and in certain places" (Gondolf, 1998, p. 146). As a result, safety planning involves helping offenders identify the circumstances under which they use violence and how they can use self-talk to de-escalate or avoid those situations. Safety planning can include the use of time-outs or leaving a situation when violence seems imminent. In fact, 53% of men who avoid reassaulting their partners after treatment used interruption methods like time-outs (Gondolf, 2000).

SUBSTANCE ABUSE TREATMENT

Research suggests that a substantial percentage of intimate partner violence offenders have substance abuse problems (Holtzworth-Munroe, Bates, Smutzler, & Sandin, 1997). Approximately 50% of males entering treatment for substance abuse or dependence have committed one or more acts of partner violence in the past year, and alcoholic males were six times more likely to commit partner violence than were nonalcoholic males (Chermack, Fuller, & Blow, 2000; O'Farrell & Murphy, 1995).

There is very limited information about how to effectively treat co-occurring substance use disorders and intimate partner violence offender behavior. As stated previously, clients in treatment may be found to have intimate partner violence offense patterns and, likewise, clients who have violent behaviors are likely to have substance abuse problems. However, a recent study suggested that only a few of the offenders in substance abuse treatment receive referrals for offending behavior (Schumacher, Fals-Stewart, & Leonard, 2003). In part, this problem can arise when there are no specific intimate partner violence treatment programs available. However, following assessment for both problems, treatment should attend to both issues with substance use being primary only when there is evidence of dependency such that even short-term absences from substances are highly improbable. Automatically referring every substance-abusing offender to substance abuse treatment before focusing on their violence is not recommended. As with other co-occurring problems (Minkoff, 2001a; 2001b), an integrated treatment approach is indicated. An integrated approach means that either a single clinician—or clinician colleagues who can share case information routinely—treat both conditions simultaneously (Minkoff, 2001b). In addition, the generally direct and confrontive approach used in intimate partner violence programs may have to be tempered with motivational approaches so that the substance abuse issues can be meaningfully engaged. Current treatment approaches to substance abuse rely on motivational interviewing (Miller & Rollnick, 2002) and the Transtheoretical Stages of Change model in order to provide effective treatment (Prochaska, DiClemente & Norcross, 1992; Prochaska, Norcross & DiClemente, 1994). These motivational approaches, built on the stages of change model, offer a way to encourage client buy-in to problems in a gradual manner, and they have been shown to be effective with offender behavior as well as substance abuse (Ginsburg, Mann, Rotgers, & Weekes, 2002). Clinicians who do not think they are competent to address both substance abuse and intimate partner violence offending behavior should refer clients with these problems to clinicians who are trained to treat them.

ANGER MANAGEMENT

Given the characteristics of intimate partner violence offenders as described in chapter 3, any treatment approach should be selected with caution and only after a thorough assessment. While the science on typologies of intimate partner offenders is very limited in its clinical usefulness, there are findings that should be carefully attended to. As noted in chapter 3, research has identified the traits associated with a group of offenders who are most likely to be most violent and harmful as well as least responsive to treatment. Some have identified this offender as antisocial, while others have described him as psychopathic or a "cobra" (Jacobson & Gottman, 1998) (see earlier section on personality disorders). The importance of these findings is that there may be major differences in how some offenders process information, experience emotions, and the ways their emotions are related to their behavior. For example, the more aggressive offender who also has lower physiological arousal in conflict, cannot be seen as an individual who "loses control" of his emotions and over-reacts. Quite the opposite, this offender is more deliberate and calculating in his abusive behavior, and clinical approaches that treat him as a captainless boat in high waves of emotion will be gravely in error. Lower arousal rates and lower heart rates may suggest lower fear levels and/or cognitive differences that mean a lesser ability to process and appreciate aversive events (Raine, 1996).

In fact, clinical assessment may reveal that an offender has these psychopathic characteristics and low arousability that are incompatible with the idea of losing control during an emotional outburst (Gottman et al., 1995). The identification of psychopathic traits can suggest a need for thoughtful treatment planning rather than administering standard clinical approaches for several reasons. First, psychopathic individuals have limited ability to use previous experience outcomes to modify their conduct (Newman, 1998; Patterson & Newman, 1993). Second, they may experience *satisfaction* rather than *anxiety* about conflict situations; so, for these clients, anger may be a useful tool rather than a problem emotion. Third, traditional psychotherapeutic support of clients' feelings may be perceived as endorsement of clients' use of anger to achieve objectives. If clinicians provide supportive comments for client expressions of anger or resentment, they may inadvertently support clients' beliefs that the anger and violence are justified. In these situations, clinicians' understanding of anger is very different from clients' understanding and the result can be an endorsement of violence rather than an expression of support for a client in stress.

Anger management is premised on the idea that a person experiences intense anger as a negative emotion and that the person needs a mechanism to bring it under control. This clinical approach may be useful for some emotionally unstable offenders, but there is, to date, no research to support the effectiveness of this intervention with intimate partner violence offenders. Given the complexities in conducting controlled trial research on the effectiveness of anger management, there is virtually no evidence to suggest the effectiveness of this approach (Novaco, 1997). In addition, it misses the boat with psychopathic individuals who do not experience anger as an unwanted emotion. The use of anger management language may have the inadvertent effect of teaching offenders how to describe themselves as "losing control" because it is more socially desirable and acceptable with this clinical explanation. If anger management approaches are used, they should only be applied when the assessment has revealed a clear pattern of emotional instability and subjective experience of anger as a negative emotion or a problem.

REFERRAL TO STRUCTURED BATTERER TREATMENT PROGRAMS

Structured intervention programs for domestic violence offenders began over two decades ago in response to what was seen by intimate partner violence experts as a lack of appropriate intervention with this population. Structured group psychoeducational approaches are specific to the problem of battering and use a standardized content. These structured programs also work closely with the court systems that refer men into treatment. In fact, the Duluth program, Domestic Abuse Intervention Project (DAIP) focused on the legal system as a key component to effective reduction of violence and programs for offenders (Pence, 2002). The Duluth approach uses education and video scenarios that are used to generate discussion by the men about what they have witnessed and how situations could be handled without violence. In addition, this program, and many other structured group approaches, uses client report logs to track control issues and actions during the week. Structured programs deal with beliefs that support violence and the cognitive errors such as negative or demeaning views of women that contribute to violence.

Group treatment has developed as the most common form of intervention for intimate partner violence offenders, in part because it expands the social networks of offenders in order to support nonviolence (a step to address contextual factors as discussed earlier), as well as providing offenders the opportunity to learn as well at teach others (Edleson & Tolman, 1992). Group treatment for intimate partner violence offending behaviors has enjoyed a clinical acceptance in much the same way that group approaches have been selected for substance abusers. Research cannot yet address the efficacy of any specific structured group treatment, but it does provide limited support for overall program effectiveness.

The effectiveness of structured offender treatment programs has been evaluated in several studies. The most rigorous of these studies includes 840 men, 618 of whom were court-referred and were the primary focus of the evaluation (Gondolf, 2001a). The study used a sample of offenders treated by four urban offender treatment programs that had been established for at least 5 years, had linkage with victim services, followed state standards of care, had a large number of clients, and used a cognitive-behavioral treatment approach. Voluntary program participants were nearly twice as likely to drop out as court-referred men (61% as compared to 33%), and they were much more likely to reassault their partners (Gondolf, 2002).

As to the effectiveness of treatment with court-referred domestic violence offenders, Gondolf reported that established, structured batterer intervention programs result in reduced rearrests for intimate partner violence. Follow-up interviews were conducted with offenders and their female partners 15 and 30 months after treatment, with a primary focus on reassault. Follow-up data were available from 413 women (67%) and 260 (42%) of the offender males (Gondolf, 2000). Forty-one percent of the men reassaulted their partners within the 30 months after treatment intake, and 21% of the men reassaulted more than once (Gondolf, 2000).

Other evaluations of offender treatment programs have resulted in mixed findings with modest program effects (Gondolf, 2001). New York City and Broward County, Florida, both participated in evaluation studies with numerous methodological problems. In general, there appear to be limited reductions in reassault 15 and 30 months after treatment intake; however, the percentages of reassault remain a reminder of the continuing danger that women experience even after their partners have been exposed to interventions.

GENERAL RECOMMENDATIONS

Clinicians who identify intimate partner violence offenders among their clients have several treatment options. Clinicians should revise their treatment plans so that "treatment as usual" takes into account the violent conduct. The treatment of depression, substance abuse, or other purely "clinical" problems may need modification based on a risk assessment that shows a pattern of intimate partner violence perpetration. It would be optimistic to assume that treatment of the clinical disorder will result in de facto treatment of the violence. However, clinicians without training in intimate partner violence will have difficulty approaching this problem in a focused way. Referral to structured offender programs should be considered as an alternative or adjunct to traditional treatment. Communities that do not have an established offender treatment program should explore resources to create one. The prevalence of intimate partner violence among clinical populations is great enough to suggest that this may be feasible even in less populous communities.

Avoidance of harm is an important goal for clinicians working with intimate partner violence offenders. The risk assessment should cue clinicians about the dangers of using inappropriate approaches like anger management as a broad-brush technique for all offenders. Clinicians should be careful to not suggest that traditional treatment of mental disorder or substance abuse will address intimate partner violence problems. In fact, some traditional treatment approaches like those that are designed to enhance self-esteem can actually result in increased aggression (Rice, 1997). Traditional treatment offers a better platform for treatment of victims than of offenders. Treatment plans can, at a minimum, focus on safety planning in every session. This attention to the safety of victims also has the ethical result of improved safety and independence of offenders, since continued assaultive behavior may cost him his freedom. Treatment aims should be focused on short-term concrete tasks, with clinicians remaining vigilant about the results of interventions throughout treatment. While continual focus on outcomes is generally recommended, the need for constant reevaluation of interventions is essential when intimate partner violence is present. This review of outcomes can include contact with collaterals and victims. Treatment should be marked by caution, with constant review of progress and clinical consultation with peers or supervisors to keep a focus on what can realistically be undertaken and what should be avoided. In this way, clinicians in mental health or substance abuse settings can practice in a safe manner to help offending clients maintain their own safety while going to greater lengths to ensure protection of the offenders' victims as well.

Chapter 5 reviewed clinical approaches for assessment and treatment of intimate partner violence offenders. The identification of offenders in clinical caseloads was discussed, and practical questions for screening and approaches to assessment were offered. **Chapter 5** also discussed the factors associated with the risk for violence among offenders and clinical guidelines for risk assessment were offered. Readers should be able to answer the following questions following a review of **chapter 5:**

- Why is identifying intimate partner violence offenders in the clinical setting a challenge?
- What factors should be considered in risk assessment with offenders?
- What is the role of survivor predictions in assessing risk levels?
- What are the key dispositional factors in measuring risk?
- What are the implications of substance abuse with respect to risk assessment?
- Which risk factors in the Monahan-Steadman model are the most likely to change rapidly?

Chapter 6

The Duties of Mental Health Professionals in Cases of Intimate Partner Violence

---

Chapter 6 focuses on the roles of mental health professionals that are unique to clinical intervention in cases of violence against women. These practice parameters are built on two predicates: that intimate partner violence is a crime, and that working with victims or offenders brings with it exposure to risk and dangerousness. The chapter sets forth "duties of care," including clinical preparation to achieve basic competency and to enable the clinician to identify and respond to violence disclosed by clients on their caseloads. A "duty to protect" involves safety planning for victims and an understanding of the appropriate use of hospitalization in cases of intimate partner violence. The "duty to warn and protect" is discussed in the context of the Tarasoff decision of 1976, and a "duty to report" relates to the legal actions required upon the disclosure of child or adult abuse by a client. Sections within **chapter 6** include the following:

- Principles of intervention in cases of intimate partner violence
- Duty of care
- Duty to protect
- Duty to warn and protect
- Duty to report

PRINCIPLES OF INTERVENTION IN CASES OF INTIMATE PARTNER VIOLENCE

The roles of clinicians addressing violence against women bring with them certain duties to the client; to the victim if the client is the offender; and to the public at large. These duties may be classified in four major groups: (1) a duty of care, (2) a duty to protect, (3) a duty to warn, and (4) a duty to report. The four areas of responsibility are convergent in many ways but are separated here to highlight burdens of professional responsibility in specific domains.

In the same way that clinicians generally operate with a theoretical basis, interventions in cases of violence against women also benefit from grounding in specific principles. An established set of principles is particularly useful in intimate partner violence because these cases are often clinically complex and at times require quick decisions in response to dangerous circumstances. Other authors have also recommended adoption of principles of care or a philosophy of treatment in intimate partner violence cases (Dutton, 1992b; Wilson, 1989). It is recommended that clinicians adhere to principles that form a foundation upon which duties can be discharged and clinical decisions constructed. These include the following seven principles:

- The first principle of care for intervention in cases of intimate partner violence cases is patterned after the Hippocratic oath, admonishing physicians to "First, do no harm." It should never be lost on a clinician that inappropriate or careless approaches to treatment with victims or offenders can result in injury or loss of life to any of the parties involved. Doing "no harm" means generic clinicians should attain, through training and other preparation, a basic level of competence to identify violence victimization in the lives of their clients, to conduct preliminary risk assessments, and to refer clients to clinicians with appropriate expertise. For clinicians with a specialization in this type of clinical practice, doing no harm means ensuring that all treatment programs are consistent with generally accepted standards of practice for intervention with victims or offenders.
- Most forms of intimate partner violence (e.g., physical assault, rape, stalking, harassment) meet states' statutory definitions for criminal behavior. This fact emphasizes the principle that intimate partner violence is unacceptable, that the infliction of

violence is the responsibility of the individual who chooses to perpetrate it, and that offenders should be held accountable for violent behavior.

- Women who are living in or who have separated from an abusive relationship often blame themselves and assume responsibility for their own victimization. The clinical remedy for this phenomena is that intervention with victims should be predicated on the principle that victims do not control and cannot be held responsible for victimization perpetrated by another person.

- Effective and appropriate interevention with women suffering from the effects of violence is not a model of pathologizing their reactions but, rather, one of empowerment. It is much more clinically useful to see reactions to life-threatening trauma as understandable in their context rather than as symptoms of a woman's pathology or disorder. This principle, in practice, ensures a more accepting and non–victim-blaming environment for treatment.

- The primary goal of treatment services for intimate partner violence offenders is the cessation of the violence that will provide for the safety of victims and their children. This goal takes priority over family reunification or the resolution of relationship issues and should be the foundation on which all treatment decisions with offenders are made. Clinicians working with offenders may wish to establish additional goals for treatment after priorization of nonviolence (e.g., improvement in employment status, resumption of child support payments, etc.), but should never lose sight of the first goal.

- The safety of clinicians who provide intimate partner violence services should be taken into consideration throughout and following the assessment and treatment process. Safety most directly relates to physical security but should also include avoidance of vicarious traumatization and other effects addressed in chapter 8. Steps to ensure clinician safety may include adoption of a protocol at an outpatient mental health office that offender services are not provided after hours when security in the building is unavailable; it may include not leaving a clinician alone in the office when victims or offenders will be seen; and it may include taking extra care to keep information private regarding where clinicians live.

- Services to victims and offenders of intimate partner violence lose an element of effectiveness when provided in isolation.

Thus, a community response (involving advocates and other criminal justice and court professionals) rather than an individual agency or clinician response is an important principle of care in intimate partner violence cases. In practice, this means clinicians are encouraged to participate in multidisciplinary teams and, with appropriate client releases of information, to discuss cases with other involved criminal justice or protective services agencies.

THE DUTY OF CARE

The incidence figures described in chapter 1 make clear that victimization is common among clinical populations, and, as a result, encountering current or historic abuse will not be a rare occurrence for any practitioner. As a result, all mental health professionals, regardless of the specific focus of their clinical practice, should prepare themselves to practice at least at a level of basic competence to identify and respond to intimate partner violence when it appears in the lives of clients on their caseloads. At a minimum, clinicians should be prepared to identify victimization through abuse-specific screening; to engage in competent risk assessment; and to refer clients appropriately if treating intimate partner violence is not their specialty practice. If referral to a clinician with a clinical specialty in intimate partner violence is not possible, the clinicians should access consultation and close clinical supervision throughout the course of treatment with the client.

Discharging the "duty of care" will require clinicians to engage in activities at two levels. First, clinicians should prepare themselves, through professional development activities (e.g., reading, education, and training), to be familiar with appropriate interventions in intimate partner violence cases in advance of ever seeing a client. Second, in addition to clinical preparation, the "duty of care" must be discharged effectively during the course of treatment intervention through application of learned principles and ongoing clinical consultation. Effective discharge of the "duty of care" will aid clinicians in ensuring safety for their clients and in avoiding any conflicts with the ethical codes of conduct. For example, enhancing practice competence through preparation will help ensure that a clinician does not practice outside the boundaries of their clinical competence and will reduce the likelihood that a clinician would ever inflict avoidable harm on a client.

DUTY TO PROTECT

Safety Planning with Victims of Intimate Partner Violence

As was discussed in chapter 4, there are three important aspects to safety planning and intervention with victims of intimate partner violence. The first involves steps to increase the victim's personal safety and that of the victim's children. The second relates to effecting psychological stabilization. The third focuses on methods for staying safe after the victim has separated from a relationship. Fulfilling a "duty to protect" by a mental health professional involves fully engaging in all three aspects of safety planning with a victim throughout the course of treatment. For clinicians working with clients who disclose the perpetration of acts of violence, the "duty to protect" would extend to steps to manage the offender's dangerousness through continuous risk assessment and steps to mitigate identified risk areas (e.g., substance use, anxiety management, etc.).

The Use and Misuse of Psychiatric Hospitalization

There is some evidence that battered women have been involuntarily committed to psychiatric hospitals despite their protestations or claims that their partners were abusing them (Gondolf, 1990; Warshaw, 1993). Clinicians need to be alert to circumstances whereby petitions for involuntary hospitalization might be used as a method of psychological control or harassment by one partner against another. A contextual approach would require a clinician conducting an evaluation for civil commitment to consider whether the behaviors of a woman are understandable and temporary reactions to violence or terror, or whether they are indicative of an underlying mental condition that requires involuntary hospitalization.

The misuse of involuntary civil commitment must also be considered with respect to intimate partner violence offenders. Criteria for involuntary hospitalization call for a mental illness (a treatable condition that has a known or knowable diagnosis and an identifiable form of care), and evidence of dangerousness. The paucity of research showing major mental illnesses among this population means that it will be a relatively rare instance in which an intimate partner violence offender will meet that criterion. While these offenders do pose differing levels of danger, this alone is not sufficient to recommend involuntary commitment. Clinicians will err if they believe that involuntary civil commitment or hospitalization of an offender will afford victims an effective measure of safety. While many units of psychiatric hospitals are locked, they are not typically sufficiently secure to prevent an offender's intended escape. In addition, involuntary commitments are typically short-lived, and an offender may be discharged quickly without the victim's knowledge. The "duty to protect" admonishes clinicians to be careful in meeting established criteria for involuntary hospitalization and to ensure that the process is not inappropriately applied in intimate partner violence cases.

DUTY TO WARN AND PROTECT

THE TARASOFF CASE

In 1969, a graduate student at the University of California at Berkeley informed his clinician that he planned to kill an unnamed but readily identifiable woman. The client conveyed to the psychologist his distress over the young woman's disinterest in him and stated that he planned to kill her upon her return from spring break. The client was temporarily hospitalized for observation, but upon his release, he went to the woman's home and, finding her alone, stabbed her to death. The young woman's name was Tatiana Tarasoff.

The landmark case of Tarasoff v. Regents of the University of California (1974, 1976) resulted from a civil lawsuit initiated by Tatiana's family against the University, the clinician, and the campus police. The Tarasoff case actually consists of two separate court decisions occurring two years apart. In 1974, the court held that clinicians have a "duty to warn" intended victims of threats made by patients. In a 1976 decision, the court altered the standard to broaden the responsibility of a clinician to use reasonable care to protect the intended victim against such danger. The expectation of clinicians arising out of the Tarasoff cases is twofold. First, they must exercise a reasonable degree of skill, knowledge, and care ordinarily possessed and exercised by members of their profession. Second, "Having exercised such a reasonable degree of skill, therapists who find that a patient poses a serious danger of violence to others bear a duty to exercise reasonable care to protect the foreseeable victim of such danger" (Tarasoff, 1976, pp. 438–439).

Clinicians who treat intimate partner violence offenders must be constantly alert to overt and subtler threats made by their clients, as the intended victim is, by definition, readily identifiable. Intimate partner violence offenders very often pose a threat to their partners, and their threats, specifically, are associated with harm. As noted in chapter 2, research has shown that an offender's threats to kill are associated with a woman's chance of physical injury from intimate partner violence (Campbell, 1986). Similarly, studies have found that a threat of violence and physical harm by the offender was the best predictor of physical violence as part of a pattern of stalking (Brewster, 2000).

DUTY TO REPORT

DUTY TO REPORT CHILD ABUSE

Mental health professionals in all states are mandated by state law to report known or suspected abuse of a child. When intervening in cases of intimate partner violence, clinicians must be acutely aware of the protection needs of children in the home, for, as indicated earlier, intimate partner violence and child abuse are correlated in 30%–70% of cases (Suh & Abel, 1990; Bowker, Arbitell, & McFerron, 1988).

If a clinician knows or suspects that a child in the home of his or her adult client is being physically or sexually abused, the duty to report is straightforward and should evoke little controversy or question. The obligation to a child who is not directly abused but who lives in the home of an adult client who is a victim of intimate partner violence is more complicated. At that point, the question is whether witnessing intimate partner violence rises to the level of child maltreatment. Clinicians who have a question regarding a child's physical or emotional status when no abuse has been directed at the child should take steps to have the child seen by a mental health professional with expertise in treating traumatized children. Such intervention should be undertaken with the involvement of the adult victim and should attend to her fears of losing her children should a child protection agency become involved in her case. At any point when a clinician suspects that the child is suffering abuse, whether from witnessing or experiencing violence, further evaluation is not the appropriate step; rather, a report to the child protection agency is called for. (See chapter 2 for a fuller discussion of the impact of intimate partner violence on child witnesses.)

Clinicians working with adult victims of intimate partner violence should also be alert to instances in which an offender uses abuse allegations against the victim as a means to harass her or to further his interests in a custody battle. If the clinician is the custody evaluator for the court, questions regarding the presence of intimate partner violence are called for, and the positive presence of intimate partner violence should impact the specific recommendations made to a court (see chapter 8 for further discussion on custody issues in cases of intimate partner violence). Evidence exists that a clinician's knowledge of intimate partner violence does not result in changes to the recommendations presented to the court, an omission that negatively impacts the welfare and protection needs of a child (Logan, Walker, Jordan, & Horvath, 2002).

DUTY TO REPORT INTIMATE PARTNER VIOLENCE

While all states have instituted mandatory reporting laws in order to protect children and vulnerable adults, a few states have also applied this statutory mandate to spouse abuse or intimate partner violence cases (Hyman et al., 1995). While the intent of this legislative policy has been to promote the protection of battered women, support for such laws and their effectiveness has been mixed. One study found that 80% of the victims of intimate partner violence believed that health professionals should have to report cases of spouse or partner abuse or violence, and just over half of the victims indicated they would have gone to a doctor or other health care provider about the violence if they knew that a professional would have had to report the abuse (Coulter & Chez, 1997). On the negative side, however, approximately 40% of the women indicated they would not seek assistance if they had prior knowledge that the professional would report the violence following their disclosure. In addition, 40% of the victims in the study worried that reportage would make their partner angrier, and a third believed that their partner would mistreat them more if a report were made. Similarly, in a study of over 1,200 abused women receiving treatment in an emergency room setting, 55.7% supported and 44.3% opposed mandatory reporting (Rodriguez et al., 2001). In general, the women supported the adoption of these mandatory interventions; however fewer seemed to perceive a benefit from the interventions, and some believed they would be less likely to report future violence as a result of these interventions.

There are important contradictions in the views of the battered women in these reported studies: while many supported mandatory reporting in general application to all women, when asked how it would impact them personally, the level of support appeared to diminish, and some indicated they would be less likely to reach out for assistance. The ambivalence of battered women to reportage and real concerns regarding dangers when reports are made need to be taken into consideration as clinicians comply with mandatory reporting laws on behalf of their clients.

REPORTING AND COMPLIANCE WITH FEDERAL LAW RELATED TO SUBSTANCE-ABUSE TREATMENT

Current federal regulations provide for strict confidentiality of the records of clients receiving services through alcohol and drug abuse treatment programs. Specifically, the *Regulations on Confidentiality of Alcohol and Drug Abuse Patient Records* (42 CFR, Part 2) provide that disclosure of any information that would identify a client as an alcohol or drug abuser is restricted. Historically, confusion has existed, as this federal regulation has appeared to conflict with state laws that mandate the reportage of known or suspected abuse or neglect. Recent changes to the federal confidentiality requirements have clarified the priority of child abuse reporting. Current regulations eliminate any restriction on compliance with state laws and allow the reporting of suspected child abuse or neglect *(Federal Register,* Vol. 52, No. 110).

Federal regulations do not specifically address the remaining conflict with state laws that mandate reports of adult abuse or neglect. As a result, clinicians in substance abuse treatment programs will need to work with the alcohol or drug abuser who is concurrently an alleged victim or perpetrator of abuse or neglect to self-report and to encourage him to request voluntary protective services.

Chapter 6 set out principles of intervention in cases of intimate partner violence designed to guide clinical work in this area. The chapter also described four duties for mental health professionals in intimate partner violence cases, including: (1) a duty of care, (2) a duty to protect, (3) a duty to warn, and (4) a duty to report (child abuse or intimate partner violence). Readers should be able to answer the following questions following a review of **chapter 6:**

- What is the primary goal of treatment for intimate partner violence offenders?
- What three steps does the "duty of care" require clinicians to be competent to perform?
- What are the two parallel duties for clinicians as set forth in the 1974 and 1976 Tarasoff decisions?
- How are these duties discharged?
- Why is the duty to report child abuse relevant in intimate partner violence cases?
- Under what circumstances does a clinician have a duty to report intimate partner violence?

Chapter 7

The Uniqueness of Mental Health Practice in the Intimate Partner Violence Domain

Chapter 7 describes how the intersection between the mental health and justice systems brings with it unique roles and responsibilities for mental health professionals, who must be attuned to the safety of clients, and cognizant of how standards of conduct typically applied to clinical practice may change in this area of work. An expanded view of who the client is and the need to work in teams rather than individual clinical practice are examples of how clinical practice can change. **Chapter 7** also describes common pitfalls encountered by clinicians in these cases, particularly as they relate to assessment, confidentiality and the management of client records, roles in court, boundary issues, and the misapplication of common clinical modalities. Finally, the chapter explores the phenomenon of "secondary traumatization"—the negative impact that clinical work in the intimate partner violence domain can have on a clinician. The sections within **chapter 7** include:

- The integration of mental health practice in the criminal justice system
- Common pitfalls encountered by clinicians in cases of violence against women
- The impact of helping: secondary traumatization

THE INTEGRATION OF MENTAL HEALTH PRACTICE IN THE CRIMINAL JUSTICE SYSTEM

By definition, intimate partner violence is criminal conduct that results in harm to a targeted person. As a result, clinicians who treat victims or offenders or who specialize in the psychological impact of trauma may find their practice intersecting with the criminal or civil justice systems. The point of intersection between the mental health and justice systems brings with it unique roles for clinicians. They must be attuned to the safety of clients and understand how standards of practice typically applied in routine clinical practice may change in application to these cases.

For example, clinicians who assess and treat offenders must take a broader view of who their client is than do typical clinicians. In addition to providing services to offenders, treating clinicians are often required to submit evaluative or progress reports to a court, a practice that in many states alters the application of laws related to confidentiality or privileged communication. Specifically, when an offender has been informed that the assessment or evaluation is for the court (i.e., when it is court ordered or court mandated), confidentiality laws related to the offender's disclosures in that limited setting are no longer applicable. Under this circumstance, the court has not become the client (in the strictest sense), but the obligation the clinician has of preparing reports for a judge who has mandated a client into treatment changes the nature of a therapy relationship with the offender-client. In addition, clinicians treating offenders are encouraged to define "client" in broad terms by maintaining a vigilant awareness of the degree to which the offender poses a risk of harm to the victim. Again, the victim is not a client in the strictest sense if the clinician is working with the offender, but the clinician incurs a legal and moral responsibility to attend to her safety when treating an offender. The duty to warn or take steps to protect intended victims from harm (discussed in chapter 6) is consistent with this broader view.

In addition to expanding the definition of "client," practice in the intimate partner violence domain also means clinicians may need to expand the number of professionals with whom they have contact on any given case. Over the past decade, professionals working in the intimate partner violence field have moved to a model of multidisciplinary team approaches, replacing single agency or clinician interventions. This model has afforded communities the opportunity to develop effective criminal justice responses to the investigation, prosecution, and treatment of intimate partner violence.

In addition to providing direct mental health services to a victim or offender, as a result, clinicians may also be asked to participate in multidisciplinary teams related to the management of interpersonal violence cases. Multidisciplinary teams, sometimes termed "coordinating councils," operate differently across the country. They may address policy and program development and the organization of protection and court services in a local community, and they may also engage in case-management functions. To the extent that a clinician participates in the latter, it is important to seek appropriate releases of information from clients before discussing any case within the context of a team setting. Clinicians who treat offenders may be excluded from case management teams, as these groups are often centered around the investigation and prosecution of a case and therefore would pose a conflict of interest to a clinician treating the offending client about whom the team was meeting.

Mental health professionals can offer unique expertise to the effective operation of multidisciplinary teams. These contributions may include the following:

- assisting a prosecutor's office in preparing a victim or the victim's children for participation in court proceedings,
- providing consultation to criminal justice professionals investigating or prosecuting intimate partner violence, (e.g., assessing the risk posed by offenders or interpreting the behaviors of victims within the context of trauma response), and
- participating with team members in needs assessments and the development of adequate offender treatment and victim support services within the community.

COMMON PITFALLS ENCOUNTERED BY CLINICIANS IN INTIMATE PARTNER VIOLENCE CASES

In addition to altering clinical practice, working with victims or offenders of intimate partner violence exposes clinicians to certain pitfalls, several of which are described here.

Common Pitfalls Faced by Mental Health Professionals

- Practice outside the boundaries of competence
- Failure to assess intimate partner violence
- Over- and underreactions to client disclosures of victimization
- Loss of client privacy by introducing clinical records in court cases
- Blurred boundaries for clinicians in the courtroom
- Overreach by clinicians testifying in court
- Overreliance on syndromal labels
- Cautions about individual psychotherapy with intimate partner violence offenders
- Cautions about marital or couples therapy
- Cautions about alcohol- and drug-abuse counseling
- Cautions about pastoral or Christian counseling

PRACTICE OUTSIDE THE BOUNDARIES OF COMPETENCE

Traditional clinical training programs have not typically included intimate partner violence in a significant way within graduate curricula. As a result, substantial numbers of clinicians enter into practice without sufficient preparation to intervene appropriately with intimate partner violence victims or offenders. Lack of graduate preparation leaves a clinician vulnerable to pitfalls resulting from practicing outside the boundaries of competence. The admonishment to psychologists found in the ethical standards of the profession is good advice to all mental health professionals: "In delivering services to clients or patients, psychologists must always be mindful that a primary obligation is to function competently. When providing services outside of one's area of competence, the risk of harm increases significantly" (Canter, Bennett, Jones, & Nagy, 1994, p. 34). The ethical standards go on to advise that simply having an "interest" in a particular area of clinical work does not necessarily qualify one to deliver services effectively or safely.

As discussed in chapter 6, it is recommended that clinicians identify victimization through abuse-specific screening; engage in competent risk assessment; and refer clients appropriately if treating intimate partner violence is not a primary area of expertise. If a clinician wishes to develop a specialty practice with victims or of-fenders, reading journal articles that provide findings from research studies or reviews of areas of the literature on intimate partner violence, attending didactic training programs on the roles and re-sponsibilities of mental health professionals in these cases, and receiving clinical supervision from a professional skilled in this spe-cialty area are recommended. Clinicians wishing to build this spe-cialty practice are also encouraged to visit local domestic violence shelters to become familiar with the services of the programs and the important perspective that victim advocates can offer to work in the intimate partner violence domain. In addition, to ensure effective practice, specialty clinicians should be knowledgeable about appli-cable laws in these cases (e.g., civil protective orders, mandatory reporting laws).

FAILURE TO ASSESS INTIMATE PARTNER VIOLENCE

As discussed in chapter 6, the presence of victimization history among a substantial number of women who seek mental health care is well documented. It does not follow, however, that clinicians routinely screen for abuse, nor that they detect abuse when working with clients (Jordan & Walker, 1994; Saunders et al., 1989). If a clinician is unaware of a client's exposure to violence, accurate lethality assessment will not be possible. In addition, if existing abuse is undetected, the clinician will also be unable to address a substantial factor effecting the client's mental health. Finally, unde-tected intimate partner violence leaves the clinician in the position of structuring a treatment intervention that could actually increase risk of harm to the client. A reasonable standard of care to avoid these pitfalls is to assess intimate partner violence among all fe-male clients.

From the legal point of view, the failure of a clinician to inquire, and to document the inquiry, about intimate partner violence can be cause for a finding of negligence just as it might be with unassessed suicidality. While not every clinician is expected to be a specialist in the treatment of intimate partner violence, concerns regarding client risk and clinician liability mean that the clinician should be able to assess the likelihood of this problem so that an appropriate referral can be made.

OVER AND UNDER-REACTIONS TO CLIENT DISCLOSURES OF VICTIMIZATION

Both novice and experienced clinicians will be exposed to clients' disclosures of graphic and severe victimization experiences. The challenge for clinicians in this circumstance is to respond in a balanced way that encourages the client to continue to disclose information at whatever level is needed. As a caring human being, it would be easy for a clinician to overreact with horror to a client's disclosure of her victimization. To do so, however, could communicate to the client that the clinician is threatened by such information and must be shielded from further disclosure. An overly emotional response could also elevate the client's existing level of fear regarding her circumstances; or it could leave her feeling more isolated and cause her to feel ashamed to reach out for assistance. At the other extreme, a completely unempathetic or matter-of-fact response to a client's disclosure could convey lack of caring and reinforce the tendency to minimize or deny victimization experience that is common to many victims. The challenge for the clinician is to strike a balance by communicating concern, care, and openness to further the exploration of the client's experience. The clinician should not suppress or deny honest human reactions to disclosures of human violence and cruelty. In fact, as will be discussed later, clinicians are encouraged to be aware of their own experience to hearing trauma stories from clients, including anger, fear, disgust, detachment, or other reactions, but should do so through discussion with supportive colleagues or supervisors outside the clinical setting. A similar balance must be achieved for clinicians learning of violence perpetration from a client. In this case, clinicians need to encourage disclosure from an offending client while remaining clear that violence is not appropriate behavior.

A second common pitfall for clinicians upon learning of current abuse from a client is to advise the client how she or he should behave. It is understandable that a therapist might want to urge a client to leave an abusive relationship immediately, divorce the violent partner, or to file criminal charges, but clinicians must be alert that doing so may encourage unsafe choices by a client. Feeling pressured by the clinician's advice, a client may act to seek an arrest warrant, for example, and may take that step before she has had adequate opportunity to take steps to be safe from offender retaliation (e.g., prepare a safety plan, move to a shelter, seek a protective order). Clinicians should also be sensitive to the fact that making choices for a client who has been victimized by an intimate partner is a form of taking control that reinforces one of the aspects of the abusive relationship. At the point of disclosure, the clinician should discuss all available sources of protection with a victim and ensure that she understands all that is available to her and can access what she wishes. The clinician should not convey that a particular solution is the only one appropriate for her.

Loss of Client Privacy by Introducing Client Information in Court Cases

Clinicians can also encounter pitfalls if they are not fully sensitive to the confidentiality of victim statements and the impact of mental health records being introduced in a court proceeding. Offenders may attempt, in both civil and criminal proceedings, to access privileged information found in mental health records of a victim (Murphy, 1998), and some have suggested that clients with victimization histories are among the most likely to have their records subpoenaed for legal proceedings (Hamby, 2004). Standardized releases of information may not adequately prepare a victim for the effect of having private information (including the mental health effects of her victimization or prior abuse history) revealed in court. At a very basic level, the release of a record in court may provide the defense with information such as a new residence or address for a victim, the very detail she most needs to conceal from the offender to ensure her safety. In addition, a defense attorney may seek evidence that a victim has suffered prior abuse as a means of discounting the victim's current claim of violence. In a domestic action, opposing counsel may seek evidence of substance abuse or depression in a victim to prove unfitness as a parent. Of course, clinicians should attempt to protect the confidentiality of a client's records, but if records have been subpoenaed or will be introduced in the court proceeding, the clinician must ensure that the victim is fully prepared for the ramifications associated with the loss of her privacy.

In order to fully inform clients regarding the circumstances under which their records could be turned over to a court, and to ensure ethical and legal clinical practice, clinicians should become informed of differences between subpoenas and court orders related to the release of records and guide their actions accordingly. For example, a subpoena is an order of the court for a witness to appear at a particular time and place to testify. (If the subpoena also requires the production of records that are in the control of the witness, it is called a "subpoena duces tecum"). A subpoena is the method used by parties in a case to obtain testimony from a witness at both depositions (where testimony under oath is taken outside of court) and at trial. Subpoenas are usually issued automatically by the court clerk upon the request of one of the parties, and they are issued prior to a hearing at which the opposing side has the opportunity to raise objections to the judge about the records being produced. If it is the view of the clinician that testimony or the production of records is not in the best interest of the client, a "motion to quash" the subpoena may be filed with the court. Upon hearing the evidence at a hearing, the court will then determine whether the testimony or records are relevant and therefore should be turned over; or whether there is not sufficient relevance or the privacy interests of the client outweigh the benefit of the materials being introduced in court. Clinicians may also request that only a particular portion of a record be turned over to the opposing counsel, and may ask that the judge conduct an in camera (out of the courtroom) review before rendering an opinion regarding the relevance of the records to the court proceeding. Specific court procedures related to records and other evidence are set out in laws and court rules specific to the state or jurisdiction in which the clinician practices and should be referenced as a guide to ethical and legal practice.

BLURRED BOUNDARIES FOR CLINICIANS IN THE COURTROOM

A second potential court-related pitfall for clinicians is the blurring of boundaries regarding their clinical relationship with an individual client and their testimony as an expert on intimate partner violence or trauma. Clinicians should be absolutely clear with clients, and with the attorney who seeks their testimony, regarding that role they are playing. If a clinician is subpoenaed to testify in court, it is important to distinguish the role of expert from treating clinician. A clinician who is treating a victim or offender should not, in most instances, be the clinician providing expert witness testimony on intimate partner violence, posttrauma response, or other matters. There is a potential conflict inherent in these roles, as the treating clinician may not be objective. In addition, testimony as an expert may result in comments made that are not in the best interest of the client or, at a minimum, that compromise the therapeutic relationship. Clinicians should be guided by the ethical standards of practice for their professions to protect both their own practice and the well being of a client. For example, the ethical standards for psychologists proscribe conflicting roles: "In most circumstances, psychologists avoid performing multiple and potentially conflicting roles in forensic matters" (Canter, Bennett, Jones, & Nagy, 1994, p. 150).

Overreach by Clinicians Testifying in Court

Clinicians who testify in court are often encouraged to provide testimony beyond their level of expertise. This may include being asked by a prosecutor or defense attorney to testify about the topic of intimate partner violence when that is not the clinician's specialty area of practice or when the clinician does not have a working command of the research literature in this area. While the clinician may be expert in trauma or forensic psychology, if they do not have a detailed working knowledge of intimate partner violence, they are advised to decline to serve as an expert or to clearly communicate the boundaries of their expertise to the defense counsel or prosecutor. As will be discussed in the following section on syndromal labels, even evaluating clinicians who are expert in intimate partner violence may also be at risk for such overreach if they testify that violence did not occur because they do not see specific evidence in the demeanor or mental status of the victim. As detailed in chapter 4, victims' reactions to physical, sexual, and psychological maltreatment vary based on numerous internal and external factors, and clinicians are cautioned regarding offering their expert opinion until they are fully informed regarding those influences. It would also be an overreach to testify that a client's current mental health problems relate to their prior victimization history instead of to a current rape, for example. This is something that may be asked of a clinician by defense counsel.

Finally, clinicians should also be cautious about testifying as an expert if they have only interviewed one of the parties to a case. This is a common pitfall in custody evaluations where intimate partner violence has occurred between the parents. There is evidence that custody evaluators are not equally skilled in evaluating for the presence of intimate partner violence and do not always ensure that the detection of abuse informs their recommendations to the court (Logan, Walker, Jordan, & Horvath, 2002). Effective expert testimony regarding the custody of a child requires evaluation of all parties and a specific determination regarding the impact of witnessing violence on the child for whom custody or visitation is being sought (see chapter 7).

RELIANCE ON SYNDROMAL LABELS

The psychological effects of violence against women have been described through development of two specific syndromes. Development of the Battered Woman Syndrome (BWS) provided a construct for beginning to understand the psychological effects of intimate partner violence (Walker, 1984, 1991). BWS was developed out of interviews with 435 women suffering from intimate partner victimization and was in part intended to redirect focus from the internal personality features of battered women to the external factor of violence that elicits psychological responses. This contextualization of a woman's emotional, cognitive and behavior reactions was viewed as less stigmatizing and victim-blaming and helped create an understanding that victimization experiences were the cause, not the result, of mental health problems for a woman (Koss et al., 1994). In the early 1970s, Burgess and Holstrom (1974) organized what they viewed to be common reactions of rape victims in a two-phase model consisting of an "acute" stage immediately following the rape, and a second, "reorganizational" phase evidenced in variable symptoms occurring in the months following. This second syndrome, named the rape trauma syndrome (RTS) originated from a study of 146 rape victims and was initially developed to assist therapists and advocates to structure their intervention with a victim following the rape. Its development was groundbreaking in characterizing a woman's reactions to rape and in providing a catalyst for future controlled empirical studies with rape victims (Frazier & Borgida, 1985; Boeschen, Sales, & Koss, 1998).

While development of the two syndromes has had extremely positive effect, use of either one in the courtroom without a clear understanding of their empirical limitations is a potential pitfall for a clinician. On the positive side, as was stated, RTS served as a spring-board for more controlled studies on rape and its psychological impact. In addition, empirical studies in the 1980s and 1990s confirmed many of the victim responses characterized in RTS, including depression, anxiety, fear, and interpersonal problems (Ellis, 1983; Resick, 1993). Nonetheless, the existence of the model itself has not been replicated in studies, and many courts have excluded testimony regarding the syndrome on the grounds that it was prejudicial to the defense of the alleged offender and could be interpreted as an expert opinion as to whether the woman was or was not raped (Koss et al., 1994).

Empirical studies have generally supported the sequelae described in the BWS (especially that of PTSD). In addition, Walker's pioneering work with BWS pushed the courts to acknowledge the influence of domestic violence on a woman and that the experience of abuse is reasonably considered an evidentiary matter in a legal case. Use of expert witness testimony using BWS also helped expand the understood meaning of self-defense beyond the narrow immediacy of fighting off a physical attack to incorporate circumstances in which the woman struck back at the offender when he appeared to be unexpectant of her aggression. Psychologically, the court was incorporating how a woman's affirmative actions were based on her appraisal of a situation as dangerous, not through the traditional legal construct of immediacy. Some have argued, however, that the process by which these positive effects in the courts were achieved on behalf of battered women carried with it a high price: that being application of a psychological construct built on the notion that a woman who acts out violently against the offender is operating under circumstances of diminished capacity (Stark, 1992). Several authors have pointed out that BWS was not intended as a diminished capacity defense, but that in application, this is the effect (Dutton, 1994).

Evaluating the clinical usefulness of these syndromes should include consideration of three questions: 1) do the symptoms associated with that syndrome represent the primary psychological responses to that type of violence; 2) it is valid to view a post-assault syndrome as a single, unitary phenomenon; and 3) does the presence of an assault syndrome mean definitively that the assault took place) (Briere, 2004; Briere & Jordan, in press). RTS and BWS fare moderately well to the first question in that most of the psychological reactions they describe have also been documented in other research. The syndromes fare less well when considering the question of a unitary phenomennon in that the type of reaction by a given victim to an assault experience will vary significantly based on a number of other internal and external factors (e.g., prior abuse, co-existing mental health problems, severity of the current assault, existence of support following the assault), it is not solely based on the assault experience. Third, the syndromes fail on the final question in that "there is very little reason to believe that the presence or absence of RTS or BWS is diagnostic of assault exposure" (Briere & Jordan, in press). In a similar critique, it hs been pointed out that there is no unified set of criteria by which to reliably determine whether the syndrome applies in a given case (Dutton, in press).

The most important guidance for clinicians to avoid the pitfalls associated with use of these syndromes in court cases is to remain mindful of their empirical limitations and avoid rendering an expert opinion regarding whether a woman has or has not been victimized based on the presence or absence of a specific cluster of psychological symptoms. Alternatively, clinical forensic hypothesis testing, which involves examining each issue in a woman's case based on its own theoretically-driven formulation and clinical assessment has been suggested (Dutton, in press). For example, as Dutton points out, ". . . a battered woman's appraisal or perception of deadly threat requires the identification of coherent pathways that are generally supported theoretically and empirically in the scientific literature and that are amenable to forensic evaluation" (Dutton, in press).

CAUTIONS ABOUT INDIVIDUAL PSYCHOTHERAPY WITH INTIMATE PARTNER VIOLENCE OFFENDERS

Group intervention has been described as the most appropriate treatment modality for intimate partner violence offenders, in part, because it expands the social networks of offenders to include men who support nonviolence (Crowell & Burgess, 1996). In individual therapy, it is difficult for therapists to remain as topic focused as is recommended in most batterer intervention programs, especially those that are based on cognitive behavioral or social learning approaches (Tolman & Bennett, 1990). Regardless of their theoretical perspectives, most clinicians tend to follow the client's lead in sessions, and the operating premises of most psychotherapies call for a client-centered or client-empowering approach. Offenders in individual therapy are remarkably adroit at shifting attention away from their behavior and on to other targets; consequently the clinician must be steadfast in insisting that the focus of therapy remains on the offender's behavior, a requirement that can tax even the most diligent of therapists. Another advantage of a group format is that it facilitates peer confrontation and peer support—two very helpful tools in working with offenders. Clients who are making progress tend to exert positive influences on those who lag behind, and they can confront each other in ways that clinicians cannot. Groups can also be topical from session to session, and one can be assured that every client has been presented with the content planned by the clinician. Finally, supportive individual therapy can too easily become a method by which the offender rationalizes his conduct if a supportive clinician unwittingly endorses violence. Unless the clinician can constantly confront the offender's thinking and rationalizations for violent behavior, individual therapy may serve to indulge the offender's traditional defenses and excuses for his conduct and should be considered a pitfall to avoid.

CAUTIONS ABOUT MARITAL OR COUPLE THERAPY

A significant number of couples seeking help for their relationship present with some evidence of intimate partner violence. In fact, in one study, 50%–70% of couples presenting for treatment at clinics reported aggression in their relationships (Cascardi, Langhinrichsen, & Vivian, 1992). The decision regarding the appropriateness of conjoint therapy should be left to the clinician following a screening for intimate partner violence—it should not be a determination based solely on the request of the clients, nor on a referral from the court. In fact, there is fairly widespread agreement that couple therapies are not appropriate with court mandated or severely violent men (see Crowell & Burgess, 1996, p. 134). As noted by one author, "Couples counseling may be suitable for some couples on a voluntary basis and after careful screening for threats and coercion, but it does not appear to be particularly practical or suitable for most court-referred cases" (Gondolf, 2002, p. 15). Clinicians must keep in mind when making a determination regarding the appropriateness of conjoint therapy that both victims and offenders tend to minimize the violence or the severity of its impact. A complete assessment and full disclosure of violence is unlikely when a victim is seated next to a violent intimate partner. This alone suggests a general rule of thumb that conjoint therapy for intimate partner violence cases is contraindicated.

The recommended approach following assessment of mild and noncontinuing violence is to proceed with couples counseling but to continuously reassess for violence or its precursors and to adjust the treatment approach accordingly so as to not prescribe increased conflict as a means of seeking relationship resolution. Likewise, adopting a position of strengthening the relationship can be a major problem if there is violence in the relationship. Caution, continually reassessed risk and openness to changing strategies is important in providing safe couples counseling. Conflicts between feminist and traditional systemic or behavioral approaches with couples have not been resolved, though some have proposed limited use of traditional approaches once the level of violence has been found to be mild and nonrecurring (Gauthier & Levendosky, 1996).

In summary, research on the safety effectiveness of couples counseling has not been conducted with sufficient controls to warrant recommended use of conjoint counseling in violent relationships (Aldarondo & Mederos, 2002). Some who propose using conjoint approaches for couples with violence accept some level of recurring violence during and after treatment (Brown & O'Leary, 1997) an idea that has little endorsement in the domestic violence field.

CAUTIONS ABOUT ALCOHOL AND DRUG ABUSE COUNSELING

As has been discussed, alcohol and drug abuse frequently co-occur with intimate partner violence. This coexistence is particularly important clinically because concurrent alcohol/drug abuse often increases the severity of intimate partner violence, and victimization in turn is related to increased substance use. Treatment models that address only one of the two problems are not only ineffective, they may risk safety for a victim and sobriety for a substance user. Alcohol and drug counselors are cautioned not to assume that a cessation of alcohol or drug use by an offender will also ensure nonviolence, as that belief is a pitfall that will lead to ineffective and risky treatment.

CAUTIONS ABOUT PASTORAL OR CHRISTIAN COUNSELING

Support and counseling from a clinician identified as a pastoral or a Christian counselor can have an extremely positive effect for a victim, as the church is a traditional and very powerful support system for many women. In addition, Christian-focused counseling can address the spiritual aspects of the victim's experience if that is of relevance or significance to her life. There is potential risk with this approach, however. If it maintains a strict adherence, without regard for the victim's safety, to the traditional Christian emphasis on valuing the marital bond, pastoral counseling may limit a victim's ability to access necessary forms of protection for herself and her children. A related problem is encountered when a pastoral counselor focuses almost exclusively on the behavior of a victim as a means to control or prevent the violence of an offender (e.g., exhorting her to be a more supportive wife or to pray for nonviolence). If a pastoral or Christian counselor avoids these types of pitfalls, the intervention can be of assistance, particularly for victims who already feel established trust with their pastoral or Christian counselor and feel safe to fully disclose their victimization. For victims who desire spiritual guidance as they deal with the trauma of the abuse, pastoral counseling can be an especially comforting form of treatment.

THE IMPACT OF HELPING: SECONDARY TRAUMATIZATION

The study of traumatic stress has evolved over the past two decades, expanding to encompass the field's growing understanding of the multiple victims who are impacted by a single trauma. A significant event in this progress was the 1980 publication of DSM-III, that included the diagnostic category of posttraumatic stress disorder (American Psychiatric Association, 1980). For the first time, a formal conceptualization existed for the common symptoms experienced by those who had faced trauma. The early focus of the trauma literature was limited to the primary victim of the incident, but over time understanding of the breadth of trauma's impact expanded to include not only those who directly experience or witness traumagenic events but also those indirectly exposed to them and their

> "The professional work centered on the relief of the emotional suffering of clients automatically includes absorbing information that is about suffering. Often it includes absorbing that suffering itself as well." (Figley, 1995, p. 2)

consequences. The DSM-IV includes, within what constitutes a sufficiently traumatic experience, the following language:

> "The essential feature of Posttraumatic Stress Disorder is the development of characteristic symptoms following exposure to an extreme traumatic stressor involving direct personal experience of an event that involves actual or threatened death or serious injury, or other threat to one's physical integrity; or witnessing an event that involves death, injury, or a threat to the physical integrity of another person; *or learning about unexpected or violent death, serious harm, or threat of death or injury experienced by a family member or other close associate* (Criterion A1)." [Italics added.] (APA, 1994, p. 424).

Clinicians who provide services to intimate partner violence victims and who are routinely exposed to the trauma stories of their clients may be included in the latter part of the criterion description.

Historically, the physical, emotional, and behavioral sequelae associated with providing human services has been described as "burnout," an occupational side-effect characterized by a chronic, progressive condition involving depersonalization, a reduced sense of personal accomplishment, and discouragement (Cherniss, 1980; Courage & Williams, 1986; Freudenberger, 1986; Kahill, 1988; Maslach, 1982; Maslach & Jackson, 1981). Burnout is a process of demoralization involving the deterioration and depletion clinicians experience from excessive work-related demands (Freudenberger, 1984), especially when working with a broad range of client populations. In recent years, however, research has focused more narrowly on the unique impact of working with clients whose stories of trauma expose clinicians to acute images of suffering, leading to development of the terms "secondary victimization" (Figley, 1993), "vicarious traumatization," (McCann & Pearlman, 1990), and "emotional contagion" (Miller, Stiff, & Ellis, 1988). More recently, Figley has suggested the term "compassion fatigue" to describe the by-product of trauma-related mental health work (Figley, 1995).

These terms may be more useful to professionals in the trauma field than the term burnout, as they highlight the unique characteristics of trauma work and because they incorporate in their conceptualizations the more sudden onset of symptoms that is common for trauma clinicians (Figley, 1995). In addition, terms such as compassion fatigue or secondary trauma focus attention on the characteristics of the work that elicit symptoms from clinicians rather than focusing on what may be perceived as weaknesses or shortcomings of clinicians themselves.

Some authors argue that secondary or vicarious traumatization is an unavoidable result of trauma counseling and observe that the nightmares, fearful thoughts, and intrusive images suffered by clinicians are very similar to the symptoms experienced by trauma victims (McCann & Pearlman, 1990). Surveys with female psychologists and counselors for sexual violence victims, for example, have found that clinicians with a higher percentage of victims of sexual violence in their caseloads experience more symptoms of posttraumatic stress (Schauben & Frazier, 1995). In one study of licensed psychologists, researchers found that working with victims of sexual violence was positively correlated with emotional exhaustion and depersonalization, a finding particularly true of younger practitioners in the study (Ackerley et al., 1988). Several researchers have identified post-trauma related symptoms in clinicians providing services to victims. For example, a study of counselors working with sexual abuse survivors found that the current percentage of victims in their client caseloads, the percentage and career total of direct service hours with those clients, and the level of exposure to graphic details regarding the sexual abuse of their clients contributed significantly to the post-trauma symptoms experienced by the clinical staff (Brady, Guy, Poelstra, & Brokaw, 1999).

Finally, a recent study of female and male counselors explored the impact of hearing traumatic material; the way in which the counselors were changed as a result; and the way they coped with the challenges of their work (Iliffe & Steed, 2000). All the counselors in the study identified a loss in confidence in their own skill and a tendency to take too much responsibility for the welfare of their clients. Both female and male counselors struggled with maintaining respect for their clients' choices, particularly those involved in a victim's return to a violent home. Counselors in the study also felt they could no longer be shocked after hearing stories of horror from their clients, and most experienced visual images of what they were told. Physical responses were reported by a number of clinicians, including a general feeling of heaviness, nausea, and feeling shaken or exhausted. Changes to cognitive schema such as feeling less secure in the world, changes to their worldview, regarding others more warily, and experiencing an increased awareness of gender power and control issues were common among intimate partner violence counselors.

Working with offenders also impacts clinicians, with some reporting that engaging abusive men in treatment is the most challenging aspect of their work (Iliffe & Steed, 2000). Almost a third of clinicians working with offenders report experiencing increases in emotional, psychological, and physical symptoms (Edmunds, 1997) and over half report becoming discouraged about client change, lowering expectations when working with sex offenders, and experiencing emotional hardening, increased anger, decreased tolerance, and an increase in confrontational behavior (Farrenkoph, 1992). Finally, clinicians working with threatening clients report becoming more cautious in personal relationships and more concerned about family safety (Ellerby, 1997). They also feel more anxious about their children's safety and are more vigilant around strangers (Jackson, Holzman, & Barnard, 1997).

CONTEXTUAL FACTORS: WHAT THE WORK BRINGS TO THE CLINICIAN

While work with trauma survivors and victims of crime can be extraordinarily rewarding, its unique demands, stresses, and responsibilities can challenge the most seasoned clinician. A clinician may be the first person outside a victim's family to hear about physical or sexual abuse in a home. A clinician may be asked to explain the "why" of unexpected trauma and destruction of life associated with violent death. Clinicians hear the anguish of children and adults who are victims or who are grieving over the loss of a loved one. They may also be exposed to vivid, graphic stories of horror and physical injury sustained by clients. Clinicians hear cold recounts by offenders of deliberately inflicting pain on another person and may be targets of the anger of a victim who cannot safely display her grief and rage in another setting. Finally, clinicians working with victims and offenders may be called upon by a court or protection agency to conduct an evaluation regarding the safety of a victim or the danger posed by an offender, recommendations that can have life-altering implications. These experiences highlight both the challenges and the rewards of therapeutic work in this area.

In the intimate partner violence arena, it is also important to consider the danger that offenders can pose to clinicians themselves. Clinicians, whether treating the victim or the offender, should be especially cautious of this risk when offering services at the point a victim leaves the offender, as the point of separation in a relationship has been associated with increased risk for a victim and may also elevate risk for others in the victim's environment. Offenders may be threatened by the work a clinician is doing with a victim, particularly if he perceives her therapy as a threat to the continuation of his relationship. A clinician may also be blamed by an offender for what he perceives to be an intrusion into his relationship and damage to his ability to control his partner. Treating or evaluating clinicians testifying in court on behalf of a victim may also be exposed to retaliation from an offender, either in advance of the testimony as a means to influence the clinician's testimony, or after the trial as a means of seeking retribution. Finally, clinicians treating offenders may also incur the anger of an offender as a result of the confrontation that is typically a part of the treatment regimen with intimate partner offenders or when they report back to a court incidents of noncompliance by the offender.

Research has documented the frustration that victims often feel when they seek the court's protection or prosecute an offender. A victim's encounter with the court system can also leave clinicians feeling frustrated by the institutional barriers within the justice system that contravene therapeutic goals and seem unjust to victim-clients. Examples of these frustrations include: seeing a victim's pleas to law enforcement for the arrest of a repetitively abusive partner go unheeded; seeing a victim's request for civil protection rejected; seeing a violent offender successfully win visitation rights to the victim's children; or seeing an offender win acquittal when the clinician believes that he should have been convicted of a crime.

Finally, clinicians may feel very ambivalent about the uncertain success of intervention with a client when she chooses to return to a home with on-going risk and violence.

"By virtue of having 'been there,' the clinician who has worked through and come to terms with his or her own abuse history may be optimally suited to provide sensitive, nondiscounting services to other survivors. In fact, the survivor-clinician may be able to understand the survivor-client's experience and responses in ways that the clinician with no such history rarely can. It is probably true, in this regard, that some of the very best abuse-focused psychotherapists are survivors who have addressed and inte-grated their own early histories." (Briere, 1992, p. 159)

ABUSE HISTORIES: WHAT THE CLINICIAN BRINGS TO THE WORK

A history of abuse in childhood is not uncommon among clinicians (Elliott & Guy, 1993; Follette, Polusny, & Milbeck, 1994; Pope, Feld-man-Summers, 1992). In a study of male and female clinicians, 17% of the clinicians (13% of male clinicians and 20% of female clinicians) reported a personal history of childhood sexual abuse; and 7.3% of males and 6.9% of females reported physical abuse histories (Nut-tall & Jackson, 1994). Including both sexual and physical abuse his-tories, the percentage increased to 21% of clinicians. Other studies report even higher rates, with 29.8% of clinicians (36% of female clinicians and 23% of male clinicians) experiencing some form of childhood trauma in one study (Follette, Polusny, & Milbeck, 1994) and in another, 33.1% of mental health professionals reporting a history of sexual or physical abuse during childhood (Pope & Feld-man-Summers, 1992). In the latter study, 36.6% of study participants reported experiencing some form of abuse during adulthood (Pope & Feldman-Summers, 1992).

Abuse histories may change the way a clinician responds to or is impacted by clinical work. For example, in one study, clinicians who had been sexually abused and/or physically abused were more likely to believe allegations of sexual abuse contained in 16 vignettes alleg-ing sexual abuse (Nuttall & Jackson, 1994). Other writers have docu-mented that trauma clinicians with personal trauma histories showed more negative effects from their professional work than those without a personal history (Pearlman & Maclan, 1995). Clini-cians with abuse histories may be at risk for two types of boundary violations: overidentifying with the client's experience through acutely empathetic responses and over disclosure, or a defense-driven underidentification with a client (Wilson & Lindy, 1994; Marvasti, 1992). Similarly, Briere (1992) points out three areas of risk for survivor-clinicians:

Overidentification occurs when the clinician reacts in an unconsciously intensified way to those aspects of the client's experience that most resemble that of the clinician. Clinicians who have not resolved their own abuse experiences may be at risk for overreacting to a client's disclosure of an event or type of abuse experience that reminds the clinician of her or his own history. At an affective level, that may include feeling intense sadness or anger; at a behavioral level it may include directing the client to take certain actions (i.e., to prosecute or confront an offender), or it may be manifested in the clinician's overinvestment in trying to comfort the client. In short, overidentification is evident when the clinician's history of abuse contributes or alters the process of therapy with the client.

Projection occurs when the clinician confuses his or her own abuse issues with those of the client. Clinicians who have not resolved their own trauma history may also be at risk of projecting their own experience or reaction to abuse onto that of the client. For example, a clinician may perceive a client as more angry than she is; may interpret the lack of an overt response to abuse experiences as resolution by the client; or may believe the client to be resistant to change when in fact the client is afraid to take certain steps based on a realistic appraisal of the threat posed by an offender.

Boundary confusion occurs when the clinician's abuse history encumbers his or her ability to discern appropriate interpersonal boundaries, particularly those of the therapeutic relationship. The most egregious boundary confusion (or violation) would be the circumstance of a sexual relationship between the clinician and the client. Boundary confusion in the intimate partner violence domain may be evidenced most commonly by clinicians who disclose details of their personal victimization during therapy with the client or by clinicians who ask overly intrusive questions.

MITIGATING THE EFFECTS OF SECONDARY TRAUMA

While clinical work in the intimate partner domain can be difficult work for clinicians, it is also replete with extremely positive and rewarding aspects, such as the meaningfulness of being part of the healing process, the joy of seeing clients change and grow, and the satisfaction associated with contributing—not only at an individual clinical level, but in the broader sense of helping society as a whole (Schauben & Frazier, 1995).

There are numerous steps that clinicians and mental health agencies can take in order to mitigate the negative effects associated with this area of mental health practice. These can include avoiding the isolation that can occur inadvertently when only one clinician in an office serves victims and offenders, or when a clinician is the only therapist in an office (Jordan & Walker, 1994). It is also important to ensure that adequate training is available to all clinicians and clinical supervisors (Iliffe & Steed, 2000; Jordan & Walker, 1994), as anxiety may be mitigated when a clinician feels a greater level of competence about how to intervene in these cases. Effective training will also reduce the likelihood that a clinician will succumb to one of the pitfalls identified in this chapter and will therefore avoid the stress associated with making an error that is harmful to a client. Clinicians and their supervisors need to discuss whether it is advisable for the clinician's caseload to be made up only of intimate partner violence clients or whether a more diverse caseload (i.e., including clients without current victimization) would help avoid some of the negative impacts of routinely hearing traumagenic material (Iliffe & Steed, 2000; Jordan & Walker, 1994). It is also recommended that trauma clinicians receive clinician supervision from a therapist with specific expertise in post-traumatic stress and trauma-related clinical work (Pearlman & Saakvitne, 1995); and that a regular time be set aside in staff meetings solely for the purpose of addressing feelings and concerns of clinical staff as a means of mediating or reducing the impact of vicarious trauma (Brady et al., 1999). Finally, debriefing sessions are recommended when a particularly difficult case is handled by a clinician or mental health agency. This may include cases of especially egregious abuse; cases in which a client dies; or cases that involve some type of harm to clinical staff. Care must be taken so as not to overwhelm clinicians with the constant presentation of traumatic material (Jordan & Walker, 1994; McCann & Pearlman, 1990).

Chapter 7 described the unique parameters of mental health practice in intimate partner violence cases. The broadening view of who the client is; the need to work in teams rather than in individual clinical practice; the management of clinical information in the court system; and the role of expert witnesses were explored. **Chapter 7** also described common pitfalls encountered by clinicians in these cases and addressed the impact on clinicians of clinical work in this area. Readers should be able to answer the following questions following a review of **chapter 7:**

- What are the risks associated with the introduction of a victim's mental health record in a court proceeding?
- Which of the "common pitfalls" do you believe are made by most mental health professionals? To which pitfall are you most susceptible?
- What are some of the challenging "contextual factors" of intimate partner violence work that can stress a clinician?
- What are the implications of having an abuse history for a clinician working with victims of intimate partner violence?
- What are three mitigators of secondary trauma?

Chapter 8

Intimate Partner Violence: A Legal Primer for Mental Health Professionals

---

Chapter 8 describes the experience of women as they enter the justice system in search of civil protection or the prosecution of the offender. The chapter focuses on the criminal justice process women encounter, including police response and how cases are prosecuted. Civil orders of protection are a key remedy for victims and are highlighted in detail in chapter 8. Finally, custody issues as they arise in the context of intimate partner violence cases and the role of evaluators are discussed in the chapter. The sections within chapter 8 include:

- The experience of intimate partner violence victims with the legal system
- Intimate partner violence as a criminal offense
- Civil protective orders for victims of intimate partner violence
- Custody issues related to intimate partner violence

THE EXPERIENCE OF INTIMATE PARTNER VIOLENCE VICTIMS WITH THE LEGAL SYSTEM

Women experiencing intimate partner violence seen by clinicians in mental health or substance abuse programs may also be involved

134

in the court system, as often these cases involve civil orders of protection, criminal prosecution, or custody or other domestic actions. Clinicians should be alert to the unique challenges women face in the court system in order to ensure that treatment plans include sufficient attention to these additional stressors in the woman's life. Court systems are, by their nature, adversarial. As noted by one author, "If one set out intentionally to design a system to provoking symptoms of posttraumatic stress disorder, it might look very much like a court of law" (Herman, 2003, page 159). Most often, victims have little control in the courtroom, with legal procedures and roles set out by civil and criminal rules and case law. While in the courtroom for hearings or trial, they are directly and visually exposed to the offender who harmed them and of whom they may still be very afraid. Whether petitioning for civil protection or testifying in a criminal case, they are asked to recount a violent episode, not in the supportive or safe environment of a therapy session, but rather to a defense attorney whose role it is to question their credibility, dispute their memory, or even to challenge whether they are telling the truth.

In addition to these psychological stressors, victims who seek court action often do so believing that the offender will attempt to retaliate against them. In fact numerous studies show that one of the primary reasons women do not seek help or intervention is because they fear retaliation (Chaudhuri & Daly, 1992; Ferraro, 1997; Mears, Carlson, Holden & Harris, 2001; Zoellner, et al., 2000). Women who seek protective orders from the court are often threatened by offenders (Fischer & Rose, 1995; Klein, 1994); and there is evidence that offenders may kidnap, seriously injure or even kill a woman in order to prevent her participation in the criminal justice process (Hart, 1991). A woman's risk may be particularly great if she is seeking court action at the same time she physically separates from the offender. As was discussed in chapter 4, separation can be an acute time of risk: the rate of intimate-offender assaults on women separated from their husbands is about three times higher than that of divorced women and about 25 times higher than that of married women (Bachman & Saltzman, 1995). Higher rates of stalking have been found after the relationship ends (Brewster, 2000; Tjaden & Thoennes, 1998), and former intimate partners have been found to be more likely than current partners to stalk women who they later killed or attempted to kill (McFarlane et al., 1999). Finally, a study

Therapists and Legal Advocacy

While the role of a therapist is not to provide legal advice, it is important to be sufficiently familiar with the legal resources available to victims in order to refer to legal advocacy assistance. As previously described, in a recent study, battered women who worked with advocates reported being more effective in accessing resources than did the women without advocates, and, as a result, were more successful in leaving the abusive situation (Sullivan, 1991).

of men incarcerated for killing their female partners found that 52% of the murders occurred when the men were separated from their intimates (Stout, 1993). Clinicians should be particularly attuned to the compounded risks when court action and separation occur simultaneously.

The court experience of a victim of intimate partner violence may also be different than a case involving assault by a stranger in that there is little question of who allegedly committed the act; rather, the dispute centers around what was done (Colb, 2001; Scheppele, 1992). In other words, in an alleged sexual offense involving intimate partners, the offender may admit to having sexual relations with the victim, but may argue that the act was consensual. As a result, trials involving intimate partners focus more heavily on "her word against his" and, often to the detriment of the victim, lend themselves to focusing more on her character than on the offender's behavior. And, as has been pointed out, "Because the defendant and victim had an intimate relationship with each other, the defendant, and therefore the defense attorney, has substantially more knowledge about the victim compared to cases in which the defendant and victim are not intimately acquainted. Thus, the defense has a great deal more 'ammunition' available to discredit the victim's testimony during trial" (Hartley, 2003, p. 415). Similarly, the structure of the law itself offers an additional challenge to women entering the court of justice, as the crimes of intimate partner abuse (particularly acts of sexual violence and stalking) involve behaviors that, in a different context, are not considered criminal acts (Jordan, Quinn, Jordan & Daileader, 2000). Consensual sex acts or frequent telephone calls,

"Although women are legally entitled to freedom from partner violence, a legal system unwilling or unable to enforce this right perpetuates victim-blaming attitudes, trivializes partner violence, and likely leaves victims of partner violence unsatisfied with the system." (Byrne, Kilpatrick, Howley, & Beatty, 1999, p. 290)

for example, are typically a positive part of an intimate relationship, but when these experiences are unwanted by a woman and cause her to be afraid, they cease to be positive and may rise to the level of a crime (Jordan, in press). The result is that statutes addressing many of the crimes involved in cases of intimate partner violence focus, not just on the offender, but also on whether the victim consented to the behavior and whether she felt afraid. This scrutiny can be particularly difficult for a victim, and discussion around this court experience should be addressed by clinicians when their clients are participating in the court system.

In addition to attempting to manage potential risk and danger, victims of intimate partner violence often encounter a justice system not entirely responsive to their experience. For example, there is evidence that the rates of arrest are very low in cases of intimate partner violence (Smith, 2001; Bourg & Stock, 1994; Avakame, Fyfe, & McCoy, 1999), as are rates of prosecution, estimated by some authors to be under 10% for domestic violence cases (Sherman, 1992). Finally, the sentencing of convicted intimate partner violence offenders has, at least until recently, been reported as quite lenient, with very few intimate partner violence offenders being required by the court to spend time in jail (Sherman, Schmidt, & Rogan, 1992). These findings may help explain why female victims of violent assault by a current or former intimate male partner report lower levels of satisfaction with the criminal justice system compared to victims of violence by nonpartners (Byrne, Kilpatrick, Howley, & Beatty, 1999). When the justice system fails to aggressively arrest, prosecute, and sentence intimate partner violence offenders, some have postulated that there is an antitherapeutic effect of the justice system in that it reinforces the perceptions of offenders that their violent behavior is acceptable or not their responsibility (Simon, 1996). These are realities of which clinicians should be aware so that they can effectively work with women whose cases interface with the court system.

INTIMATE PARTNER VIOLENCE AS A CRIMINAL OFFENSE

The majority of victimization experienced by women in intimate relationships falls into the realm of criminal law: whether as an assault, rape, harassment, terroristic threat, stalking or other similar offenses (psychological abuse is the one form of victimization that can rarely be criminally prosecuted). While the law considers acts of intimate partner violence criminal, not all victims of intimate partner violence contact the police, even when they perceive a need for law enforcement protection. As few as 7%–14% of intimate partner assaults are reported to the police agencies (Kantor & Straus, 1987), and only approximately 16% of rapes are reported to law enforcement agencies (Kilpatrick, Edmonds, & Seymour, 1992). A number of factors influence whether a woman contacts the police for help, but studies show she is more likely to do so when the abuse she experienced was severe or occurred very frequently (Bowker, 1984) and in cases in which she was injured in the attack (Bachman & Coker, 1995). Women in longer-term abusive relationships may be less likely to reach out (Abel & Suh, 1987), as is the case with women with less education (Bachman & Coker, 1995). Finally, the likelihood of calling the police increases if the violence was witnessed by a child or other relative (Berk, Berk, Newton, & Loseke, 1984).

Over the past 20 years, numerous studies have been undertaken to determine whether arresting an intimate partner violence offender is an effective criminal justice response—in other words, whether it reduces recidivism. In short, it appears that arresting the offender can be an effective deterrent if law enforcement agencies are monitored and evaluated (Bourg & Stock, 1994). A coordinated community approach combining police making arrests and the use of mandated treatment by the courts has also been found to be a more effective deterrent (Syers & Edleson, 1992), and arrests may be more effective if undertaken in conjunction with other interventions, such as providing victims with transportation to shelters, offering legal and social services, and involving victims more directly in the decision to arrest the offender (Sherman, Schmidt, & Rogan, 1992).

Even if an offender is arrested, that does not mean that a victim's case will proceed to trial; in fact, prosecution rates are extremely low in these cases (Sherman, 1992). Some suggest that low prosecution rates result from the fact that victims are often ambivalent about whether they want their partner to go to jail. As a result, it follows that the rate of wanting to drop criminal charges is significantly greater in intimate partner violence than in other criminal cases (Ford & Regoli, 1993; Lerman, 1986). Clinicians working with clients prosecuting offenders should be aware that the major reasons for the attrition in these cases include the lack of social support by family or friends, substance abuse problems for the woman, confusion with the process, frustration with the slowness of the process, paralyzing fear, and conflict in the mind of the victim as to whether the offender should go to jail (Bennett,Goodman, & Dutton, 1999). These factors can be incorporated into an effective treatment plan by establishing goals for increasing social support or clinically addressing substance abuse, fear, or other relevant issues. In one study, 27% of offenders arrested on victim complaints reassaulted the victim prior to trial (Ford & Regoli, 1998), a reminder of the reality on which a victim's fear is often based.

As with the case of arrest, the implementation of a coordinated community approach to the prosecution of intimate partner violence cases appears to have a positive effect. Studies have found that lower criminal recidivism on the part of intimate partner offenders is associated with the cumulative effects of successful prosecution, probation, monitoring, and court-ordered counseling (Buzawa, Hotaling, & Klein, 1998; Murphy, Musser, & Maton, 1998).

CIVIL PROTECTIVE ORDERS FOR VICTIMS OF INTIMATE PARTNER VIOLENCE

Given that the criminal justice system cannot always afford victims maximum protection, and given the reticence of some victims to participate in criminal proceedings for fear of offender retaliation (Hart, 1996), the development of a civil remedy to supplement or even replace criminal prosecution has been an important reform for victims of intimate partner violence. The primary civil remedy available in these cases is a civil court order of protection. Prior to passage of civil protective order legislation, victims of intimate

Therapists should seek information regarding the specific provisions of their state's protective order law from advocates in intimate partner violence programs, prosecutors, or the local court system.

partner violence had to initiate divorce actions before restraining orders and their protections could be made available. This process was unwieldy and financially out of reach for some victims; it afforded no protection for nonmarried victims, and restraining orders did not offer many of the advantages of protective orders, such as providing for immediate enforcement (i.e., arrest). In 1976, Pennsylvania passed a law providing for temporary orders of protection in intimate partner violence cases (Chaudhuri & Daly, 1992), and currently, all states have enacted laws authorizing the issuance of civil or criminal protective orders (U.S. Department of Justice, 2002).

The primary purpose of the civil restraining order is to protect victims from further abuse,—setting it apart from the criminal justice system, which is intended to punish the offender. For the purposes of most state protective order statutes, intimate partner violence is generally defined as physical injury, sexual violence, or the infliction of fear of being victimized in these ways (Finn, 1991), but clinicians will need to access the specific statutory definition found in the laws of their local jurisdictions.

Most women who seek protective orders do so in response to experiencing serious violence for an extended period of time, not after the first time they are assaulted. In one study, for example, women had suffered from violence for almost 2.5 years before reaching out for court assistance (Harrell & Smith, 1996). More than 40% of the women in another study had experienced severe physical abuse at least every few months, and nearly one quarter had suffered abusive behavior for more than 5 years (Keilitz et al., 1998). Over one third of those women had been threatened or injured with a weapon; more than half had been beaten or choked; and almost all had been intimidated through threats, stalking, and harassment.

While states differ in the specific type of protections or remedies they offer victims through protective orders, most often, offenders are prohibited from the following:

- committing further acts of violence
- directly communicating with the victim (or, in some states, members of the victim's family)

- going near the residence of the victim (Carlson, Harris, & Holden, 1999)

Some states also allow courts to require offenders to move from the victim's or shared residence, and some address temporary custody or support of children the couple have in common. States also differ on who is eligible to receive protective orders, but typically include spouses, former spouses, persons who live or have lived together, and persons who have a child in common (Gist et al., 2001). Some states allow other family members to access protective orders. Not all states allow dating partners to seek protective orders, an unfortunate exclusion given the findings of one study in which found that 28% of women seeking protection had experienced appreciable threats of abuse, actual physical assault, and stalking, but were denied orders, most often because they did not live with the offender (Gist et al., 2001).

Civil orders of protection are first issued on an ex parte basis, meaning that the victim can petition the court without the offender being present. Clinicians should encourage victims to be as detailed as possible when filling out a petition in order to fully inform the court of the danger they face, remembering that this may be difficult for those victims who are uncomfortable fully disclosing their victimization or who may not be fully capable of articulating fear. Notably, it is often women who have experienced the most severe violence who are most likely to minimize the extent of their victimization (Dunham & Senn, 2000). Clinicians are cautioned not to specifically advise a victim client what to write on a petition for a protective order (as some states might define that action as the unauthorized practice of law), but a discussion within the context of a therapy session or a referral to a victim advocate for assistance with the protective order process is highly appropriate.

Following a woman's request for a protective order, if the court believes that the violence described exposes her to future or imminent harm, a temporary ex parte order will be issued by the court. Within a time frame set by the respective state's law, a hearing will be held at which the offender will have the legal right to be heard and to argue against an order being entered if he so chooses. If the court continues to believe, after the full hearing, that intimate partner violence has occurred and that future danger exists, an order of longer duration (typically more than a year) is entered. If an offender violates a protective order, he may be arrested or may face

Not all women who obtain a temporary protective order go on to seek a permanent order of protection. For example, one study found that one fourth of women with temporary orders did not go on to seek permanent orders, because the offender went to counseling (Harrell & Smith, 1996). This finding emphasizes the importance of initial and ongoing risk assessment for therapists treating intimate partner violence offenders.

contempt of court, depending on the specific provisions within that state's laws. Most states have made violation of protective orders a criminal offense, and many states allow law enforcement officers to arrest for violations of protective orders without a warrant (Crowell & Burgess, 1996).

In 1994, Congress passed a federal law (Violence Against Women Act, 18 U.S.C. § 2265, 1994), which, among other provisions, made intimate partner violence—related civil orders of protection enforceable across state lines. This means that if a client receives her protective order in one state and then flees to, works in, or travels to another state, the conditions of that order may be enforced in the second state. Under the Constitution of the United States, this so-called "full faith and credit" is given by the court of one state to most final court decisions issued by another state. This is also true for other documents not issued by the court, such as driver's licenses, marriage licenses, and death certificates.

Research examining whether protective orders keep women safe from further violence offers mixed results. Some authors suggest that protective orders are successful in stopping subsequent violence, reporting that 86–92% of the time, the violence stopped after the protective order was issued (Kaci, 1994; Keilitz et al., 1998). In addition to a decrease in acts of violence subsequent to the issuance of protective orders, studies have found victims reporting life improvements, feeling better about themselves, and feeling safer because they had protective orders in place (Keilitz et al., 1998). Other research is not nearly so optimistic, however, with 60% of women in a 2-year follow-up study reporting some form of reabuse, including severe violence (29%), other physical violence (24%), threats of violence, acts of property damage (43%), and psychological abuse

Mutual Orders of Protection

Mutual orders are those issued against both the victim and the offender. They are criticized for exposing victims to danger and being unfair to their interests. Specific problems resulting from mutual orders include these:

- They are based on misconceptions, myths, gender bias and incorrect theories about intimate partner violence.
- They send the wrong message regarding accountability, the message given being that there is mutual accountability rather than that the primary aggressor is in the wrong.
- They send the wrong message to children in the home regarding who is at fault, and they further empower the offender.
- Mutual orders result in questions for law enforcement as to who should be arrested, and too often, this leads to a victim's being arrested.
- Victims may lose full faith and credit recognition for their order, and, as such, may not be able to seek enforcement if they flee to another state.
- Mutual orders may violate the victim's due process rights, since she will not have been served prior to the court hearing, and the order typically does not state the basis on which the order has been entered against her. (Zorza, 1999)

(57%) (Harrell & Smith, 1996). The point for clinicians is that while protective orders may have the effect of deterring some acts of future violence, by themselves, this remedy is not sufficient to completely protect the life and property of intimate partner violence victims.

Certain characteristics of cases involving protective orders are associated with a risk of the order being violated. For example, very low socioeconomic status is associated with risk of the reabuse of the victim; and women in short-term relationships may be at greater risk of reabuse than those in longer-term relationships because offenders may believe they have more to lose from continuing abuse after a protective order has been issued against them (Carlson, Harris, & Holden, 1999). Women with children are also more likely than women without children to experience reabuse; in fact, in one study, the odds of reabuse for women who have biological children with the offender was nearly four times higher than for couples without children (Carlson, Harris, & Holden, 1999).

Other risk factors associated with reabuse include the following (Harrell & Smith, 1996):

- The more severe the abuse experienced by the victim over the past year, the more likely she is to suffer revictimization after the protective order is issued.
- The persistence in the pattern of violence is also a predictor of reabuse.
- Women living separately from the offender are at greater risk of revictimization, which again points to the danger associated with the point of separation in violent relationships.
- The level of resistance evidenced by the offender to having the order entered is not only related to reabuse, it is also related to the severity of the reabuse, the likelihood of property damage, and the likelihood of future psychological abuse of the victim.
- If the police arrest the man at the time of an incident, the likelihood of severe violence over the following year is decreased.

For clinicians, knowledge that an offender strenuously objected to the issuance of a protective order, that there are children in the home, that the victim is separated from the offender, that there has been severe and persistent abuse over the previous year, and that the victim is subject to other risk factors previously noted should highlight the need for additional, thorough, and concrete safety planning.

CUSTODY ISSUES RELATED TO INTIMATE PARTNER VIOLENCE

Notwithstanding the common myth that women stay in abusive relationships, there is significant evidence that violent relationships end in divorce. In one study, almost two thirds (63%) of the battered women left the offender within 2 years of the study (Campbell, Miller, Cardwell, & Belknap, 1994). Similarly, studies show that violence early in marriage almost doubles the risk of divorce, with 82% of couples separating within 2 years (after 4 years, 93% of couples experiencing severe violence separated, 46% of couples experiencing moderate violence separated, and 38% of nonviolent couples separated) (Bradbury & Lawrence, 1999). In that a significant number of divorcing couples have children in common, both courts and clinicians will see disputes regarding custody. In a recent study, child custody evaluators reported that 37% of their referrals involved allegations of intimate partner violence (Bow & Boxer, 2003).

There is evidence that, in addition to experiencing threats to their own safety, women separated from an abusive partner experience threats of custody disputes (30%), threats of harm to their children (10%), and threats to abduct their children (17%) (Mechanic, Weaver, & Resick, 2000). Some have suggested that in custody disputes, the legal system becomes a further mechanism by which the offender harasses and attempts to exert control over the victim (Bow & Boxer, 2003; Shalansky, Erickson, & Henderson, 1999; Zorza, 1995). For example, offenders may attempt to secure child custody or unlimited child visitation in order to maintain control or dominance over her (Quirion, Lennett, Lind, & Tuck, 1997). When a woman seeks custody of her children, counter claims from offenders are common; and when abuse allegations are made, counter allegations are often the response. Abusive partners may attempt to coerce a spouse into accepting a lower financial payment in exchange for maintaining custody of the children (Lonsdorf, 1991), and, in fact, women who are successful in retaining custody of their children may be given child support awards that are insufficient for the actual cost of raising children (Epenshade, 1984; Weitzman, 1985; Wishik, 1986). It is in this context that women go to court to end a violent marriage and seek custody of children they have in common with the offender. It is also in this context that clinicians are called upon to provide evaluations for the court of the fitness of parents and to make recommendations regarding custody and visitation.

In 1994, in recognition of the risk an intimate partner offender can pose to children, the National Council of Juvenile and Family Court Judges issued the Model Code on Domestic and Family Violence, which included this statement: "It is detrimental to the child and not in the best interest of the child to be placed in sole custody, joint legal custody, or joint physical custody with the perpetrator of family violence" (National Council of Juvenile and Family Court

Judges, 1994, p. 33). Similarly, a number of states have amended the law to include a rebuttable presumption that it is not in the best interest of the child to be placed, either through sole or joint custody, with an intimate partner offender, and a majority of state legislatures have revised their laws to include the presence of intimate partner violence as a factor to be considered when judges make custody and visitation decisions (Roberts & Kurst-Swanger, 2002). Three approaches have generally been adopted in most states' statutes: a rebuttable presumption that it is not in the best interest for child custody to be given to an intimate partner violence offender; factor tests, which encourage judges to weigh the impact of domestic violence in determining a child's best interest; or no statutory reference to intimate partner violence (Levin & Mills, 2003).

Custody evaluators face the significant challenge of striking a balance between the child's safety, the child's need for parental contact, and the rights of both parents. Assessments conducted in the course of custody evaluations that detect the presence of intimate partner violence and evaluate its impact can result in recommendations to a court for custody or visitation arrangements that are most likely to ensure a child's safety and well being. Unfortunately, evaluating clinicians do not always consider the existence of intimate partner violence when making recommendations to the court regarding custody and visitation, an omission that can place both the child and the adult victim at risk (Logan, Walker, Jordan, & Horvath, 2002). In general, criticisms of child custody evaluators have included five perceived pitfalls: (1) having insufficient basic knowledge about intimate partner violence, (2) failing to use collateral sources and record reviews, (3) overreliance on psychological testing, (4) failing to consider intimate partner violence as a major issue in custody determination by assuming that allegations are exaggerated or fabricated, or (5) operating with a bias in favor of male offenders (Bow & Boxer, 2003).

When conducting evaluations of all family members in order to prepare a report for the court, evaluating clinicians must take care not to overpathologize trauma symptoms that may be experienced by victims of intimate partner violence (Koss et al., 1994). As was discussed in chapter 4, moderate levels of depression, sleeplessness, hypervigilance, or other sequelae are normal reactions to traumatic exposure and, while relevant, do not translate into unfitness as a parent. Conversely, evaluating clinicians are cautioned not to underestimate the pathology of a batterer who may appear more functional at the time of the evaluation than the victim does because he has not been exposed to violence or had other trauma inflicted upon him (Walker & Edwall, 1987). Offenders may be very adept at projecting a nonabusive image to evaluators and to the court (Bancroft & Silverman, 2002). In addition, it is important not to assume that a victim's reticence to allow custody or visitation for an abusive partner is simply an attempt to be derisive or an attempt to alienate the children from their father. It may reasonably result from fear for the children's or the victim's safety. This is extremely important when custody evaluators are working with a family that has a history of violence, because women who attempt to protect themselves and their children have been labeled as "alienating" the children from their father (Doyne et al., 1999). In one study, over three fourths of evaluators believed that attempts to alienate the child from the other parent was an important reason for denying sole or joint custody to a parent (Ackerman & Ackerman, 1996).

The National Center for State Courts Resource Handbook for Judges and Court Managers (1997) offers guidelines for custody evaluations when intimate partner violence is present. Thes guidelines include following:

- Identify the existence, nature, and potential consequences of intimate partner violence within the family and document any collaborating evidence.
- Identify the strengths, vulnerabilities, and needs of all other members of the family.
- Develop a plan for custody and visitation that builds on the strengths of each family member and that will serve the best interests of the children.
- If intimate partner violence is a factor in the dispute, develop a plan that addresses the potential dangers of continuing contact between the victim and the batterer, and any need to restrict visitation (pp. 36–37).

If an evaluating clinician does not possess expertise in intimate partner violence and childhood trauma, it is important to seek consultation or additional supervision so that the safety of threatened family members and the children is fully explored in the recommendations (APA, 1994; Association of Family and Conciliation Courts,

1994). Evaluators should also review patterns and history of violence, including criminal histories, and should seek copies of any protective orders that have been issued in the case (Stahl, 1999). In addition, clinicians should note that there is a greater risk of future violence when there is a history of violence; when there has been no treatment for violence; when the offender blames others for his behavior, denies problems, or both; and when the perpetrator is consumed or obsessed with the victim (Stahl, 1999). In fact, the presence of intimate partner violence should result in a full risk assessment with the victim and the offender (as suggested in chapter 4 and chapter 5, respectively). Furthermore, the extent to which offenders have or do not have empathy for the effect of the violence on the children is also an important factor for evaluators to consider (Stahl, 1999).

Chapter 8 described the experience of victims of intimate partner violence as they enter the justice system. The chapter focused on the criminal justice process that women encounter, including police response and how cases are prosecuted. The use and effectiveness of civil orders of protection were also highlighted in detail in **chapter 8**. Finally, custody issues as they arise in the context of intimate partner violence cases were discussed briefly in the chapter. Readers should be able to answer the following questions following a review of **chapter 8:**

- What are three unique differences between the way intimate partner violence and other cases are handled in the criminal justice system?
- What factors might make a victim reticent to contact law enforcement to report victimization?
- What are the primary conditions provided by protective orders?
- What are the factors associated with risk of violation of protective orders?
- What are the four recommended components of a custody evaluation?

References

Abbey, A., Clinton-Sherrod, A. M., McAuslan, P., Zawacki, T., & Buck, P. O. (2003). The relationship between quantity of alcohol consumed and the severity of sexual assaults committed by college men. *Journal of Interpersonal Violence, 18*, 813–833.

Abbott, J., Johnson, R., Koziol-McLain, J., & Lowenstein, S. R. (1995). Domestic violence against women: Incidence and prevalence in an emergency department population. *Journal of the American Medical Association, 273*, 1763–1767.

Abel, E. M., & Suh, E. K. (1987). Use of police services by battered women. *Social Work, 32*, 526–528.

Acierno, R., Resnick, H. S., Kilpatrick, D. G., Saunders, B. E., & Best, C. L. (1999). Risk factors for rape, physical assault, and posttraumatic stress disorder in women: Examination of differential multivariate relationships. *Journal of Anxiety Disorders, 13*, 541–563.

Ackerley, G. D., Burnell, J., Holder, D. C., & Kurdek, L A. (1988). Burnout among licensed psychologists. *Professional Psychology: Research and Practice, 19*(6), 624–631.

Ackerman, M. J., & Ackerman, M. (1996). Child custody evaluation practices: A 1996 survey of psychologists. *Family Law Quarterly, 30*(3), 565–586.

Aldarondo, E., & Mederos, F. (2002). *Programs for men who batter: Intervention and prevention strategies in a diverse society.* Kingston, NJ: Civic Research Institute.

Aldarondo, E., & Straus, M. A. (1994). Screening for physical violence in couple therapy: Methodological, practical, and ethical considerations. *Family Process, 33*, 425–439.

Amato, P., & Rogers, S. (1997). A longitudinal study of marital problems and subsequent divorce. *Journal of Marriage and the Family, 59*, 612-124.

American Psychiatric Association (1980). *Diagnostic and statistical manual of mental disorders* (3rd ed.). Washington, D.C.: Author.

American Psychiatric Association. (1994). *Diagnostic and statistical manual of mental disorders* (4th ed.). Washington, DC: Author.

American Psychiatric Association, (2000). *Diagnostic and Statistical Manual of Mental Disorders* (4th ed.). Text Revision. Washington, DC: American Psychiatric Press.

American Psychological Association. (1994). *Guidelines for child custody evalua-tions in divorce proceedings.* Washington DC: American Psychological Association.

APA Presidential Task Force on Violence and the Family. Washington, DC: American Psychological Association; 1996: 51–52.

Anderson, D. K., Saunders, D. G., Yoshihama, M., Bybee, D., & Sullivan, C. M. (2003). Long-term trends in depression among women separated from abusive partners. *Violence Against Women 9*(7), 807–838.

Appel, A. E., & Holden, G. W. (1998). The co-occurrence of spouse and physical child abuse: A review and appraisal. *Journal of Family Psychology, 12,* 578–599.

Arbuckle, J., Olson, L., Howard, M., Brillman, J., Anctil, C., & Sklar, D. (1996) Safe at home: Domestic violence and other homicides among women in New Mexico. *Annals of Emergency Medicine, 27,* 210–215.

Arellano, C. (1996). Child maltreatment and substance use: a review of the literature. *Substance Use & Misuse, 31*(7), 927–935.

Arias, I., & Pape, K. T. (1999). Psychological abuse: Implications for adjustment and commitment to leave violence partners. *Violence and Victims, 14,* 55–67.

Association of Family and Conciliation Courts (1994). Model standards of prac-tice for child custody evaluation. *Family and Conciliation Courts Review, 32,* 504.

Astin, M. C., Lawrence, K. J., & Foy, D. W. (1993). Posttraumatic stress disorder among battered women: Risk and resiliency factors. *Violence and Victims, 8,* 17–28.

Avakame, E. F., Fyfe, J. J., & McCoy, C. (1999). Did you call the police? What did they do? An empirical assessment of Black's theory of mobilization of law. *Justice Quarterly, 16,* 765–792.

Bachman, R., & Coker, A. (1995). Police involvement in domestic violence: The interactive effects of victim injury, offender's history of violence, and race. *Violence and Victims, 10,* 91–106.

Bachman, R., & Saltzman, L. (1995). Violence against women: Estimates from the redesigned survey. NCJ-154348. Washington, DC: Bureau of Justice Statis-tics, U.S. Department of Justice.

Bailey, J. E., Kellerman, A. L., Somes, G. W., Banton, J. G., Rivara, F. P., & Rushforth, N. P. (1997). Risk factors for violent death of women in the home. *Archives of Internal Medicine, 157,* 777–782.

Bancroft, L., & Silverman, J. G. (2002). *The batterer as parent: Addressing the impact of domestic violence on family dynamics.* Thousand Oaks, CA: Sage.

Bandura, A. (1986). *Social foundations of thought and action: A social cognitive theory.* Englewood Cliffs, NJ: Prentice Hall.

Bandura, A. (1999). Social cognitive theory of personality. In L. A. Pervin & O. P John (Eds.), *Handbook of personality theory and research* (2nd ed.,)pp. 154–196). New York: Guilford Press.

Barnett, O. W., & Fagan, R. W. (1993). Alcohol abuse in male spouse abusers and their female partners. *Journal of Family Violence, 8,* 1–25.

Barratt, E. S. (1994). Impulsiveness and aggression. In J. Monahan & H.J. Stead-man (Eds.), *Violence and mental disorder: Developments in risk assessment* (pp. 61–79). Chicago: University of Chicago Press.

Basile, K. D. (2002). Prevalence of wife rape and other intimate partner sexual coercion in a nationally representative sample of women. *Violence and Victims, 17*(5), 511–524.

Beasley, R., & Stoltenberg, C. D. (1992). Personality characteristics of male spouse abusers. *Professional Psychology: Research and Practice, 23,* 310–317.

Beckham, J., Moore, S., Feldman, M., Hertzberg, M., Kirby, A. & Fairbank, J. (1998). Health status, somatization, and severity of post-traumatic stress disorder in Vietnam combat veterans with post-traumatic stress disorder. *American Journal of Psychiatry, 155,* 1565–1569.

Belle, D. (1990). Poverty and women's mental health. *American Psychologist, 45,* 385–389.

Bennett, L., & Lawson, M. (1994). Barriers to cooperation between domestic violence and substance abuse programs. *Families in Society, 75,* 277–286.

Bennett, L., Goodman, L., & Dutton, M. A. (1999). Systemic obstacles to the criminal prosecution of a battering partner: A victim perspective. *Journal of Interpersonal Violence, 14*(7), 761–772.

Bennice, J. A., Resick, P. A., Mechanic, M., & Astin, M. (2003). The relative effects of intimate partner physical and sexual violence on post-traumatic stress disorder symptomatology. *Violence and Victims, 18*(1), 87–94.

Bergen, R. K. (1995). Surviving wife rape: How women define and cope with the violence. *Violence Against Women, 1,* 117–138.

Bergen, R. K. (1996). Wife rape: Understanding the response of survivors and service providers. Thousand Oaks, CA: Sage.

Bergman, B., & Brismar, B. (1991). Suicide attempts by battered wives. *Acta Psychiatrica Scandinavia, 83,* 380–384.

Bergman, B., Larsson, B., Brismar, B., & Klang, M. (1987). Psychiatric morbidity and personality characteristics of battered women. *Acta-Psychiatrica-Scandinavica, 76,* 678–683.

Berk, R. A., Berk, S. F., Newton, P. J., & Loseke, D. R. (1984). Cops on call: Summoning the police to the scene of spousal violence. *Law and Society Review, 18,* 479–498.

Bernat, J. A., Ronfeldt, H. M., Calhoun, K. S., & Arias, I. (1998). Prevalence of traumatic events and peritraumatic predictors of posttraumatic stress symptoms in a nonclinical sample of college students. *Journal of Traumatic Stress, 11*(4), 645–664.

Billingsley, A. (1992). *Climbing Jacob's ladder: The enduring legacy of African American families.* New York: Simon & Schuster.

Bjerregaard, B. (2000). An empirical study of stalking victimization. *Violence and Victims, 15* (4), 389–406.

Bland, P. (1997, Winter). Strategies for improving women's safety and sobriety. *The Source, 50,* 1–6.

Bourg, S., & Stock H. V. (1994). A review of domestic violence arrest statistics in a police department using a pro-arrest policy: Are pro-arrest policies enough? *Journal of Family Violence, 9*(2), 177–189.

Bow, J. N., & Boxer, P. (2003). Assessing allegations of domestic violence in child custody evaluations. *Journal of Interpersonal Violence, 18*(12), 1394–1410.

Bowker, L. H. (1984). Battered women and the police: A national study of usage and effectiveness. *Police Studies, 7,* 84–93.

Bowker, L. H., Arbitell, M., & McFerron, J. R. (1988). On the relationship between wife beating and child abuse. In K. Yllo & M. Bogard (Eds.), *Feminist perspectives on wife abuse* (pp. 158–174). Newbury Park, CA: Sage.

Bowlby, J. (1977). The making and breaking of affectional bonds: I: Aetiology and psychopathology in the light of attachment theory. *British Journal of Psychiatry, 130,* 201–210.

Bradbury, T., & Lawrence, E. (1999). Physical aggression and the longitudinal course of newlywed marriage. In X. Arriaga & S. Oskamp (Eds.), *Violence in intimate relationships* (pp. 181–202). Thousand Oaks, CA: Sage.

Brady, J. L., Guy, J. D., Poelstra, P. L., & Brokaw, B. F. (1999). Vicarious traumatization, spirituality, and the treatment of sexual abuse survivors. *Professional Psychology: Research and Practice, 30*(4), 386–393.

Brady, K. T., Killeen, T., Saladin, M. E., Dansky, B., & Becker, S. (1994). Comorbid substance abuse and posttraumatic stress disorders: Characteristics of women in treatments. *American Journal on Addictions, 3,* 160–164.

Brecklin, L.R. (2002). The role of perpetrator alcohol use in the injury outcomes of intimate assaults. *Journal of Family Violence, 17*(3), 185–197.

Breslau, N., Davis, G., Andreski, P., & Peterson, E. (1991). Traumatic events and posttraumatic stress disorder in an urban population of young adults. *Archives of General Psychiatry, 48,* 216–222.

Breslau, N., Davis, G., Peterson, E., & Schultz, L. (1997). Psychiatric sequelae of posttraumatic stress disorder in women. *Archives of General Psychiatry, 54,* 81–87.

Brewin, C.R., Andrews, B., & Valentine, J. D. (2000). Meta-analysis of risk factors for posttraumatic stress disorder in trauma-exposed adults. *Journal of Consulting and Clinical Psychology, 68,* 748–766.

Brewster, M. P. (2000). Stalking by former intimates: Verbal threats and other predictors of physical violence. *Violence and Victims, 15,* 41–54.

Briere, J. (1989). *Therapy for adults molested as children: beyond survival.* New York: Springer Publishing.

Briere, J. N. (1992). *Child abuse trauma: Theory and treatment of the lasting effect.* Newbury Park, CA: Sage.

Briere, J. N. (1995). *Trauma symptom inventory professional manual.* Odessa, FL: Psychological Assessment Resources.

Briere, J. N. (1997). Psychological assessment of adult posttraumatic states. Washington, DC: American Psychological Association.

Briere, J. (2004). *Psychological assessment of posttraumatic states: Phenomenology, diagnosis, and measurement, 2nd Edition.* Washington, DC: American Psychological Association.

Briere, J. N., & Jordan, C. E. (in press). Violence against women: Outcome complexity and implications for treatment. *Journal of Interpersonal Violence.*

Briere, J., & Spinazzola, J. (in press). Phenomenology and psychological assessment of complex posttraumatic states. *Journal of Traumatic Stress.*

Briere, J. N., & Zaidi, L. Y. (1989). Sexual abuse histories and sequelae in female psychiatric emergency room patients. *American Journal of Psychiatry, 146,* 1602–1606.

Brown, P. D., & O'Leary, K. D. (1997). Wife abuse in intact couples. In G. Kaufman Kantor & J. L. Jasinski (Eds.), *Out of the darkness: contemporary perspectives on family violence* (pp. 194–207). Thousand Oaks, CA: Sage Publications.

Browne, A. (1987). when battered women kill. New York: The Free Press.

Browne, A., & Williams, K. (1993) Gender, intimacy and lethal violence: Trends from 1967 through 1987. *Gender and Society, 7,* 78–98.

Burgess, A. W., & Holstrom, L. L. (1974). Rape trauma syndrome. *American Journal of Psychiatry, 133,* 981–986.

Buzawa, E., Hotaling, G., & Klein, A. (1998). The response to domestic violence in a model court: Some initial findings and implications. *Behavioral Sciences and the Law, 16,* 185–206.

Byrne, C. A., Kilpatrick, D. G., Howley, S. S., & Beatty, D. (1999). Female victims of partner versus nonpartner violence: Experiences with the criminal justice system. *Criminal Justice and Behavior, 26*(3), 275–292.

Cadoret, R. J., O'Gorman, T. W., Troughton, E. & Heywood, E. (1985). Alcoholism and antisocial personality: Interrelationships, genetic and environmental factors. *Archives of General Psychiatry, 42,* 161-167.

Campbell, J. C. (1986). Nursing assessment for risk of homicide with battered women. *Advances in Nursing Science, 8*(4), 36–51.

Campbell, J. C. (1989). Women's responses to sexual abuse in intimate relationships. *Women's Health Care International, 8,* 335–347.

Campbell, J. C. (1992) "If I can't have you, no one can": Power and control in homicide of female partners. In J. Radford & D. E. H. Russell (Eds.), *Femicide: The politics of woman killing* (pp. 99–113). New York: Twayne.

Campbell, J. C. (1995). Prediction of homicide of and by battered women. In Campbell, J. C. (Ed.), *Assessing dangerousness: Violence by sexual offenders, batterers, and child abusers* (pp. 96–113). Thousand Oaks, CA: Sage.

Campbell, J., & Alford, P. (1989). The dark consequences of marital rape. *American Journal of Nursing,89*(7), 946–949.

Campbell, J., Jones, A. S., Dienemann, J., Kub, K. Schollenberger, J., O'Campo, P., Gielen, A. C., & Wynne, C. (2002). Intimate partner violence and physical health consequences. *Archives of Internal Medicine, 162,* 1157–1163.

Campbell, J. C., Kub, J., Belknap, R. A., & Templin, T. N. (1997). Predictors of depression in battered women. *Violence Against Women, 3*(3), 271–293.

Campbell, J., Miller, P., Cardwell, M., & Belknap, R. (1994). Relationship status of battered women over time. *Journal of Family Violence, 9*(2), 99–111.

Campbell, J. C., & Soeken, K. L. (1999) Forced sex and intimate partner violence: Effects on women's risk and women's health. *Violence Against Women, 5*(9), 1017–1035.

Campbell, J. C., Sullivan, C. M., & Davidson, W. S. (1995). Depression in women who use domestic violence shelters: A longitudinal analysis. *Psychology of Women's Quarterly, 19,* 237–255.

Campbell, J. D., Webster, D., Koziol-McLain, J., Block, C., Campbell, D., Curry, M. A., Gary, F., Glass, N., McFarlane, J., Sachs, C., Sharps, P., Ulrich, Y., Wilt, S., Manganello, J., Xu, X., Schollenberger, J., Frye, V., & Laughon, K. (2003). Risk factors for femicide in abusive relationships: Results from a multisite case control study. *American Journal of Public Health, 93*(7), 1089–1097.

Campbell, R., & Raja, S. (1999). The secondary victimization of rape victims: Insights from mental health professionals who treat survivors of violence. *Violence and Victims, 14,* 261–275.

Canter, M. B., Bennett, B. E., Jones, S. E., & Nagy, T. F. (1994). *Ethics for psychologists: A commentary on the APA ethics code.* Washington, DC: American Psychological Association:

Cantrell, P. J., MacIntyre, D. I., Sharkey, K. J., & Thompson, V. (1995). Violence in the marital dyad as a predictor of violence in peer relationships of older adolescents/young adults. *Violence and Victims, 10,* 35–41.

Carlson, B. E. (1984). Children's observations of interpersonal violence. In A. Roberts (Ed.), Battered women and their families (pp.147–167). New York: Springer Publishing.

Carlson, B. E., McNutt, L., & Choi, D. Y. (2003). Childhood and adult abuse among women in primary health care: Effects on mental health. *Journal of Interpersonal Violence, 18*(8), 924–941.

Carlson, M. J., Harris, S. D., & Holden, G. W. (1999). Protective orders and domestic violence: Risk factors for re-abuse. *Journal of Family Violence, 14*(2), 205–226).

Carmen, E. H., Rieker, P. P., & Mills, T. (1984). Victims of violence and psychiatric illness. *American Journal of Psychiatry, 141,* 378–383.

Cascardi, M., Langhinrichsen, J., & Vivian, D. (1992). Marital aggression: Impact, injury, and health correlates for husbands and wives. *Archives of Internal Medicine, 152,* 1178–1184.

Cascardi, M., Mueser, K. T., DeGirolomo, J., & Murrin, M. (1996). Physical aggression against psychiatric inpatients by family members and partners: A descriptive study. *Psychiatric Services, 47,* 531–533.

Cascardi, M. & O'Leary, K. D. (1992). Depressive symptomatology, self-esteem, and self-blame in battered women. *Journal of Family Violence 7,* 249–259.

Cascardi, M., O'Leary, K., & Schlee, K. (1999). Co-occurrence and correlates of posttraumatic stress disorder and major depression in physically abused women. *Journal of Family Violence, 14*(3), 227–249.

Chaudhuri, M., & Daly, K. (1992). Do restraining orders help? Battered women's experience with male violence and legal process. In E. Buzawa &C. Buzawa(Eds.), *Domestic violence: The criminal justice response.* (pp. 227–252). Thousand Oaks, CA: Sage Publications.

Chermack, S. T., Fuller, B. E. & Blow, F. C. (2000). Predictors of expressed partner and non-partner violence among patients in substance abuse treatment. *Drug and Alcohol Dependence, 58,* 43–54.

Cherniss, C. (1980). Staff burnout: Job stress in the human services. Beverly Hills, CA: Sage.

Chilcoat, H., & Breslau, N. (1998). Posttraumatic stress disorder and drug disorders. *Archives of General Psychiatry, 55,* 913–917.

Clark, A. H., & Foy, D. W. (2000). Trauma exposure and alcohol use in battered women. *Violence Against Women, 6*(1), 37–48.

Coben, J., Forjuoh, S., & Gondolf, E. (1999). Injuries and health care use in women with partners in batterer intervention programs. *Journal of Family Violence, 14,* 1, 83–94.

Coccaro, E. F., & Kavoussi, R. J. (1996). Neurotransmitter correlates of impulsive aggression. In D. M. Stoff & R. B. Cairns (Eds), *Aggression and violence: Genetic, neurobiological, and biosocial perspectives* (pp. 67–85). Mahwah, NJ: Lawrence Erlbaum Associates, Publishers.

Cohen, L., & Felson, M. (1979). Social change and crime rate trends: A routine activity approach. *American Sociological Review, 44,* 588–608.

Cohen, M. A., & Miller, T. R. (1998). The cost of mental health care for victims of crime. *Journal of Interpersonal Violence, 13*(1), 93–110.

Coker, A. L., Walls, L. G., & Johnson, J. E. (1998). Risk factors for traumatic physical injury during sexual assaults and female victims. *Journal of Interpersonal Violence, 13,* 605-620.

Coker, A. L., Smith, P. H., Bethea, L., King, M. R., & McKeown, R. E. (2000). Physical health consequences of physical and psychological intimate partner violence. *Archives of Family Medicine, 9,* 451–457.

Colb, S. F. (2001). "Whodunit" versus "what was done": When to admit character evidence in criminal trials. *North Carolina Law Review, 79,* 939–992.

Coleman, F. L. (1997). Stalking behavior and the cycle of domestic violence. *Journal of Interpersonal Violence, 12,* 420–432.

Collins, J., Kroutil, L., Roland, E., & Moore-Gurrera, M. (1997). I ssues in the linkage of alcohol and domestic violence services. In M. Galanter (Ed.), *Recent developments in alcoholism,* (Vol. 13, pp. 387–405). New York: Plenum.

Cooper, M., & Eaves, D., (1996). Suicide following homicide in the family. *Violence and Victims, 11*(2), 99–112.

Coulter, M. L., & Chez, R. A. (1997). Domestic violence victims support mandatory reporting: For others. *Journal of Family Violence, 12,* 349–356.

Courage, M. M., & Williams, D. M. (1986). An approach to the study of burnout in professional care providers in human service organizations. *Journal of Social Service Research, 10*(1), 7–22.

Covington, S. (1997). Women, addiction, and sexuality. In L. Straussner & E. Zelvin (Eds.), *Gender and addictions: Men and women in treatment* (pp. 79–95). Northvale, NJ: Jason Aronson.

Cox, C. E., Kotch, J. B., & Everson, M. D. (2003). A longitudinal study of modifying influences in the relationship between domestic violence and child maltreatment. *Journal of Family Violence, 18*(1), 5–17.

Dannenberg, A. L., Carter, D. M., Lawson, H. W., Ashton, D. M., Dorfman, S. F., & Graham, E. H. (1995). Homicide and other injuries as causes of maternal death in New York City, 1987 through 1991. *American Journal of Obstetrics and Gynecology, 172,* 1557–1564.

Dansky, B. S., Saladin, M. E., Brady, K. T., & Kilpatrick. D. G. (1995). Prevalence of victimization and posttraumatic stress disorder among women with substance use disorders: Comparison of telephone and in-person assessment samples. *International Journal of the Addictions, 30,* 1079–1099.

Davidson, J. R., & Foa, E. B. (1993). Posttraumatic stress disorder: DSM-IV and beyond. Washington, DC: American Psychiatric Press.

Davidson, L. M., & Baum, A. (1990). Posttraumatic stress in children following natural and human-made trauma. In L. M. Davidson & A. Baum (Eds.), Handbook of developmental psychopathology (pp. 251–259). New York: Plenum.

Davis, K. E., Ace, A., & Andra, M. (2000) Stalking perpetrators and psychological maltreatment of partners: Anger-jealousy, attachment insecurity, need for control, and break-up context. *Violence and Victims, 15*(4), 407–425.

Davis, K. E., Coker, A. L., & Sanderson, M. (2002). Physical and mental heath effects of being stalked for men and women. *Violence and Victims, 17* (4), 429–443.

De Becker, G. (1997). The gift of fear: Survival signals that protect us from violence. Boston: Little, Brown.

Diaz-Olavarrieta, C., Campbell, J. C., Garcia de la Cadena, C., Paz, F., & Villa, A. (1999). Domestic violence against patients with chronic neurologic disorders. *Archives of Neurology, 56,* 681–685.

Douglas, K. S., & Dutton, D. G. (2001). Assessing the link between stalking and domestic violence. *Aggression and Violent Behavior, 6,* 519–546.

Doyne, S., Bowermaster, J., Meloy, J., Dutton, D., Jaffe, P., Temko, S., et al. (1999). Custody disputes involving domestic violence: Making children's needs a priority. *Juvenile and Family Court Journal, 50,* 2, 1–12.

Dunham, K., & Senn, C. Y. (2000). Minimizing negative experiences: Women's disclosure of partner abuse. *Journal of Interpersonal Violence, 15*(3), 251–261.

Dunn, G., Ryan, J., & Dunn, C. (1994). Trauma symptoms in substance abusers with and without histories of childhood abuse. *Journal of Psychoactive Drugs, 26*(4), 357-360.

Dutton, D. G. (1994). Behavioral and affective correlates of borderline personality organization in wife assaulters. *International Journal of Criminal Justice and Behavior, 17,* 26-38.

Dutton, D. G. (1995a). Trauma symptoms and PTSD-like profiles in perpetrators of intimate abuse. *Journal of Traumatic Stress, 8,* 299–316.

Dutton, D. G. (1995b). Intimate abusiveness. *Clinical Psychology: Science and Practice, 2,* 207–224.

Dutton, D. G. (1998). The abusive personality: Violence and control in intimate relationships. New York: Guilford.

Dutton, D. G. Saunders, K., Starzomsky, A. & Bartholomew, K. (1994). Intimacy-anger and insecure attachment as precursors of abuse in intimate relationships. *Journal of Applied Social Psychology, 24,* 1367–1387.

Dutton, M.A. (1992a). Treating battered women in the aftermath stage. Special issue: Psychotherapy in independent practice: Current issues of clinicians. *Psychotherapy in Private Practice, 10,* 93–98.

Dutton, M. A. (1992b). Empowering and healing the battered woman: A model for assessment and intervention. New York: Springer Publishing.

Dutton, M. A. (1992c). Assessment and treatment of PTSD among battered women. In D. Foy (Ed.), *combat veterans, battered women, adult and child sexual assaults Treating PTSD: procedures for.* (pp. 69–98). New York: Guilford

Dutton, M. A. (in press). Complexity of women's responses to violence: Response to Briere and Jordan. *Journal of Interpersonal Violence.*

Dutton, M. A., & Dionne, D. (1991). Counseling and shelter for battered women. In M. Steinman (Ed.), *Woman battering: Policy responses* (pp. 113–130). Cincinnati, OH: Anderson.

Dutton, M. A., Haywood, Y., & El-Bayoumi, G. (1997). Impact of violence on women's health. (41–56). In S. Gallant, G. Puryear Keita, and R. Royak-Schaler (Eds), Health care for women: Psychological, social, and behavioral influences. Washington, DC: American Psychological Association.

Easton, C., Swan, S., & Sinha, R. (2000). Motivation to change substance use among offender of domestic violence. *Journal of Substance Abuse Treatment, 19,* 1–9.

Eberle, P. A. (1982). Alcohol abusers and non-users: A discriminant analysis of differences between two subgroups of batterers. *Journal of Health and Social Behavior, 23,* 260–271.

Eby, K., Campbell, J., Sullivan, C., & Davidson, W. (1995). Health effects of experiences of sexual violence for women with abusive partners. *Health Care for Women International, 16,* 563–576.

Eckhart, C. I., Barbour, K. A., & Davidson, G. C. (1998). Articulated thoughts of martially violent and nonviolent men during anger arousal. *Journal of Consulting and Clinical Psychology, 66,* 259–269.

Edleson, J. L. (1999). Children's witnessing of adult domestic violence. *Journal of Interpersonal Violence, 14,* 839–870.

Edleson, J. L, & Tolman, R. M. (1992). *Intervention for men who batter: An ecological approach.* Newbury Park, CA: Sage Publications.

Edmunds, S. B. (1997). The personal impact of working with sex offenders. In S. B. Edmunds (Eds.), *Impact: Working with sexual abusers* (pp. 11–29). Brandon, VT: Safer Society Press.

Ellerby, L. (1997). Impact on clinicians: Stressors and providers of sex offender treatment. In S. B. Edmunds (Eds.), *Impact: Working with sexual abusers* (pp. 51–60). Brandon, VT: Safer Society Press.

Elliott, D. M. (1992). Traumatic Events Survey. Unpublished psychological test. Los Angeles:Harbor-UCLA Medical Center.

Elliott, D., & Guy, J. (1993). Mental health professionals' versus nonmental health professionals' childhood trauma and adult functioning. *Professional Psychology: Research and Practice, 24,* 83–90.

Ellis, D., & DeKeseredy, W. S. (1997). Rethinking estrangement, interventions, and intimate femicide. *Violence Against Women, 3,* 590–609.

Ellis, E. M. (1983). A review of empirical rape research: Victim reactions and response to treatment. *Clinical Psychology Review, 3,* 473–490.

Engels, M. L., & Moisan, D. (1994). The Psychological Maltreatment Inventory: Development of a measure of psychological maltreatment in childhood for use in adult clinical settings. *Psychological Reports, 74,* 595–604.

Epenshade, T. (1984). The economic consequences of divorce. *Journal of Marriage and the Family, 41,* 615–625.

Epstein, J., Saunders, B., Kilpatrick, D., & Resnick, H. (1998). PTSD as a mediator between childhood rape and alcohol use in adult women. *Child Abuse and Neglect, 22,* 223–234.

Escamilla, A. G. (1998). A cognitive approach to anger management treatment for juvenile offenders. *Journal of Offender Rehabilitation, 27,* 199–208.

Fantuzzo, J., Boruch, R., Beriama, A., Atkins, M., & Marcus, S. (1997). Domestic violence and children: Prevalence an risk in five major US cities. *Journal of the American Academy of Child and Adolescent Psychiatry, 36,* 116–122.

Fantuzzo, J., McDermott, P, & Lutz, M. N. (1999). Clinical issues in the assessment of family violence involving children. In R. T. Ammerman and M. Hersen (Eds.), Assessment of family violence: A clinical and legal sourcebook (2d ed.) (pp. 10–23). Baltimore: John Wiley and Sons.

Farr, K. A. (2002). Battered women who were "being killed and survived it": Straight talk from survivors. *Violence and Victims, 17*(3), 267–281.

Ferraro,K. J. (1997). Battered women: Strategies for survival. In A. P. Cardarelli (Ed.), *Violence between intimate partners: Patterns, causes and effects* (pp. 124–143). Boston: Allyn & Bacon.

Farrenkopf, T. (1992). What happens to therapists who work with sex offenders. *Journal of Offender Rehabilitation, 18*(3/4), 217–223.

Figley, C. R. (1993). Compassion stress and the family therapist. *Family Therapist News,* 1–8.

Figley, C. R. (1995). Compassion fatigue as secondary traumatic stress disorder: An overview. In C. R. Figley (Ed.), *Compassion fatigue: Coping with secondary traumatic stress disorder in those who treat the traumatized* (pp. 1–20). New York: Brunner/Mazel.

Fildes, J., Reed, L., Jones, N., Martin, M., & Barrett, J. (1992). Trauma: The leading cause of maternal death. *Journal of Trauma, 32,* 643–645.

Fillmore, M., Dixon, M., & Schweizer, T. (2000). Alcohol affects processing of ignored stimuli in a negative priming paradigm. *Journal of Studies on Alcohol, 61,* 571–578.

Fillmore, M., & Vogel-Sprott, M. (1999). An alcohol model of impaired inhibitory control and its treatment in humans. *Experimental and Clinical Psychopharmacology, 7*(1), 49–55.

Finkelhor, D. (1979). *Sexually victimized children.* New York: Free Press.

Finkelhor, D. (1984). Child sexual abuse: New theory and research. New York: Free Press.

Finkelhor, D., & Yllo, K. (1985). License to rape: *Sexual abuse of wives.* New York: Holt, Rinehart & Winston.

Fischer, K., & Rose, M. (1995). When enough is enough: Battered women's decision making around court orders of protection. *Crime and Delinquency, 41*(4), 414–429.

Flett, G. L. & Hewitt, P. L. (2002). In C. Wekerle & A. Wall, (Eds.), The violence and addiction equation: Theoretical and clinical issues in substance abuse and relationship violence (pp. 64–97). New York: Taylor & Francis Group.

Fleury, R., Sullivan, C., & Bybee, D. (2000). When ending the relationship does not end the violence: Women's experiences of violence by former partners. *Violence Against Women, 6,* 12, 1363–1383.

Foa, E. B., Cascardi, M., Zoellner, L. A., & Feeny, N. C. (2000). Psychological and environmental factors associated with partner violence. *Trauma, Violence, & Abuse, 1*(1), 67–91.

Foa, E. B., Zinbarg, R., & Rothbaum, B. O. (1992). Uncontrollability and unpredictability in posttraumatic stress disorder. *Psychological Bulletin, 10,* 218–238.

Follette, V. M., Polusny, M. M., & Milbeck, K. (1994) Mental health and law enforcement professionals' trauma history, psychological symptoms, and impact of providing services to child sexual abuse survivors. Professional Psychology: *Research and Practice, 25*(3), 275–282.

Follingstad, D. R., Brennan, A. F., Hause, E. S, Polek, D. S., & Rutledge, L. L. (1991). Factors moderating physical and psychological symptoms of battered women. *Journal of Family Violence, 6,* 81–95.

Follingstad, D. R., Hause, E. S., Rutledge, L. L., & Polek, D. S. (1992). Effects of battered women's early responses on later abuse patterns. *Violence and Victims, 7*(2), 109–128.

Follingstad, D. R., Laughlin, J. E., Polek, D. S., Rutledge, L. L., & Hause, E. S. (1991). Identification of patterns of wife abuse. *Journal of Interpersonal Violence, 6*(2), 187–204.

Follingstad, D. R., Rutledge, L. L., Berg, B. J., Hause, E. S., & Polek, D. S. (1990). The role of emotional abuse in physically abusive relationships. *Journal of Family Violence 5*(2), 107–120.

Ford, D. A., & Regoli, J. (1993). The criminal prosecution of wife assaulters: Process, problems, and effects. In N. Zoe Hilton (Ed.), *Legal responses to wife assault: Current trends and evaluation* (pp. 127–164). Newbury Park, CA: Sage.

Ford, D. A., & Regoli, J. (1998). The Indianapolis domestic violence prosecution experiment. In American Bar Association & U.S Department of Justice (Eds.), *Legal interventions in family violence: Research findings and policy implications* (Report No. NCJ-171666, pp. 62–62). Washington, DC: U.S. Government Printing Office.

Freudenberger, H. J. (1984). Burnout and job dissatisfaction: Impact on the family. In J. C. Hansen & S. H. Cramer (Eds.), *Perspectives on work and the family* (pp. 95–105). Rockville, MD: Aspen.

Freudenberger, H. J. (1986). The issues of staff burnout in therapeutic communities. *Journal of Psychoactive Drugs, 18*(2), 247–251.

Gauthier, L. M. & Levendosky, A. A. (1996). Assessment and treatment of couples with abusive male partners: Guidelines for therapists. *Psychotherapy, 33,* 403–417.

Gazmararian, J. A., Lazorick. S., Spitz, A. M., Ballard, T. J., Saltzman, L. E., & Marks, J. S. (1996). Prevalence of violence against pregnant women: A review of the literature. *Journal of the American Medical Association, 275,* 1915–1920.

Gelles, R. (Ed.) (1979). *Family violence.* Beverly Hills, CA: Sage Publications.

Gil, D. G. (1970). Violence against children: Physical abuse in the United States. Cambridge, MA: Harvard University Press.

Gillespie, C. (1989). Justifiable homicide: Battered women, self-defense, and the law. Columbus: Ohio State University Press.

Gil-Rivas, V., Fiorentine, R., & Anglin, D. (1996). Sexual abuse, physical abuse, and posttraumatic stress disorder among women participating in outpatient drug abuse treatment. *Journal of Psychoactive Drugs, 28*(1), 95–102.

Ginsburg, J. I. D., Mann, R. E., Rotgers, F. & Weekes, J. R. (2002). In W. R. Miller & S. Rollnick, (Eds.), *Motivational Interviewing* (2nd ed., pp. 333–346). New York: Guilford Press.

Gist, J. H., McFarlane, J., Malecha, A., Fredland, N., Schultz, P., & Willson, P. (2001). Women in danger: Intimate partner violence experienced by women who qualify and do not qualify for protective order. *Behavioral Sciences and the Law, 19,* 637–647.

Gleason (1993). Mental disorders in battered women: An empirical study. *Violence and Victims, 8,*53–68.

Golding, J. M. (1999). Intimate partner violence as a risk factor for mental disorders: A meta-analysis. *Journal of Family Violence, 14*(2), 99–132.

Gondolf, E. W. (1990). *Psychiatric responses to family violence.* Lexington, MA: Lexington Books.

Gondolf, E. W. (1998). Assessing woman battering in mental health services. Thousand Oaks, CA: Sage Publications.

Gondolf, E. W. (1999). MCMI-III results for batter program participants in four cities: Less "pathological" than expected. *Journal of Family Violence, 14*(1), 1–17.

Gondolf, E. W. (2000a). How batterer program participants avoid reassault. *Violence Against Women,6*(11), 1204–1222.

Gondolf, E. W. (2000b). A 30-month follow-up of court-referred batterers in four cities. *International Journal of Offender Therapy and Comparative Criminology, 44*(1), 111–128.

Gondolf, E. W. (2001a). Final report: an extended follow-up of batterers and their partners. Indiana, PA: Mid-Atlantic Training Institute.

Gondolf, E. W. (2001b). Limitations of experimental evaluation of batterer programs. *Trauma, Violence, and Abuse, 2*(1), 79–88.

Gondolf, E. W. (2002). *Batterer intervention systems: Issues, outcomes and recommendations.* Thousand Oaks, CA: Sage Publications.

Gondolf, E. W., Fisher, E., & McFerron, J. R. (1988). Racial differences among shelter residents: A comparison of Anglo, Black, and Hispanic battered women. *Journal of Family Violence, 3,* 39–51.

Gondolf, E. W., & Foster, R. (1991). Wife assault among V.A. alcohol rehabilitation patients. *Hospital and Community Psychiatry, 42,* 74–79.

Goodman, L.A., Dutton, M.A., & Bennett, L. (2000). Predicting repeat abuse among arrested batterers: Use of the Danger Assessment Scale in the criminal justice system. *Journal of Interpersonal Violence, 15*(1), 63–74.

Goodman, L. A., Dutton, M. A., & Harris, M. (1997). The relationship between violence dimensions and symptom severity among homeless, mentally ill women. *Journal of Traumatic Stress, 10,* 51–70.

Goodman, L. A., Koss, M. P., Fitzgerald, L. F., Russo, M. F., & Keita, G. P. (1993). Male violence against women: Current research and future directions. *American Psychologist, 48,* 1054–1058.

Goodman, L. A., Salyers, M. P., Mueser, K. T., Rosenberg, S. D., Swartz, M., Essock, et al. 2001). Recent Victimization in women and men with severe mental illness: Prevalence and correlates. *Journal of Traumatic Stress, 14*(4), 615–632.

Gottman, J. M, Jacobson, N. S. Rushe, R. H., Shortt, J. W., Babcock, J., La Taillade, J. J. & Waltz, J. (1995). The relationship between heart rate reactivity, emotionally aggressive behavior, and general violence in batterers. *Journal of Family Psychology, 9,* 227–248.

Graham-Bermann, S. A. (1998). The impact of woman abuse on children's social development. In G. W. Holden, R. Geffner, & E. N. Jouriles, (Eds.), Children exposed to marital violence: Theory, research, and applied issues (pp. 21–54). Washington, DC: American Psychological Association.

Grant, B., Harford, T., Dawson, D., Chou, P., Dufour, M. & Pickering, R. (1994). Prevalence of DSM-IV alcohol abuse and dependence: United States 1992. *Alcohol Health Research World, 18*(3), 243–248.

Greenfield, L.A., Rand, M.R., Craven, D., Flaus, P.A., Perkins, C.A., Ringel, C., et al. (1998). *Violence by intimates: Analysis of data on crimes by current or former spouses, boyfriends, and girlfriends* (NCJ-167237). Washington, DC: Department of Justice, Bureau of Justice Statistics.

Hall, D. M. (1998). Victims of stalking. In R. Meloy (Ed), *The psychology of stalking* (pp. 113–137). San Diego: Academic Press.

Hamberger, L., & Hastings, J. (1986). Personality correlates of men who abuse their partners: A cross-validational study. *Journal of Family Violence, 1*(4), 323–341.

Hamberger, L., & Hastings, J. (1988). Personality characteristics of spouse abusers: A controlled comparison. *Violence and Victims, 3,* 31-48.

Hamberger, L., & Hastings, J. (1991). Personality correlates of men who batter and nonviolent men: Some continuities and discontinuities. *Journal of Family Violence, 6,* 131–147.

Hamby, S. L. (2004). The spectrum of victimization and the implications for health. In K. A. Kendall-Tackett (Ed.), Health consequences of abuse in the family : a clinical guide for evidence-based practice (p. 7–27). Washington, DC: American Psychological Association Press.

Hampton, R, Oliver, W., & Magarian, L. (2003). Domestic violence in the African American community: An analysis of social and structural factors. *Violence Against Women, 9*(5), 533–557.

Hansen, M., Harway, M., & Cervantes, N. (1991). Therapists' perceptions of severity in cases of family violence. *Violence and Victims, 6*(3), 225–235.

Hanson, R. K. (1990) The psychological impact of sexual assault on women and children: A review. *Annals of Sex Research, 3,* 187–232.

Harmon, R., Rosner, R. & Owens, H. (1998). Risk appraisal and management of violent behavior. *Psychiatric Services, 4,* 236–249.

Harrell, A., & Smith, B.E. (1996). Effects of restraining orders on domestic violence victims. In Buzawa, E., and Buzawa, C. (Eds.), *Do Arrests and Restraining Orders Work?* (pp. 214–242). Sage: Thousand Oaks, CA.

Harris, G., Rice, M., & Quinsey, V. (1993). Violent recidivism of mentally disordered offenders: The development of a statistical prediction instrument. *Criminal Justice and Behavior, 20,* 315–335.

Hart, B. (1991). Domestic violence intervention system: A model for response to women abuse. In *Confronting Domestic Violence: Effective Police Response.* Harrisburg, PA: Pennsylvania Coalition Against Domestic Violence.

Hart, B. (1994). Lethality and dangerousness assessments. *Violence Update, 4*(10), 7–8.

Hart, B. (1996). Battered women and the criminal justice system. In Buzawa, E., and Buzawa, C. (Eds.), Do Arrests and Restraining Orders Work? (pp. 98–114). Thousand Oaks, CA: Sage Publications.

Hart, B., & Stuehling, J. (1992). *Personalized safety plan.* Reading, PA: Pennsylvania Coalition Against Domestic Violence.

Hart, S., & Brassard, M. R. (1991). Psychological maltreatment: Progress achieved. *Development and Psychopathology, 3,* 61–70.

Hart, S., Hare, R., & Forth, A. (1994). In J.Monahan & H. J. Steadman (Eds.), *Violence and mental disorder: Developments in risk assessment* (pp. 81–100). Chicago: University of Chicago Press.

Hartley, C.C. (2003). A therapeutic jurisprudence approach to the trial process in domestic violence felony trials. *Violence Against Women, 9*(4), 410–437.

Heckert, D. A. & Gondolf, E. W. (2000). Assessing assault self-reports by batterer program participants and their partners. *Journal of Family Violence, 15*(2), 181–197.

Heckert, D. A. & Gondolf, E. W. (2002). *Predicting levels of abuse and reassault among batterer program participants (Final Report).* Washington, DC: The National Institute of Justice.

Heilbrun, K. (2001). Principles of Forensic Mental Health Assessment. New York, NY: Kluwer Academic/Plenum Publishers.

Helton, A. S., McFarlane, J., & Anderson, E. T. (1987). Prevention of battering during pregnancy: Focus on behavioral change. *Public Health Nursing, 4*(3), 166–174.

Henning, K., & Klesges, L. M. (2003). Psychological abuse reported by court-involved battered women. *Journal of Interpersonal Violence, 18*(8), 857–871.

Henning, K., Leitenberg, H., Coffey, P., Turner, T., & Bennett, R. T. (1996) Long-term psychological and social impact of witnessing physical conflict between parents. *Journal of Interpersonal Violence, 11*(1), 35–51.

Herbert, T. B., Silver, R. C., & Ellard, J. (1991). Coping with an abusive relationship: How and why do women stay? *Journal of Marriage and the Family, 53,* 211–325.

Herman, J. L. (1992). Trauma and Recovery: The aftermath of violence—from domestic abuse to political terror. New York: BasicBooks.

Herman, J. L. (2003). The mental health of crime victims: Impact of legal intervention. *Journal of Traumatic Stress, 16*(2), 159–166.

Heyman, R. E, O'Leary, K. D. & Jouriles, E. N. (1995). Alcohol and aggressive personality styles: Potentiators of serious physical aggression against wives? *Journal of Family Psychology, 9,* 44–57.

Hilton, N. Z. (1992). Battered women's concerns about their children witnessing wife assault. *Journal of Interpersonal Violence, 7*(1), 77–86.

Hindelang, M., Gottfredson, M., & Garofalo, J. (1978). Correlates of delinquency: The illusion of discrepancy between self-report and official measures. *American Sociological Review, 44,* 995–1014.

Holden, G. W., & Ritchie, K. L. (1991). Linking extreme marital discord, child rearing, and child behavior problems: Evidence from battered women. *Child Development, 62,* 311–327.

Holtzworth-Munroe, A., Bates, L., Smutzler, N., & Sandin, E. (1997). A brief review of the research on husband violence: Part I: Maritally violent versus nonviolent men. *Aggression and Violent Behavior, 2*(1), 65–99.

Holtzworth-Munroe, A., Meehan, J. C., Herron, K. Rehman, U. & Stuart, G. L. (2003). Do subtypes of maritally violent men continue to differ over time? *Journal of Consulting and Clinical Psychology, 71,* 728–740.

Holtzworth-Munroe, A., & Stuart, G. L. (1994). Typologies of male batterers: Three subtypes and the differences among them. *Psychological Bulletin, 116*(3), 476–497.

Hotton, T. (2001). Spousal violence after marital separation. *Juristat, 21,* 1-19.

Housekamp, B. M, & Foy, D. W. (1991). The assessment of posttraumatic stress disorder in battered women. *Journal of Interpersonal Violence, 6,* 367–375.

Hughes, H. M. (1988). Psychological and behavioral correlates of family violence in child witnesses and victims. *American Journal of Orthopsychiatry, 58,* 77–90.

Hughes, H. M. (1997). Research concerning children of battered women: Clinical implications. In R. Geffner, S. B. Sorenson, & P. K. Lundberg-Love (Eds.), *Violence and sexual abuse at home: Current issues, interventions, and research in spousal battering and child maltreatment* (pp. 225–244), Binghamton, NY: Haworth.

Hughes, H. M., & Graham-Bermann, S. A. (1998). Children of battered women: Impact of emotional abuse on development and adjustment. *Journal of Emotional Abuse, 1,* 23–50.

Hughes, H. M., Graham-Bermann, S. A., & Gruber, G. (2001). Resilience in children exposed to domestic violence. In S. A. Graham-Bermann & J. Edleson (Eds.), *Domestic violence in the lives of children: The future of research, intervention, and social policy* (pp. 67–90). Washington, DC: American Psychological Association.

Hughes, H. M., & Luke, D. A. (1998). Heterogeneity in adjustment among children of battered women. In G. W. Holden, R. Geffner, & E. N. Jouriles, (Eds.), *Children exposed to marital violence: Theory, research, and applied issues* (pp. 185–221). Washington, DC: American Psychological Association.

Hughes, H., Parkinson, D., & Vargo, M. (1989). Witnessing spouse abuse and experiencing physical abuse: A "double whammy"? *Journal of Family Violence, 4,* 197–209.

Huss, M. T., & Langhinrichsen-Rohling, J. (2000). Identification of the psychopathic batterer: The clinical, legal and policy implications. *Aggression and Violent Behavior, 5*(4), 403–422.

Huss, M. T., Leak, G. K. and Davis, S. F. (1993). A validation study of the Novaco Anger Inventory. *Bulletin of the Psychonomic Society, 31,* 279–281.

Huth-Bocks, A. C., Levendosky, A. A., & Semel, M. A. (2001). The direct and indirect effects of domestic violence on young children's intellectual functioning. *Journal of Family Violence, 16*(3), 269–290.

Hyman, A., Schillinger, D., & Lo, B. (1995). Laws mandating reporting of domestic violence: Do they promote patients well-being? *Journal of the American Medical Association, 273*(22), 1781–1787.

Iliffe, G., & Steed, L. G. (2000). Exploring the counselor's experience of working with perpetrators and survivors of domestic violence. *Journal of Interpersonal Violence, 15*(4), 393–412.

Jackson, K. E., Holzman, C., & Barnard, T. (1997). Working with sex offenders: The impact on practitioners. In S. B. Edmunds (Ed.), *Impact: Working with sexual abusers* (pp. 61–73). Brandon, VT: Safer Society Press.

Jacobson, N. S., & Gottman, J. M. (1998). *When men batter women: New insights into ending abusive relationships.* New York: Simon & Schuster.

Jacobson, N. S., Gottman, J. M., Gortner, E., Berns, S., & Shortt, J. U. (1996). Psychological factors in the longitudinal course of battering: When do the couples split up? When does the abuse decrease? *Violence and Victims, 11*(4), 371–392.

Jaffe, P. G., Wolfe, D., & Wilson, S. (1990). *Children of battered women.* Newbury Park, CA: Sage.

Jones, A. (1994). *Next time she'll be dead: Battering and how to stop it.* Boston, Mass: Beacon Press.

Jordan, C. E. (in press). Intimate partner violence and the justice system: An examination of the interface. *Journal of Interpersonal Violence.*

Jordan, C. E., Logan, TK, Walker, R., & Nigoff, A. (2003). Stalking: An examination of the criminal justice response. *Journal of Interpersonal Violence, 18*(2), 148–165.

Jordan, C. E., Quinn, K., Jordan, B., & Daileader, C. R. (2000) Stalking: Cultural, clinical and legal considerations. *Brandeis Law Journal, 38* (3), 513–579.

Jordan, C. E. & Walker, R. (1994). Guidelines for handling domestic violence cases in community mental health centers. *Hospital and Community Psychiatry, 45,* 2, 147–151.

Jouriles, E. N., & Norwood, W. D. (1995). Physical aggression toward boys and girls in families characterized by the battering of women. *Journal of Family Psychology, 9,* 69–78.

Jouriles, E. N., Mehta, P., McDonald, R., & Francis, D.J. (1997). Psychometric properties of family members' reports of parental physical aggression toward clinic-referred children. *Journal of Consulting and Clinical Psychology, 65,* 309–318.

Kaci, J. H. (1994). Aftermath of seeking domestic violence protective orders: The victim's perspective. *Journal of Contemporary Criminal Justice, 10,* 201–219.

Kahill, S. (1988). Interventions for burnout in the helping professionals: A review of the empirical evidence. *Canadian Journal of Counseling Review, 22*(3), 310–342.

Kantor, G. K., & Straus, M. A. (1987). The "Drunken Bum" theory of wife beating. *Social Problems, 34,* 213–231.

Kaplan, M. L., Asnis, G. M., Lipschitz, D. S., & Chorney, P. (1995). Suicidal behavior and abuse in psychiatric outpatients. *Comprehensive Psychiatry, 36,* 229–235.

Kaufman, Kanter, G., & Asdigian, N. (1997). When women are under the influence does drinking or drug use by women provoke beatings by men? In M. Galanter (Ed.), *Recent developments in alcoholism.* New York: Plenum Press.

Keilitz, S. L., Davis, C., Efkeman, H. S., Flango, C., & Hannaford, P. L. (1998). Civil protection orders: Victims' views on effectiveness. National Institute of Justice Research Preview, U.S. Department of Justice.

Kellermann, A. L., & Mercy, J. A. (1992). Men, women and murder: Gender-specific differences in rates of fatal violence and victimization. *Journal of Trauma, 33,* 1–5.

Kellermann, A. L., Rivara, F. P., Rushforth, N. B., Banton, J. G., Reay, D. T., Francisco, J. T., Locci, A. B., Prodzinski, J., Hackman, B. B., & Somes, G. (1993). Gun ownership as a risk factor for homicide in the home. *New England Journal of Medicine, 329,* 1084–1091.

Kemp, A., Green, B. L., Hovanitz, C., & Rawlings, E. I. (1995). Incidence and correlates of posttraumatic stress disorder in battered women: Shelter and community samples. *Journal of Interpersonal Violence, 10*(1), 43–55.

Kendall-Tackett, K. A. (2003). Treating the long-term health effects of childhood abuse: A guide for mental health, medical and social services professionals. New York: Civil Research Institute.

Kessler, R. C., Sonnega, A., Bromet, E., Hughes, M., & Nelson, C. B. (1995). Posttraumatic stress disorder in the National Comorbidity Survey. *Archives of General Psychiatry, 52,* 1048–1060.

Khan, F. I., Welch, T. L., & Zillmer, E. A. (1993) MMPI-2 profiles of battered women in transition. *Journal of Personality Assessment, 60,* 100–111.

Khantzian, E. (1990). Self-regulation and self-medication factors in alcoholism and the addictions: Similarities and differences. *Recent Developments in Alcoholism, 8,* 255–271.

Khantzian, E. (1997). The self-medication hypothesis of substance use disorders: a reconsideration and recent applications. *Harvard Review of Psychiatry, 4*(5), 231–244.

Kilpatrick, D., Acierno, R., Resnick, H., Saunders, B., & Best, C. (1997). A 2-year longitudinal analysis of the relationship between violent assault and substance use in women. *Journal of Consulting and Clinical Psychology, 65*(5) 834–847.

Kilpatrick, D., Acierno, R., Saunders, B., Resnick, H., & Best, C. (2000). Risk factors for adolescent substance abuse and dependence: Data from a national sample. *Journal of Consulting and Clinical Psychology, 68*(1), 19–30.

Kilpatrick, D. G., Best, C. L., Saunders, B. E., & Veronen, L. J. (1988). Rape in marriage and in dating relationships: How bad is it for mental health? *Annals of the New York Academy of Sciences, 528,* 335–344.

Kilpatrick, D. G., Edmonds, C. N., & Seymour, A. (1992). Rape in America: A report to the nation. Arlington, VA: National Victim Center & Medical University of South Carolina.

Kilpatrick, D. G., Resick, P. A., & Veronen, L. J. (1981) Effects of rape experience: A longitudinal study. *Journal of Social Issues, 37,* 105–120.

Kilpatrick, D., & Resnick, H. (1993). Posttraumatic stress disorder associated with exposure to criminal victimization in clinical and community populations. In J. Davidson & E. Foa (Eds.), Posttraumatic stress disorder: associated DSM-IV and beyond. (pp. 147–172.). Washington (DC): American Psychiatric Press.

Kilpatrick, D., Resnick, H., & Acierno, R. (1997). Health impact of interpersonal violence: Implications for clinical practice and public policy. *Behavioral Medicine, 23,* 79–85.

Kilpatrick, D., Resnick, H., Saunders, B., & Best, C. (1998). Victimization, posttraumatic stress disorder, and substance use and abuse among women. In C. Wetherington & A. Roman (Eds.), *Drug addiction research and the health of women* (pp. 285–307). National Institute on Drug Abuse. Rockville, (MD): National Institute of Health. U.S. Department of Health and Human Services.

Kilpatrick, D., Saunders, B., Veronen, L., Best, C., & Von, J. (1987). Criminal victimization: Lifetime prevalence, reporting to the police, and psychological impact. *Crime and Delinquency, 334,* 479–489.

Kilpatrick, D., & Williams, L. (1997). Post-traumatic stress disorder in child witnesses to domestic violence. American *Journal of Orthopsychiatry, 67,* 639–64.

Kimerling, R., & Calhoun, K. S. (1994). Somatic symptoms, social support, and treatment seeking among sexual assault victims. *Journal of Consulting and Clinical Psychology, 62,* 333–340.

Klein, A. R. (1994). *Spousal/partner assault: A protocol for the sentencing and supervision of offenders.* Boston: Production Specialties.

Kocot, T., & Goodman, L. (2003). The roles of coping and social support in battered women's mental health. *Violence Against Women, 9*(3), 323–346.

Koss, M. P. (1992). The underdetection of rape: Methodological choices influence incidence estimates. *Journal of Social Issues, 48,* 61–75.

Koss, M. P., Goodman, L. A., Browne, A., Fitzgerald, L. F., Keita, G. P., & Russo, N. F. (1994). *Male violence against women at home, at work, and in the community.* Washington, DC: American Psychological Association.

Kropp, P. R., Hart, S. D., Webster, C. D., & Eaves, D. (1999). *Spousal assault risk assessment guide: User's manual.* North Tonawanda, NY: Multi-Health Systems.

Kubany, E. S., Leisen, M. B., Kaplan, A. K., & Kelly, M. (2000). Validation of the Distressing Event Questionnaire (DEQ): A brief diagnostic measure of posttraumatic stress disorder. *Psychological Assessment, 12,* 192–209.

Kurz, D. (1996). Separation, divorce, and woman abuse. *Violence Against Women, 2*(1), 63–81.

Kushner, M., Abrams, K. & Borchardt, C. (2000). The relationship between anxiety disorders and alcohol use disorders: A review of major perspectives and findings. *Clinical Psychology Review, 20,* 2, 149–171.

Kyriacou, D. N., McCabe, F., Anglin, D., Lapesarde, K., & Winer, M. R. (1998). Emergency department-based study of risk factors for acute injury from domestic violence against women. *Annals of Emergency Medicine, 31,* 502–506.

Langan, P. A., & Innes, C. A. (1986). Preventing domestic violence against women. Washington DC: U.S. Department of Justice, Bureau of Justice Statistics.

Leonard, K. E., & Quigley, B. M. (1999). Drinking and marital aggression in newlyweds: An event-based analysis of drinking and the occurrence of husband marital aggression. *Journal of Studies on Alcohol, 60,* 537–545.

Lerman, L. (1986). Prosecution of wife beaters: Institutional obstacles and innovations. In M. Lystad (Ed). *Violence in the home: Interdisciplinary perspectives* (pp. 251–295). New York: Brunner/Mazel.

Lerner, C. F., & Kennedy, L. T. (2000). Stay-leave decision making in battered women: Trauma, coping and self-efficacy. *Cognitive Therapy and Research, 24,* 215–232.

Leserman, J., Li, D., Drossman, D. A., Hu, Y.J. B. (1998). Selected symptoms associated with sexual and physical abuse among female patients with gastrointestinal disorders: The impact on subsequent health care visits. *Psychological Medicine, 28,* 417–425.

Letourneau, E. J., Holmes, M., Chasendunn-Roark, J. (1999). Gynecologic health consequences to victims of interpersonal violence. *Women's Health Issues, 9,* 115–120.

Levin, A., & Mills, L. G. (2003). Fighting for child custody when domestic violence is at issue: Survey of state laws. *Social Work, 48*(4), 463–470.

Litrownik, A. J., Newton, R., Hunter, W. M., English, D., & Everson, M. D. (2003). Exposure to family violence in young at-risk children: A longitudinal look at the effects of victimization and witnessed physical and psychological aggression. *Journal of Family Violence, 18* (1), 59–73.

Litwack, T. R., & Schlesinger, L. B. (1987). Assessing and predicting violence: Research, law, and applications. In I. B. Weiner and A. K. Hess (Eds.), *Handbook of forensic psychology* (pp. 205–257). New York: Wiley.

Loeber, R, Farrington, D. P., Stouthamer-Loeber, M. & van Kammen, W. B. (1998). Antisocial behavior and mental health problems: explanatory factors in childhood and adolescence. Mahwah, NJ: Lawrence Erlbaum Associates.

Logan, TK, Leukefeld, C., & Walker, B. (2000). Stalking as a variant of intimate violence: Implications from a young adult sample. *Violence and Victims, 15*(1), 91–110.

Logan, TK, Nigoff, A., Walker, R., & Jordan, C. E. (2002). Stalker profiles with and without protective orders: Do protective orders make a difference in reoffending or criminal justice processing? *Violence and Victims, 17*(5), 541–553.

Logan, TK, Walker, R., Cole, J., & Leukefeld, C. (2002). Victimization and substance use among women: contributing factors, interventions, and implications. *Review of General Psychology, 6, 4,* 325–397.

Logan, TK, Walker, R., Jordan, C. E., & Campbell, J. (2004). An integrative review of separation and victimization among women: consequences & implications. *Trauma, Violence and Abuse, 5(2),* 143–193.

Logan, TK, Walker, R., Jordan, C. E., & Horvath, L. (2002). Child custody evaluations and domestic violence: Case comparisons. *Violence and Victims, 17*(6), 719–742.

Lonsdorf, B. (1991). The role of coercion in affecting women's inferior outcomes in divorce: Implications for researchers and therapists. In C. Everett (Ed.), The consequences of divorce: Economic and custodial impact on children and adults. Binghamton, NY: Haworth Press, Inc.

Loring, M. T. (1994). Emotional abuse. New York: Lexington.

Lurigio, A. J., & Resick, P. A. (1990). Healing the psychological wounds of criminal victimization: Predicting postcrime distress and recovery. In A. J. Lurigio, W. G. Skogan, & R. C. Davis (Eds.), *Victims of crime: Problems, policies, and programs* (pp. 51–67). Newbury Park, CA: Sage.

Mackey, T., Sereika, S. M., Weissfeld, L. A., Hacker, S. S., Zender, J. F., & Heard, S. L. (1992). Factors associated with long-term depressive symptoms of sexual assault victims. *Archives of Psychiatric Nursing, 6,* 10–25.

Magdol, L. Moffitt, T. E., Caspi, A. & Silva, P. A. (1998). Developmental antecedents of partner abuse: A prospective-longitudinal study. *Journal of Abnormal Psychology, 107,* 375–389.

Maiden, P. (1997). Alcohol dependence and domestic violence: Incidence and treatment implications. *Alcoholism Treatment Quarterly, 15*(2), 31–50.

Maiuro, R. Cahn, T., Vitaliano, P., Wagner, B. C & Zegree, J. B. (1988). Anger, hostility, and depression in domestically violent versus generally assaultive men and nonviolent control subjects. *Journal of Consulting and Clinical Psychology, 56,* 17–23.

Malinosky-Rummell, R., & Hansen, D. J. (1993). Long-term consequences of childhood physical abuse. *Psychological Bulletin, 114,* 68–79.

Margolin, G. (1998). Effects of domestic violence on children. In P. K. Trickett & C. J. Schellenbach, (Eds.), *Violence against children in the family and in the community* (pp. 57–102). Washington, DC: American Psychological Association.

Marshall, L. L. (1994a). Psychological abuse of women: Sex distinct clusters. *Journal of Family Violence, 11*(4), 379–409.

Marshall, L. L. (1994b). Physical and psychological abuse. In W. R. Cupach & B. H. Spitzberg (Eds.), *The dark side of interpersonal communication.* NJ: Hillsdale.

Marshall, L. L. (1999). Effects of men's subtle and overt psychological abuse on low-income women. *Violence and Victims, 14*(1), 69–88.

Martin, S. E., & Bachman, R. (1997). The relationship of alcohol to injury in assault cases. In Galanter, M. (Ed.), *Recent Developments in Alcoholism* (Vol. 13). New York: Plenum Publishing.

Martin, S. E. & Bachman, R. (1998). The contribution of alcohol to the likelihood of completion and severity of injury in rape incidents. *Violence Against Women, 4,* 694-712.

Marvasti, J. (1992). Psychotherapy with abused children and adolescents. In J. Brandell (Ed.), *Countertransference in psychotherapy with children and adolescents* (pp. 191–214). Northvale, NJ: Jason Aronson.

Maslach, C. (1982). *The burnout: The cost of caring*. Englewood Cliffs, N.J: Prentice-Hall.

Maslach, C., & Jackson, S. E. (1981). The measurement of experienced burnout. *Journal of Occupational Behavior, 2*(2), 99–113.

McCann, L., & Pearlman, L. A. (1990). Vicarious traumatization: A framework for understanding the psychological effects of working with victims. *Journal of Traumatic Stress, 3*(1), 131–149.

McCarthy-Tucker, S., Gold, A. & Garcia, E. (1999). Effects of anger management training on aggressive behavior in adolescent boys. *Journal of Offender Rehabilitation, 29,* 129–141.

McCauley, J., Kern, D., Kolodner, K., Dill, L., Schroeder, A., DeChant, H., Ryden, J., Bass, E., & Derogatis, L. (1995). The "battering syndrome": Prevalence and clinical characteristics of domestic violence in primary care internal medicine practices. *Annals of Internal Medicine, 123*(10), 744–781.

McCormick, R. & Smith, M. (1995). Aggression and hostility in substance abusers: The relationship to abuse patterns, coping styles, and relapse triggers. *Addictive Behaviors, 20*(5) 555–562.

McFarlane, J. M., Campbell, J. C., Wilt, S., Sachs, C. J., Ulrich, Y., Xu, X. (1999) Stalking and intimate partner femicide. *Homicide Studies, 3*(4), 300–316.

McFarlane, J., Parker, B., & Soeken, J. (1995). Abuse during pregnancy: Frequency, severity, perpetrators and risk factors of homicide. *Public Health Nursing, 12,* 284–289.

McFarlane, J., Parker, B., & Soeken, J. (1996). Abuse during pregnancy: Associations with maternal health and infant birth weight. *Nursing Research, 45*(1), 37–42.

McFarlane, J., Parker, B., Soeken, J., & Bullock, L. (1992). Assessing for abuse during pregnancy: Severity and frequency of injuries and associate entry into prenatal care. *Journal of the American Medical Association, 267,* 2370–2372.

McGuire, K. & Pastore, A. L. (Eds.). (1996). *Sourcebook of criminal justice statistics 1995* (NCJ-176356). Washington, DC: Bureau of Justice Statistics, U.S. Department of Justice.

Mears, D. P., Carlson, M. J., Holden, G. W., & Harris, S. D. (2001). Reducing domestic violence revictimization : The effects of individual and contextual factors and type of legal intervention. *Journal of Interpersonal Violence, 16*(12), 1260–1283.

Mechanic, M. B., Weaver, T. L, & Resick, P. A. (2000). Intimate partner violence and stalking behavior: Exploration of patterns and correlations in a sample of acutely battered women. *Violence and Victims, 15,* 55–72.

Mederos, F. (2002). Changing our vision of intervention-the evolution of programs for physically abusive men. In E. Aldarondo & F. Mederos (Eds), Programs for men who batter: Intervention and prevention strategies in a diverse society (pp. 2–23). Kingston, NJ: Civic Research Center.

Meloy, J. R. (1996) Stalking (Obsessional Following): A review of some preliminary studies. *Aggression and Violent Behavior 1* (2), 147–162.

Meloy, J. R. (1998). *The psychology of stalking: Clinical and forensic perspectives.* San Diego: Academic Press.

Meloy, J. R., & Gothard, S. (1995). Demographic and clinical comparison of obsessional followers and offenders with mental disorders. *American Journal of Psychiatry, 152*(2), 258–263.

Mercy, J. A., & Saltzman, L. E. (1989). Fatal violence among spouses in the United States, 1976–1985. *American Journal of Public Health, 79,* 595–599.

Mertin, P., & Mohr, P. B. (2002). Incidence and correlates of posttrauma symptoms in children from backgrounds of domestic violence. *Violence and Victims, 17*(5), 555–567.

Migeot, M., & Lester, D. (1996). Psychological abuse in dating, locus of control, depression, and suicidal preoccupation. *Psychological Report, 79,* 682.

Miller, B. A., & Downs, W. R. (1993). The impact of family violence on the use of alcohol by women. *Alcohol Health and Research World, 17,* 137–143.

Miller, K. I., Stiff, J. B., & Ellis, B. H. (1988). Communication and empathy as precursors to burnout among human service workers. *Communication Monographs, 55*(9), 336–341.

Miller, M., & Morris, N. (1988). Predictions of dangerousness: An argument for limited use. *Violence and Victims, 3,* 263–284.

Miller, W. R. & Rollnick, S. (2002). *Motivational interviewing* (2nd ed.). New York: Guilford Press.

Mills, J. F., Kroner, D. G. and Forth, A. E. (1998). Novaco Anger Scale: Reliability and validity within an adult criminal sample. *Assessment, 5,* 237–248.

Milner, J. S.,, & Campbell, J. C. (1995). Prediction issues for practitioners. In J. C,. Campbell, (Ed.), *Assessing dangerousness: Violence by sexual offenders, batterers, and child abusers* (pp. 20–40). Thousand Oaks, CA: Sage.

Minkoff, K. (2001a). Program components of a comprehensive integrated care system for seriously mentally ill patients with substance disorders. In, H. R. Lamb, (Ed.), *Best of new directions for mental health services* (New Directions for Mental Health, # 91). San Fransisco: Jossey-Bass.

Minkoff, K. (2001b). Developing standards of care for individuals with co-occurring psychiatric and substance use disorders. *Psychiatric Services. 52,* 597–599.

Monahan, J., & Steadman, H. J. (Eds.) (1994). *Violence and mental disorder: Developments in risk assessment.* Chicago: University of Chicago Press.

Moore, T. E., & Pepler, D. J. (1998). Correlates of adjustment in children at risk. In G. W. Holden, R. Geffner, & E. N. Jouriles, (Eds.), *Children exposed to marital violence: Theory, research, and applied issues* (pp. 157–184). Washington, DC: American Psychological Association.

Moracco, K., Runyan, W. W, & Butts, J. D. (1998). Femicide in North Carolina, 1991–1993: A statewide study of patterns and precursors. *Homicide Studies, 2,* 422–446.

Moscicki, E. K., O'Carroll, P., Rae, D. S., Locke, B. Z., Roy, A., & Regier, D. A. (1988) Suicide attempts in the Epidemiologic Catchment Area study. *Yale Journal of Biology and Medicine, 61,* 259–268.

Mullen, P., & Pathé, M. (1994). Stalking and the pathologies of love. *Australian and New Zealand Journal of Psychiatry, 28,* 469–477.

Mullen, P. E., Pathé, M. & Purcell, R. (2000). Stalkers and their victims. Cambridge, England: Cambridge University Press

Mullen, P. E., Pathé, M., Purcell, & Stuart, G. W. (1999). Study of stalkers. *American Journal of Psychiatry, 156*(8), 1244–1249.

Murdoch, D., Phil, R. & Ross, D. (1990). Alcohol and crimes of violence: Present issues. *International Journal of the Addictions, 25,* 1065–1081.

Murphy, C., Meyer, S. & O'Leary, K. (1993). Family of origin violence and MCMI-II psychopathology among partner assaultive men. *Violence and Victims, 8,* 165–176.

Murphy, C., Meyer, S. & O'Leary, K. (1994). Dependency characteristics of partner assaultive men. *Journal of Abnormal Psychology, 103,* 729–735.

Murphy, C. M., Musser, P. H., & Maton, K. I. (1998). Coordinated community intervention for domestic abusers: Intervention system involvement and criminal recidivism. *Journal of Family Violence, 13*(3), 263–284.

Murphy, C. M., & O'Leary, K. D. (1989). Psychological aggression predicts physical aggression in early marriage. *Journal of Consulting and Clinical Psychology, 57,* 579–582.

Murphy, W. (1998). Minimizing the likelihood of discovery of victims' counseling records and other personal information in criminal cases: Massachusetts gives a nod to a constitutional right to confidentiality. *New England Law Review, 32*(4).

National Center for State Courts (1997). *Domestic Violence and child custody disputes: A resource handbook for judges and court managers.* Williamsburg, VA: National Center for Sate Courts.

National Council of Juvenile and Family Court Judges (1994). The model code on domestic and family violence. Reno, NV: Author.

Newcomb, M., Vargas-Carmona, J., & Galaif, E. (1999). Drug problems and psychological distress among a community sample of adults: Predictors, consequences, or confound? *Journal of Community Psychology, 27*(4), 405–429.

Newman, J. P. (1998). Psychopathic behavior: An information processing perspective. In J. D. Cooke, A. E.Forth, & R. D. Hare (Eds.), *Psychopathy: Theory, research, and implications for society* (pp. 81–104). Dordrecht, Netherlands: Kluwer Academic Publishers.

Norris, J., Nurius, P. & Dimeff, L. (1996). Through her eyes: Factors affecting women's perception of and resistance to acquaintance sexual aggression threat. *Psychology of Women Quarterly, 20,* 123–145.

Novaco, R. W. (1994). Anger as a risk factor for violence. In J. Monahan & H. J. Steadman (Eds.), Violence and mental disorder: Developments in risk assessment (pp. 21–59). Chicago: University of Chicago Press.

Novaco, R. W. (1997). Remediating anger and aggression with violent offenders. *Legal and Criminological Psychology, 2,* 77–88.

Nuttall, R., & Jackson, H. (1994). Personal history of childhood abuse among clinicians. *Child Abuse & Neglect, 18*(5), 455–472.

O'Carroll, P. W., & Mercy, J. A. (1986). Patterns and recent trends in Black homicide. In D. F. Hawkins, (Ed.), *Homicide among Black Americans* (pp. 29–42). Lanham, MD: University Press of America.

O'Farrell, T. J. & Murphy, C. M. (1995). Marital violence before and after alcoholism treatment. *Journal of Consulting and Clinical Psychology, 63,* 256–262.

Ogloff, J. R. P. (1996). A legal perspective on impulsivity: Some cautionary comments on the genesis of a clinical construct. In C. D. Webster & M. A. Jackson, (Eds), *Impulsivity: Theory, assessment and treatment* (pp. 63–81). New York: Guilford Press.

O'Keefe, M. (1995). Predictors of child abuse in maritally violent families. *Journal of Interpersonal Violence, 10,* 3–25.

O'Leary, K.D., Malone, J., & Tyree, A. (1994). Physical aggression in early marriage: Prerelationship and relationship effects. *Journal of Consulting and Clinical Psychology, 62,* 594–602.

O'Leary, K. D., Vivian, D., & Malone, J. (1992). Assessment of physical aggression against women in marriage: The need for multimodal assessment. *Behavioral Assessment, 14*(1), 5–14.

Orava, T. A., McLeod, P. J. & Sharpe, D. (1996). Perceptions of control, depressive symptomatology, and self-esteem of women in transition from abusive relationships. *Journal of Family Violence, 11,* 167–186.

Ozer, E. J., Best, S. R., Lipsey, T. L., & Weiss, D. S. (2003). Predictors of posttraumatic stress disorder and symptoms in adults: A meta-analysis. *Psychological Bulletin, 129*(1), 52–73.

Palarea, R. E., Zona, M. A., Lane, J. C., & Langhinrichsen-Roling, J. (1999). The dangerous nature of stalking: Threats, violence and associated risk factors. *Behavioral Sciences and the Law, 17,* 269–283.

Pan, H., Neidig, P. & O'Leary, D. (1994). Predicting mild and severe husband-to-wife physical aggression. *Journal of Consulting and Clinical Psychology, 62,* 975–981.

Pathé, M. & Mullen, P. (1997). The impact of stalkers on their victims. *British Journal of Psychiatry, 170,* 12–17.

Patterson, C. M. & Newman, J. P. (1993). Reflectivity and learning from aversive events: Toward a psychological mechanism for the syndromes of disinhibition. *Psychological Review, 100,* 716–738.

Pearlman, L. A., & MacIan, P. S. (1995). Vicarious traumatization: An empirical study of the effects of trauma work on trauma therapists. *Professional Psychology: Research and Practice, 26*(6), 558–565.

Pearlman, L. A., & Saakvitne, K. W. (1995). Trauma and the therapist: Countertransference and vicarious traumatization in psychotherapy with incest survivors. New York: Norton.

Pence, E. (2002). The Duluth domestic abuse intervention project. In E. Aldarondo. & F. Mederos, (Eds.), *Programs for men who batter: Intervention and prevention strategies in a diverse society* (pp. 6-1–6-46). Kingston, NJ: Civic Research Institute.

Pernanen, J. (1991). Alcohol in Human Violence. New York: Guilford.

Peterson, J., Rothfleisch, J., Zelazo, P., & Pihl, R. (1990). Acute alcohol intoxication and cognitive functioning. *Journal of Studies on Alcohol, 51,* 114–122.

Pickens, R. W. Svikis, D. S. McGue, M. & LaBuda, M. C. (1995). Common genetic mechanisms in alcohol, drug, and mental disorder comorbidity. *Drug and Alcohol Dependence, 39,* 129–138.

Pihl, R. O. & Hoaken, P. N. S. (2002). Biological bases of addiction and aggression in close relationships. In C. Wekerle & A. Wall, (Eds.), *The violence and addiction equation: Theoretical and clinical issues in substance abuse and relationship violence* (pp. 25–43). New York: Taylor & Francis Group.

Plichta, S. B. (1996). Violence and abuse: Implications for women's health. In M. M. Falik & K. S. Collins (Eds.), *Women's health: The Commonwealth Survey* (pp. 237–272), Baltimore: Johns Hopkins University Press.

Plichta, S. B. (in press). Intimate partner violence and physical health consequences: Policy and practice implications. *Journal of Interpersonal Violence.*

Plichta, S. B., & Weisman, C. S. (1995). Spouse or partner abuse, use of health services, and unmet need for medical care in U.S. women. *Journal of Women's Health, 4,* 45–53.

Pope, K., & Feldman-Summers, S. (1992). National survey of psychologists' sexual and physical abuse history and their evaluation of training and competence in these areas. *Professional Psychology: Research and Practice, 23,* 353–361.

Pressman, B. (1984). Family violence: Origins and treatment. Guelph, Ontario: University of Guelph Office for Educational Practice.

Pressman, B. (1989). Treatment of wife-abuse: The case for feminist therapy. In B. Pressman, , G.Cameron, & M. Rothery, (Eds.), *Intervening with assaulted women: Current theory, research and practice,* (pp. 21–45). Hillsdale, NJ: Lawrence Erlbaum Associates.

Prochaska, J. O., DiClemente, C. C. & Norcross, J. C. (1992). In search of how people change: Applications to addictive behaviors. *American Psychologist. 47,* 1102–1114.

Prochaska, J. O., Norcross, J. C. & DiClemente, C. C. (1994). Changing for good. New York: Avon Books.

Quigley, B. M., & Leonard, K. E. (1996). Resistance of husband aggression in the early years of marriage. *Violence and Victims, 11*(4), 355–370.

Quirion, P., Lennett, J., Lind, K., & Tuck, C. (1997). Protecting children exposed to domestic violence in contested custody and visitation litigation. *Boston Public Interest Law Journal, 6,* 501.

Raine, A. (1996). Autonomic nervous system activity and violence. In D. M. Stoff & R. B. Cairns, (Eds), *Aggression and violence: Genetic, neurobiological, and biological perspectives* (pp. 145–168). Mahwah, NJ: Lawrence Erlbaum Associates, Publishers.

Raine, A., Buchsbaum, M. S., Stanley, J. Lottenberg, S. Abel, L. & Stoddard, J. (1994). Selective reductions in prefrontal glucose metabolism in murderers. *Biological Psychiatry, 36,* 365–373.

Rand, M., & Strom, K. (1997) *Violence-related injuries treated in hospital emergency departments* (Bureau of Justice Statistics special report). Washington, DC: U.S. Department of Justice.

Rasche, C. E. (1995). Minority women and domestic violence: The unique dilemmas of battered women of color. In B. R. Price & N. J. Sokoloff (Eds.), *The criminal justice system and women: Offenders, victims, and workers* (2nd ed.) (pp. 246–261). New York: McGraw-Hill.

Rennison, C. M., & Welchans, S. (2000). *Bureau of Justice statistics special report: Intimate partner violence.* Washington, DC: U.S. Department of Justice.

Resick, P. A. (1990) Victims of sexual assault. In A. J. Lurigio, W. G. Skogan, & R. C. Davis (Eds.), *Victims of crime: Problems, policies, and programs* (pp. 69–85). Newbury Park, CA: Sage.

Resnick, H., Kilpatrick, D., Dansky, B., Saunders, B., & Best, C. (1993). Prevalence of civilian trauma and posttraumatic stress disorder in a representative national sample of women. *Journal of Consulting & Clinical Psychology, 61,* 984–991.

Rice, M. E. (1997). Violent offender research and implications for the criminal justice system. *American Psychologist, 52,* 414–423.

Riggs, D. S., Kilpatrick, D. G., & Resnick, H. (1992). Long-term psychological distress associated with marital rape and aggravated assault: A comparison to other crime victims. *Journal of Family Violence, 7*(4), 283–296.

Ringel, C. (1997). *Criminal victimization 1996: Changes 1995–96 with trends 1993–96.* (NCJ-165812). Washington, DC: Bureau of Justice Statistics, U.S. Department of Justice.

Roberts, A. R., & Kurst-Swanger, K. (2002). Court responses to battered women and their children. In A. R. Roberts (Ed.), *Handbook of domestic violence intervention strategies: Policies, programs, and legal remedies* (pp. 127–146). New York: Oxford University Press.

Roberts, G. L., Lawrence, J. M., O'Toole, B. I., & Raphael, B. (1997). Domestic violence in the emergency department: Two case-control studies of victims. *General Hospital Psychiatry, 19,* 5–11.

Rodriguez, M. A., McLoughlin, E. Nah, G., & Campbell, J. C. (2001). Mandatory reporting of domestic violence injuries to the police: What do emergency department patients think? *Journal of the American Medical Association, 286*(5) 580–583.

Roizen, J. (1997). Epidemiological issues in alcohol-related violence. In M. Galanter (Ed.), *Recent developments in alcoholism:* (Vol. 13, Alcoholism and violence) (pp. 7–41). New York: Plenum.

Rosenbaum, A., & O'Leary, K. D. (1981). Marital violence: characteristics of abusive couples. *Journal of Consulting and Clinical Psychology, 49,* 63–71.

Rossman, B. B. R. (2001). Longer term effects of children's exposure to domestic violence. In Graham-Bermann & Edleson (Eds.), *Domestic violence in the lives of children* (pp. 35–65). Washington, D.C.: American Psychological Association.

Rothschild, B., Dimson, C., Storaasil, R. & Clapp, L (1997). Personality profiles of veterans entering treatment for domestic violence. *Journal of Family Violence, 12,* 259–273.

Russell, D. E. H. (1982). *Rape in marriage.* New York: Macmillan.

Sabourin, T. C., Infante, D. A., & Rudd, J. E. (1993). Verbal aggression in marriages: A comparison of violent, distressed but nonviolent, and nondistressed couples. *Human Communication Research, 20,* 245–267.

SAMSHA (Substance Abuse and Mental Health Services Administration). (1997). *Substance abuse treatment and domestic violence.* Department of Health and

Human Services: Center for Substance Abuse Treatment. (TIP #25, DHHS Publication No. SMA 97-3163). Rockville, MD: U.S. Government Printing Office.

SAMSHA (Substance Abuse and Mental Health Services Administration). (1998). *Services research outcomes study.* Department of Health and Human Services. Office of Applied Studies (Analytic Series: A-5). Rockville, MD: U.S. Government Printing Office.

Sanderlin, T. K. (2001). Anger management counseling with the antisocial personality. *Annals of the American Psychotherapy Association, 4*(3), 9–11.

Sato, R. A., & Heiby, E. M. (1992). Correlates of depressive symptoms among battered women. *Journal of Family Violence, 7,* 229–245.

Saunders, B. E. (2003). Understanding children exposed to violence: Toward an integration of overlapping fields. *Journal of Interpersonal Violence, 18*(4), 356–376.

Saunders, B. E., Kilpatrick. D. G., & Resnick, H. S. (1989). Brief screening for lifetime history of criminal victimization at mental health intake: A preliminary study. *Journal of Interpersonal Violence, 4,* 267–277.

Saunders, D. G. (1982). Counseling the violent husband. In P. A Keller & L. G. Ritt (Eds.), *Innovations in Clinical Practice: A Sourcebook* (Vol. 1) (pp. 16–29). Sarasota, FL: Professional Resource Exchange.

Saunders, D. G. (1992). A typology of men who batter: Three types derived from cluster analysis. *American Journal of Orthopsychiatry, 62,* 264–275.

Saunders, D. G. (1994). Posttraumatic stress symptom profiles of battered women: A comparison of survivors in two settings. *Violence and Victims, 9,* 31–44.

Saunders, D. G. (1995). Prediction of wife assault. In Campbell, J. C. (Ed.), *Assessing dangerousness: Violence by sexual offenders, batterers, and child abusers* (pp. 68–95). Thousand Oaks, CA: Sage.

Saunders, D. G. (1999). In R. T. Ammerman & M. Hersen (Eds.), *Assessment of family violence: A clinical and legal sourcebook.* Baltimore: John Wiley & Sons.

Saunders, D. G., Hamberger, K., & Hovey, M. (1993). Indicators of woman abuse based on a chart review at a family practice center. *Archives of Family Medicine, 2,* 537–543.

Schauben, L. J., & Frazier, P. A. (1995). Vicarious trauma: The effects on female counselors of working with sexual violence survivors. *Psychology of Women Quarterly, 19,* 49–64.

Schechter, S. (1987). *Guidelines of mental health practitioners in domestic violence cases.* Washington, DC: National Coalition Against Domestic Violence. Scheppele, K. L. (1992). Just the facts, ma'am: Sexualized violence, evidentiary habits, and the revision of truth. *New York Law Review, 37,* 123–172.

Schumacher, J. A., Fals-Stewart, W. & Leonard, K. E. Domestic violence treatment referrals for men seeking alcohol treatment. *Journal of Substance Abuse Treatment, 24,* 279–283.

Sev'er, A. (1997). Recent or imminent separation and intimate violence against women. *Violence Against Women, 3,* 566–589.

Shalansky, C., Ericksen, J., & Henderson, A. (1999). Abused women and child custody: The ongoing exposure to abusive ex-partners. *Journal of Advanced Nursing, 29*(2), 416–426.

Shalev, A. Y. (1996). Stress versus traumatic stress: From acute homeostatic reactions to chronic psychopathology. In B. A. van der Kolk, A. C. McFarlane & L.Weisaeth (Eds.), *Traumatic Stress* (pp. 77–101). New York: Guilford Press.

Sherman, L. (1992). The influence of criminology on criminal law: Evaluating for misdemeanor domestic violence. *Journal of Criminal Law and Criminology, 85*(1), 901–945.

Sherman, L. W., Schmidt, J. D., Rogan, D. P. (1992). *Policing domestic violence: Experiments and dilemmas.* New York: Free Press.

Shields, N. M., & Hanneke, C. R. (1983). Battered wives' reactions to marital rape. In D. Finkelhor, R. J. Gelles, G. T. Hotaling, & M. A. Straus (Eds.), *The dark side of families: Current family violence research* (pp. 131–148). Beverly Hills, CA: Sage.

Shields, N. M., Resick, P. A., & Hanneke, C. R. (1990). Victims of marital rape. In R. T. Ammerman & M. Hersen (Eds.), *Treatment of Family Violence* (pp. 165–182). New York: John Wiley.

Silvern, L., & Kaersvang, L., (1989). The traumatized children of violent marriages. *Child Welfare, 68,* 421–436.

Silvern, L., Karyl, J., Waelde, L., Hodges, W.F., Starek, J., Heidt, E.,et al. (1995). Retrospective reports of parental partner abuse: Relationships to depression, trauma symptoms and self-esteem among college students. *Journal of Family Violence, 10,* 177–201.

Simon, L. M. J. (1996). A therapeutic jurisprudence approach to the legal processing of domestic violence cases. In D. B. Wexler & B. J. Winick, (Eds.), *Law in a Therapeutic Key: Developments in Therapeutic Jurisprudence* (pp. 243–285). Durham, NC: Carolina Academic Press.

Slagle, D. A. (1990). Psychiatric disorders following closed head injury: An overview of biopsychosocial factors and their etiology and management. *International Journal of Psychiatry in Medicine, 21*(1), 1–35.

Smith, A. (2001). Domestic violence laws: the voices of battered women. *Violence and Victims, 16*(1), 91–110.

Smith, P. H., Tessaro, I., & Earp, J. (1995). Women's experiences with battering: A conceptualization from qualitative research. *Women's Health Issues, 5,* 173–182.

Snyder, D. K., & Fruchtman, L. A. (1981). Differential patterns of wife abuse: A data-based typology. *Journal of Consulting and Clinical Psychology, 49,* 878–885.

Sorenson, S. B., & Telles, C. A. (1991). Self-reports of spousal violence in a Mexican-American and non-Hispanic White population. *Violence and Victims, 6,* 3–15.

Spitzberg, B. (2002). The tactical topography of stalking victimization and management. Trauma, *Violence, & Abuse, 3*(4), 261–288.

Spitzberg, B., Nicastro, A., & Cousins, A. (1998). Exploring the interactional phenomenon of stalking and obsessive relational intrusion. *Communication Reports, 11,* 33–47.

Spitzberg, B. & Rhea, J. (1999). Obsessive relational intrusion and sexual coercion victimization. *Journal of Interpersonal Violence, 14,* 1, 3–20.

Stahl, P. (1999). *Complex issues in child custody evaluations.* Thousand Oaks, CA: Sage.

Stark, E., & Flitcraft, A. (1988). Women and children at risk: A feminist perspective on child abuse. *International Journal of Health Services, 18,* 97–118.

Stark, E., & Flitcraft, A. (1996). Preventing gendered homicide. In E. Stark & A. Flitcraft (Eds.), *Women at risk: Domestic violence and women's health* (pp. 121–153). Thousand Oaks, CA: Sage.

Steinmetz, S.K. (1978). Violence between family members: A review of the recent literature. *Marriage and Family Review, 1*(3), 3–16.

Stermac, L., Del Bove, G., & Addison, M. (2001). Violence, injury, and presentation patterns in spousal sexual assaults. *Violence Against Women, 7(11),* 1219–1233.

Sternberg, K. J., Lamb, M. E., Greenbaum, C., Cicchetti, D., Dawud, S., Cortes, R. M. Krispin, O., & Lorey, F. (1993). Effects of domestic violence on children's behavioral problems and depression. *Developmental Psychology, 29*(1), 44–52.

Stets, J. E. (1990). Verbal and physical aggression in marriage. *Journal of Marriage and the Family, 52,* 501–514.

Stets, J. E., & Straus, M. A. (1990). Gender differences in reporting of marital violence and its medical and psychological consequences. In M. A. Straus & R. J. Gelles (Eds.), *Physical violence in American families: Risk factors and adaptation to violence in 8,145 families* (pp. 151–165). New Brunswick, NJ: Transaction.

Stewart, S. (1996). Alcohol abuse in individual exposed to trauma: a critical review. *Psychological Bulletin, 120*(1), 83–112.

Stith, S. M. & Hamby, S. L. (2002). The anger management scale: Development and preliminary psychometric properties. *Violence and Victims, 17*(4), 383–402.

Stout, K. D. (1993). Intimate femicide: A study of men who have killed their mates. *Journal of Offender Rehabilitation, 19,* 81–94.

Straus, M. A. (1979). Measuring family conflict and violence: The conflict tactics scale. *Journal of Marriage and the Family, 41,* 75–88.

Straus, M. A. (1989). Assaults by wives on husbands: Implications for primary prevention of marital violence. Debate at the annual meeting of the American Society of Criminology, Reno, NV.

Straus, M. A. (1990). The national family violence surveys. In M. A. Straus & R. J. Gelles (Eds.), *Physical violence in American families: Risk factors and adaptation to violence in 8,145 families* (pp. 3–16). New Brunswick, NJ: Transaction.

Straus, M. A. (1992). Children as witness to marital violence: A risk factor for lifelong problems among a nationally representative sample of American men and women. In D. F. Schwarz (Ed.), *Children and violence.* Columbus, OH: Ross Laboratories.

Straus, M. A., & Gelles, R. (1990). Physical violence in American families: Risk factors and adaptation to violence in 8,145 families. New Brunswick, NJ: Transaction.

Straus, M. A., Gelles, R., & Steinmetz, S. (1980). Behind closed doors: Violence in the American family. Garden City, NY: Anchor Press.

Straus, M. A., & Smith, C. (1990). Family patterns and child abuse. In M. A. Straus & R. J. Gelles, (Eds.), Physical violence in American families: Risk factors adaptations to violence in 8,145 families (pp. 245–261), New Brunswick, NJ: Transaction.

Sugarman, D. B., & Hotaling, G. T. (1997). Intimate violence and social desirability: A meta-analytic review. *Journal of Interpersonal Violence, 12,* 275–290.

Suh, E., & Abel, E. (1990). The impact of spousal violence on the children of the abused. *Journal of Independent Social Work, 4,* 27–34.

Sullivan, C. M. (1991). The provision of advocacy services to women leaving abusive partners. *Journal of Interpersonal Violence, 6*(1), 41–54.

Sullivan, C., & Bybee, D. (1999). Reducing violence using community-based advocacy for women with abusive partners. *Journal of Consulting and Clinical Psychology, 67,* 1, 43–53.

Sullivan, J., & Evans, K. (1994). Integrated treatment for the survivor of childhood trauma who is chemically dependent. *Journal of Psychoactive Drugs, 26*(4), 369–378.

Surtees, P. G (1995). In the shadow of adversity: The evolution and resolution of anxiety and depressive disorder. *British Journal of Psychiatry, 166,* 583–594.

Swanson, J. W. (1994). Mental disorder, substance abuse, and community violence: An epidemiological approach. In J. Monahan & H. J. Steadman (Eds.), *Violence and mental disorder: Developments in risk assessment* (pp. 101–136). Chicago, IL: University of Chicago Press.

Swendsen, J., & Merikangas, K. (2000). The comorbidity of depression and substance use disorders. *Clinical Psychology Review, 20*(2), 173–189.

Syers, M., & Edleson, J. L. (1992). The combined effects of coordinated criminal justice intervention in woman abuse. *Journal of Interpersonal Violence, 7*(4), 490–502.

Szinovacz, M., & Egley, L. (1995). Comparing one-partner and couple data on sensitive marital behaviors: The case of marital violence. *Journal of Marriage and the Family, 57,* 995–1010.

Tajima, E. A. (2002). Risk factors for violence against children: Comparing homes with and without wife abuse. *Journal of Interpersonal Violence, 17,* 122–149.

Tarasoff *v.* Regents of the University of California, 118 Cal. Rptr. 129, 529P. 2d 553 (1974).

Tarasoff *v.* Regents of the University of California, 17 Cal. 3d 425 (1976).

Taylor, L., Zuckerman, B., Harik, V., & Groves, B. (1994). Witnessing violence by young children and their mothers. *Journal of Developmental and Behavioral Pediatrics, 15*(2), 120–123.

Testa, M., & Dermen, K. (1999). The differential correlates of sexual coercion and rape. *Journal of Interpersonal Violence, 14*(5), 548–562.

Testa, M. & Livingston, J. (2000). Alcohol and sexual aggression: Reciprocal relationships over time in a sample of high-risk women. *Journal of Interpersonal Violence, 15,* 4, 413–427.

Testa, M., & Parks, K. (1996). The role of women's alcohol consumption in sexual victimization. *Aggression and Violent Behavior, 1*(3), 217–234.

Thompson, M. P., Kaslow, N. J., & Kingree, J. B. (2002). Risk factors for suicide attempts among African American women experiencing recent intimate partner violence. *Violence and Victims, 17*(3), 283–295.

Thompson, M. P., Saltzman, L. E., & Johnson, H. (2001). Risk factors for physical injury among women assaulted by current or former spouses. *Violence Against Women 7*(8), 886–899.

Tjaden, P. & Thoennes, N. (1998). *Stalking in America: Findings from the national violence against women survey* (NCJ-1669592). Washington, DC: National Institute of Justice, Centers for Disease Control and Prevention. Bureau of Justice Statistics, U.S. Department of Justice.

Tjaden, P. & Thoennes, N. (2000). Prevalence and consequences of male-to-female and female-to-male intimate partner violence as measured by the National Violence Against Women Survey. *Violence Against Women, 6*(2), 142–161.

Tolman, R. M., & Bennett, L. W. (1990). A review of quantitative research on men who batter. *Journal of Interpersonal Violence,5*(1), 87–118.

Torres, S. (1991). A comparison of wife abuse between two cultures: Perception, attitudes, nature, and extent (Special Issue). *Issues in Mental Health Nursing: Psychiatric Nursing for the 90's: New Concepts, New Therapies, 12,* 113–131.

True, W. R., & Pitman, R. (1999). Genetics and posttraumatic stress disorder. In P. A. Saigh & J. D. Bremmner (Eds.), *Posttraumatic stress disorder: A comprehensive text* (pp. 144–159 Boston, MA: Allyn & Bacon.

Tutty, L. M., Bidgood, B. A., & Rothery, M. A. (1993). Support groups for battered women: Research on their efficacy. *Journal of Family Violence, 8*(4), 325–343.

Ullman, S. E., Karabatsos, G., & Koss, M. P. (1999b). Alcohol and sexual aggression in a national sample of college men. *Psychology of Women Quarterly, 23,* 673–689.

U.S. Department of Justice (2002). *Enforcement of protective orders* (NCJ-189190). Washington, DC: Author.

Van den Bree, M. B. M., Svikis, D. S. & Pickens, R. W. (2000). Antisocial personality and drug use disorders-Are they genetically related? In D. H. Fishbein, (Ed.), *The science, treatment, and prevention of antisocial behaviors: Application to the criminal justice system* (pp. 8-1–8-19). Kingston, NJ: Civic Research Institute.

Virkkunen, M. & Linnoila, M. (1996). Serotonin and glucose metabolism in impulsively violent alcoholic offenders. In D. M. Stoff & R. B. Cairns, (Eds.), Aggression and violence: genetic, neurobiological, and biosocial perspectives (pp. 87–99). Mahwah, NJ: Lawrence Erlbaum Associates, Publishers.

Vitanza, S., Vogel, L. D. M., & Marshall, L. L. (1995). Distress and symptoms of posttraumatic stress disorder in abused women. *Violence and Victims, 10,* 23–24.

Volkow, N. D., Tancredi, L. R., Grant, G., Gillespie, H., Valentie, A., Mullani, N., Wang, G-J. & Hollister, L. (1995). Brain glucose metabolism in violent psychiatric patients: A preliminary study. *Psychiatry Research: Neuroimaging, 61,* 243–253.

Walker, L. E. (1984). *The battered woman syndrome.* New York: Springer Publishing.

Walker, L. E. (1991). Post-traumatic stress disorder in women: Diagnosis and treatment of battered woman syndrome. *Psychotherapy, 28,* 21–29.

Walker, L. E. (1994). *Abused women and survivor therapy: A practical guide for the psychotherapist.* Washington, DC: American Psychological Association.

Walker, L. E., & Edwall, G. E. (1987). Domestic violence and determination of visitation and custody in divorce. In D. J. Sonkin (Ed.), *Domestic violence on trial: Psychological and legal dimensions of family violence* (pp. 127–154), New York: Springer Publishing.

Wall, A-M. & McKee, S. (2002). Cognitive social learning models of substance use and intimate partner violence. In C. Wekerle & A-M Wall (Eds.), *The violence and addiction equation* (pp. 123–152). New York: Taylor & Francis Group.

Wallace, A. (1986). *Homicide: The social reality.* Sydney, Australia: New South Wales Bureau of Crime and Statistics.

Waltz, J., Babcock, J.C., Jacobson, N.S., & Gottman, J. M. (2000). Testing a typology of batterers. *Journal of Consulting and Clinical Psychology, 68,* 658–669.

Warshaw, C. (1989). Limitations of the medical model in the care of battered women. *Gender & Society, 3,* 506–517.

Warshaw, C. (1993). Domestic violence: Challenges to medical practice. *Journal of Women's Health, 2,* 73–80.

Webster, C. D. & Jackson, M. A. (1997). A clinical perspective on impulsivity. In C. D. Webster & M. A. Jackson, (Eds.), *Impulsivity: theory, assessment and treatment* (pp. 13–31). New York: Guilford Press.

Weisz, A. N., Tolman, R. M., & Saunders, D. G. (2000). Assessing the risk of severe domestic violence: The importance of survivors' predictions. *Journal of Interpersonal Violence, 15*(1), 75–90.

Weitzman, L. (1985). *The divorce revolution.* Free Press: New York.

West, C. G., Fernandez, A., Hillard, J. R., Schoof, M., & Parks, J. (1990) Psychiatric disorders of abused women at a shelter. *Psychiatric Quarterly, 61,* 295–301.

Wexler, D. B. (2000). Domestic *violence 2000: An integrated skills program for men.* New York: W.W. Norton & Company.

Whatley, M. A. (1993). For better or worse: The case of marital rape. *Violence and Victims, 8*(1), 29–39.

White, J. W., & Koss, M. P. (1991). Courtship violence: Incidence in a national sample of higher education students. *Violence and Victims, 6,* 247–256.

Widiger, T. A., & Trull, T. J. (1994). Personality disorders and violence. In J.Monahan & H. J. Steadman (Eds.), *Violence and mental disorder: Developments in risk assessment* (pp. 203–226). Chicago: University of Chicago Press.

Widom, C. S. (1989). Does violence beget violence? A critical examination of the literature. *Psychological Bulletin, 106,* 3–28.

Widom, C. & Toch, H. (2000). The contribution of psychology to criminal justice education. In D. H. Fishbein (Ed.), *The Science, Treatment, and Prevention of Antisocial Behaviors* (pp. 3-1–3-19),. Kingston, NJ: Civic Research Center.

Wills, T. & Filer, M. (1996). Stress-coping model of adolescent substance use. In T. Ollendick and R. Prinz (Eds.), *Advances in clinical and child psychology* (18) (pp. 91-132). New York: Plenum Press,

Wills, T., & Hirky, E. (1996). Coping and substance abuse: A theoretical model and review of the evidence. In M. Zeidner & N. Endler (Eds.), *Handbook of coping: Theory, research, and application.* New York: Wiley.

Wilson, J. P. (1989). *Trauma, transformation, and healing: An integrative approach to theory research, and post-traumatic therapy.* New York: Brunner/Mazel.

Wilson, J. P., & Keane, T. M. (Eds.) (1996). *Assessing psychological trauma and PTSD.* New York: Guilford Press.

Wilson, J., & Lindy, J. (1994). *Countertransference in the treatment of PTSD.* New York: Guilford Press.

Wilson, M., & Daly, M. (1993). Spousal homicide risk and estrangement. *Violence and Victims, 1,* 3–16.

Wishik, H. (1986). Economics of divorce: An exploratory study. *Family Law Quarterly, 20,* 79–107.

Wonderlich, S. A., Beatty, W. W., Christie, D. W. & Staton, R. D. (1993). Personality characteristics of men who physically abuse women. *Hospital and Community Psychiatry, 44,* 54–58.

Zoellner, L. A., Feeny, N. C., Alvarez, J., Watlington, C., O'Neill, M. L., Zager, R. & Foa, E. B. (2000). Factors associated with completion of the restraining order process in female victims of partner violence. *Journal of Interpersonal Violence, 15*(10), 1081–1099.

Zorza, J. (1995). How abused women can use the law to help protect their children. In E. Peled, P. Jaffe, & J. Edleson (Eds.), *Ending the cycle of violence: Community response to children of battered women* (pp. 147–169). Thousand Oaks, CA: Sage Publications.

Zorza, J. (1999). What is wrong with mutual orders of protection? *Domestic Violence Report,* June/July.

Index